the

body

SACRED

About the Author

Dianne Sylvan has been a practicing Wiccan since the age of sixteen. She is the author of *The Circle Within: Creating a Wiccan Spiritual Tradition* as well as numerous articles for Pagan publications including *NewWitch* and the *Witches' Calendar*. Dianne is co-priestess of Grove of Starlight Coven and founder of the fledgling EarthDance tradition. She teaches Wicca, Runes, ecstatic dance, and other magical pursuits in the midst of her writing projects and life as a Witch in Austin, Texas.

To Write to the Author

If you wish to contact the author or would like more information about this book, please write to the author in care of Llewellyn Worldwide and we will forward your request. Both the author and publisher appreciate hearing from you and learning of your enjoyment of this book and how it has helped you. Llewellyn Worldwide cannot guarantee that every letter written to the author can be answered, but all will be forwarded. Please write to:

Dianne Sylvan
℅ Llewellyn Worldwide
2143 Wooddale Drive, Dept. 0-7387-0761-9
Woodbury, MN 55125-2989, U.S.A.
Please enclose a self-addressed stamped envelope for reply,
or $1.00 to cover costs. If outside U.S.A., enclose
international postal reply coupon.

Many of Llewellyn's authors have websites with additional information and resources. For more information, please visit our website at http://www.llewellyn.com.

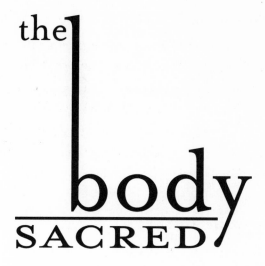

the body

SACRED

DIANNE SYLVAN

Llewellyn Publications
Woodbury, Minnesota

First Edition
First Printing, 2005

Book design and layout by Joanna Willis
Cover design by Gavin Dayton Duffy
Cover image © 2005 by ThinkStock
Editing by Valerie Valentine

Llewellyn is a registered trademark of Llewellyn Worldwide, Ltd.

Library of Congress Cataloging-in-Publication Data
Sylvan, Dianne, 1977-
    The body sacred / Dianne Sylvan.—1st ed.
        p. cm.
    Includes bibliographical references and index.
    ISBN 0-7387-0761-9
        1. Witchcraft. 2. Body image in women—Miscellanea. I. Title

BF1572.B63S95 2005
299'.94--dc22
                                                                2005045144

Llewellyn Publications
A Division of Llewellyn Worldwide, Ltd.
2143 Wooddale Drive, Dept. 0-7387-0761-9
Woodbury, MN 55125-2989, U.S.A.
www.llewellyn.com

Printed in the United States of America

CONTENTS

ACKNOWLEDGMENTS

Special thanks go out to all the women who so obligingly responded to my prodding and survey questions about their self-esteem and body image. Some of those women's words pepper the pages of this book; the rest served as inspiration and valuable insight.

So to S1ren, the Jess, Shana, Anise, Debi, Jewel, Terri, Kylara, Raene, Metis, Kelli, Aislin, and Bethany . . . I offer my never-ending appreciation.

Thanks also to the women of my pantheon of personal role models who, each in her own way and most without ever having met me, lifted me out of body image bondage and into the realizations that brought this book into being. They include Margaret Cho, Yasmine Galenorn, Inga Muscio, Maya Angelou, Tori Amos, Ani DiFranco, and a whole host of others, as well as my friends, lovers, coven sisters, and extended tribe who are quite happy to let me dance, eat ice cream cones, wear anything or nothing, and claw the sheets to my dark little Scorpio heart's content.

And last of all, but foremost, thanks to the Star of Light, my strength and sustenance; and of course to Jeff for saving my life once, and saving my sanity every day. Hail and welcome, my Lady and Lord, and blessed be.

ABOUT THIS BOOK
AND ITS AUTHOR

The Body Sacred is a book about our bodies. It's about how we treat them, and moreover, how we *should* treat them. It's about what it really means to say "Thou art Goddess," and how we can take the thread of that meaning and spin it around our lives to bind up the gaping wounds that society and self-hate have created in our minds, hearts, and spirits.

This book is written primarily for women, though I am perfectly aware that men have plenty of body image problems of their own. I, however, am a woman. I can't write a book for men any more than I could write one for Baptists. I don't have the hubris to pretend I can understand the male perspective except through the lens of my own, and it's not exactly the most objective in the world. Just as I said in my first book, *The Circle Within,* Wiccan men need to stand up and write; they need to create ritual and community as much as women do. We can't do it for you. A man reading this might learn something valuable about the challenges women face, or he might not; regardless, I would love to see this topic explored for men by a male author.

Along those lines, most of the rituals and exercises herein focus on the Goddess rather than the God. This is simply because, again, this book is about women, and as women it's important that we find images of deity we can identify with. Notable exceptions occur in chapters 2 and 7, but for the most part we'll be emphasizing feminine deity as a path back to our own sacred femininity. If you feel more comfortable working with both masculine and feminine divinity equally, by all means alter the rituals and invocations to reflect that.

In my own practice, the Lord and Lady each have areas of my life that they seem to specialize in, but neither is more important than the other. For the purposes of this book, however, the spotlight will mostly be on her. As such, when I say "the Goddess" I do not mean both Lord and Lady under one convenient header. Some Wiccans use one title or the other to speak of both faces of deity at once; I do not do that. When I say "Goddess," I mean "Goddess." If I am speaking of both I usually say deity, the gods, the Divine, and so on.

While we're on the subject of vocabulary, a quick note: I also do not use the words "Wicca" and "Witchcraft" interchangeably, though I know many people do. It is my view that Wicca is a religion, and Witchcraft is an art; you don't have to be Wiccan to be a Witch, or vice versa. Magic is an important part of Wicca, but casting a circle doesn't make you a Witch any more than baking a cake makes you a pastry chef. I consider myself both a Wiccan priestess and a Witch, and both of those titles were hardearned and walk hand in hand on my path.

Something else to keep in mind is that this is not a book about dieting or exercise. I don't believe in diets. To be frank, I think they're utter crap, and I'll talk about that a bit more later on. I am not here to tell you what to eat or how many miles to jog. I will discuss our relationship with food and eating, and how it affects our body image, but there is no food plan in these pages and no convenient log for you to copy and check off how many calories or glasses of water you've had today. I don't really care about any of that; if you want to live off nothing but Krispy Kreme donuts and Red Zinger tea, more power to you. I hope,

Interesting [handwritten margin note]

however, that after reading this book you might think twice before you do that to yourself.

Besides, I'm not a nutritionist, a personal trainer, a counselor, or any handy designation with a diploma on the wall. Nothing I say should be considered medical advice, because I am definitely *not* a doctor. I am a Wiccan priestess, a child and servant of the Goddess and God, a woman, a writer, and a Witch.

I am also fat, by society's standards. According to diet industry statistics, I should be dead right now, although my vitals and chemistry are spot-on normal, whatever that is. As a woman of size in a world of stupid, I've had to deal with more catty comments, name calling, sidelong looks into my grocery basket, helpful diet suggestions from total strangers, and outright disgust than you can imagine . . . unless you're like me. Fat discrimination is a comical idea to a lot of people—it's not real unless it's directed at you. In fact, fat jokes are one of the few kinds of cruelty that is still perfectly acceptable in conversation.

In fact, if you go by the ideals set forth in advertising and on television, I should be a suicidal virgin with no friends that sits around in her muumuu eating donuts and watching *Jerry Springer.*

Sorry to disappoint you.

(Not that I haven't eaten my share of donuts, mind you . . . but I don't own a muumuu, never have. And one nice thing about the Pagan community is that the big girls get as many sultry looks over the Beltaine fire as the thin ones do; I've known a number of larger women whose tents should have a revolving flap. And one more thing—if you ever catch me watching *Jerry Springer*, please back over me with my car.)

Fat isn't the only thing I want to bring into the spotlight, however. A good two-thirds of women in our wondrous modern age wish they could change something about their bodies, and for many, that wish dances the dangerous borders of obsession. Maybe when you see your reflection you think your hair is too straight, your skin too dark, you're too tall, or too short. Maybe you think being in a wheelchair renders you asexual. Maybe you are too ashamed of what happened to you as a child to feel anything from the neck down. Maybe getting old scares the hell out of you, so you deny it with every fiber of your will.

If you've ever had a "fat day," I'm writing for you. If you've ever decided not to go after a promotion because the other candidate is a tall skinny blonde, I'm writing for you. If you've ever wished that bathing in bleach would make you white, or that ironing your hair would make it straight, or that having a doctor hack into your face would make you young again, I'm writing for you.

I'm writing for me, too.

You may be tempted to think, reading my words and experiences, that I'm somehow done with body image issues, that I've dealt with it and am now above it all. Nothing could be further from the truth. I struggle with self-acceptance every day, and some days I do a lot better than others. Some days I look in the mirror and want to crawl back in bed until they invent a cure for RDU (Really Damned Ugly) syndrome. Some days I think I'm the sexiest Witch in Austin. Most days fall somewhere in between, closer to the latter end of the scale.

I don't trust experts. I don't believe that anyone who writes a book about an issue like this has completely, 100 percent left it behind. I certainly don't want you to believe I'm better or more advanced spiritually or emotionally than you are because I'm the one typing and you're the one reading. It may be that I've thought about these things more, or know how to put them into words in a way others can relate to; it may be that I just have a big mouth. I'll let you be the judge.

You will find a lot of my personal life in these pages. I really didn't see any other way to talk about this subject than to haul out my skeletons and dress them up for the parade. I plan to be rather open about the subjects herein, when necessary. You won't find lurid details about my sex life (which, I can tell you right now, has been pretty lurid at times), but you will find the truth about my own struggles with beauty, sexuality, and self-acceptance, so that hopefully you will realize we all face the same kinds of pain and all have to unlearn the same poisonous lessons.

Americans like to declare war on things. We have the War on Drugs, the War on Poverty, and so on, none of which tend to be terribly successful; there is, however, another war going on that will probably never get equal coverage on CNN—the body war. We have declared war on our own bodies, naming them the enemy, vowing to conquer their messy habits and uncontrollable aging, their size and shape and sheer mass. We have invented thousands of weapons for this war that range from plastic surgery to hair transplants to low-carb bread (which should be an oxymoron, in my opinion, emphasis on *moron*).

We will, however, never win this war.

Our bodies fight back. Diets fail spectacularly for 90 percent or more of those who try them. Our hormones ensure that all the makeup in the world won't stop wrinkles, menopause, and sagging breasts. Go ahead, have that pound or two sucked out of your butt; another three pounds will be more than happy to step in and fill the void. It's funny, really, how pointless most of our efforts turn out to be, because in the end, nature will have her way, or simply send us heart attacks for our trouble.

I am writing this from the trenches. I am not standing on a hill a mile away from the battle where the blood is obscured by smoke and the cries of the wounded have blended into distant cacophony. I am struggling with you up the hill, losing ground almost as often as I gain it . . . but here, amidst the swinging swords and fat-gram counters, I have found something truly remarkable: a resistance.

You'll find these outlaw women everywhere, and in fact a lot of them are Pagans. They're the brave souls who have thrown down their arms, stripped off their armor, and shattered the mirror with their shields. Instead of wasting their time hating their bodies, they enjoy them; they

I want to do that

move and eat and dress and behave as if every second of every day is a blessing and a gift, and when you see them, the first thing you think is, "Thou art Goddess."

These women are the ones who aren't afraid to get up and dance. They look you straight in the eye, flash a dazzling smile, and wear whatever they damn well please, because they aren't afraid of what you think of them. They aren't afraid of anything, really, because they have come to accept and understand the single perfect truth of the universe: it's all God. There can be nothing truly ugly if the Goddess is beautiful, because we are all cells in her body, as much a part of her as sunset and moonrise, ocean and anthill.

Humor me for a moment. Imagine that you are one of these outlaw goddesses, that your spine is unbent with shame over how you look, that you treat your body as the sacred instrument it is. Imagine loving yourself without reservation, just for a moment.

Now stand up, put your hands on your hips, and recite the following invocation, which you may be pleased to note is almost the only thing in this book that rhymes:

Lady of the shining moon,
Lady of the starlit eyes,
Lady of the rocky shore,
And Lady of the thunder thighs,
Holy are thine ancient groves,
Holy is thy swaying grass,
Holy are thy sheltering wings,
And holy is thy big, fat ass.

As soon as you're done being either amused or horrified, read on.

One question you may have is this: there are already a number of excellent books out there on women and body image, many of which can be found in the recommended reading section at the end of each chapter, so why do I feel the need to add another? The reason is that all of these books have one thing in common: they are written from the perspective of someone still living in the dominant paradigm of our society, Western religion and the antiquated mentality of Newtonian physics.

What exactly that means, we'll get to shortly, but the quick version is this: Wiccans, by virtue of our view of deity, see the world of form, including our bodies, differently than most other people in the West. Our relationship with the Divine, with the universe, with life, is a breed apart from what most of us were raised with—not necessarily better or worse, just different. The majority of us are not born to Wicca, or any other Pagan faith; we have to completely change how we look at ourselves and the world when we convert, and that is not easy. It amazes me that more hasn't been written about it. When you become a Wiccan, your universe turns on its head, and you have to realign your perceptions, which means it's not such a simple thing to switch from "I'm a fat slug, I need to start Atkins tomorrow, how many calories were in that salad?" to "I am a divine being, the hands of the Lord and Lady on Earth, and the body I have been given is a blessing, and a dead sexy one at that."

That is why I wrote this book, to address that change of mentality as it affects how we perceive our bodies and our place in the world. The old ways of seeing no longer apply to us—we need no longer be bound by the "power-over" systems of consumerist society. As Wiccans, we have a whole new set of resources to help us live the fullest, most fabulous lives we possibly can . . . but before we can dance, we have to shrug off the weight of not-good-enough and learn how to stand and walk. We can rip off the mask, look in the mirror, and see the Goddess grinning back as she says, "It's about time you got here."

How to Use *The Body Sacred*

I am not a theorist. I feel that my job is not to talk your ear off about a concept and then leave it at that, but to speak my piece and then give you ideas and tools to *do* something about it all. Where my words leave off is where your real work begins; I can't drag you kicking and screaming into a good relationship with your body. The hard part is all up to you.

That in mind, the chapters that follow contain as many exercises, ritual ideas, and meditations as I could stuff into them. It's not enough to think I'm a genius (or an idiot) and then close the book and forget about it all. Take what you see here, try it on, take it apart, and make it your own. Most importantly, don't take what I say as any sort of gospel; I can only speak for myself and my experience. My brand of Wicca may be vastly different from yours, but I hope that won't keep you from finding something useful here. I am not the official Wicca spokesmodel, and thank the Lady for that. I look really stupid in a tiara.

The first two chapters of *The Body Sacred* deal with the underlying problems of our society's view of the body, and how Wiccan theology and philosophy offer a magical and beautiful alternative to the warfare we've been trained for. After that, we'll discuss a series of archetypes, each one representing a different aspect of your relationship with the body sacred:

The Reflection—self-perception

The Mother—nourishment and self-care

The Healer—wellness and energy

The Lover—sexuality and sensuality

The Dancer—movement and spiritual ecstasy

The Crone—aging and the Blood Mysteries

Each of these archetypes embodies both the positive and negative expression of these parts of our lives. The Mother, for example, governs how we nourish and care for our bodies, so she is responsible for both that relaxing bubble bath you took last night and the half-gallon of mint-chocolate-chip you inhaled immediately afterward. In each chapter, we will explore how to work with that aspect of ourselves, using the tools that most Wiccans already work with—ritual, magic, meditation, and so on.

Some of the archetypes may not be a problem for you. You may have no difficulty whatsoever with the Crone, who counsels us toward aging gracefully. You may need help with all six. It's important to re-member not to think of them as separate people, but as layers of your life and spirit, each one necessary to craft a whole, fulfilled woman.

Each chapter contains ritual ideas and so forth, as well as stories of goddesses (and humans) that embody each archetype. While I am not a hard polytheist, I am also firmly against the "Plug-and-Play Deity" approach to Wicca, where you pick a goddess because she's related to what you want, and invoke her without knowing a thing about her or her culture. The stories here are meant to serve as inspiration for you to go out and learn more if a particular Lady calls to you.

One last point. It should be pretty obvious by now that this is not a Wicca 101 book. I am assuming, as I generally do with my writing, that you have either already decided to make this your path, or you at least know enough about it to read without scratching your head every other paragraph. I don't write slanted toward any particular tradition, but I am leaning more toward what you might call American Eclectic Wicca than the older traditions that are a lot more structured and formal. I feel I should also mention that I do not assume or expect you to have read any of my other work in order to read this one; many of the themes in *The Body Sacred* are similar to those in my first book, though here they take on a different perspective and slightly different purpose. Blessed be.

I found God in myself and I loved her . . . I loved her fiercely

NTOZAKE SHANGE

o n e

THE
fall from grace

To cast off the shroud of self-hatred, stand up, and reclaim the sanctity of our bodies from the utter insanity that has gripped Western culture is to announce to the world that your self-worth will not be bought and sold at cosmetics counters and plastic surgeons' offices, that you have seen through the smokescreen that the diet and beauty industry has pulled over the eyes of women all around you . . . that you are no longer a commodity, but a manifestation of divine grace, blessed just as you are.

> For us to have self-esteem is truly an act of revolution . . . and our revolution is long overdue.
> MARGARET CHO

Advertisers, diet chains, and makeup companies all have a vested interest in making sure that never happens. From childhood we are taught by magazines and television that no matter how we were born, no matter how we grow, we are simply not good enough the way we are . . . but, if we just buy this or that product, we could be so much better. Shell out your money to Jenny Craig, Slim-Fast, and Cover Girl and you too can achieve the American dream—the body of a white twelve-year-old girl (with twenty-five-year-old breasts) that never ages.

Never mind the size of your frame, the texture of your hair, the fact that all the women of your family have two things in common—a recipe for the world's best meatloaf and an ass like two watermelons in a sack. No matter what shape you are, no matter what your genetic destiny or ethnic heritage, the idyllic life of the American Stick Woman can be yours . . . for a price.

From an outside perspective, say, that of a historian in a few hundred years studying us the way we study the Middle Ages, the fact that women pay upwards of three thousand dollars to have bags of saltwater sewn into their chests and fat sucked out of their butts is so incredibly ridiculous-sounding it doesn't seem real.

> In the Middle Ages, they had guillotines, stretch racks, whips and chains. Nowadays, we have a much more effective torture device called the bathroom scale.
>
> STEPHEN PHILLIPS

Of course, bleeding people with leeches to suck the evil humors out didn't seem all that crazy in medieval England, either.

We are no longer chattel to our fathers and husbands, but we allow our spirits to be sold into slavery for the price of a size-six wardrobe.

The body war is the consequence of our progress as women, as our potential and our position run head-on into each other. It's a distraction technique—keep women worried about their butt size, and they'll be too busy (and too hungry) to take over the world. Recent advertising would have us believe that we've already gained total equality, and therefore as liberated women we should now work to be "the best women we can be," which usually means buying makeup, dressing a certain way, and eating a certain way. On average, women still make less money than men, but a larger percentage of our income goes to support the diet and cosmetic industries. We participate in our own oppression.

In the pyramid of human needs as envisioned by philosophers and psychologists such as Abraham Maslow, physical needs like food and

shelter are the very basis of our sense of self. Achievement, self-actu-
alization, and spirituality are the higher levels; until our physical sense
of self is secure, we cannot progress up the ladder. That makes good
sense—it's hard to meditate if you are out on the streets with no shoes
in winter. Likewise, if we stay stuck in a mindset in which appearance
takes priority, we keep ourselves on the bottommost rung, unable to
think of anything else. It's difficult to reach enlightenment or the Sen-
ate floor if you do nothing but stare in the mirror and berate your
own face.

To be a woman in this world is to stand in the middle of a storm,
screaming to be heard above the thunder of voices that tell us we are
ugly, inadequate, and inferior.

Little girls are dieting at age nine.

The average American model is 5'11" and weighs 117 pounds. The
average American woman, however, is 5'4" and weighs 140 pounds.

There are, at this moment, approximately ten million women and
one million men who have either anorexia, bulimia, or both.

The United Nations Development Program estimates that the essential nutritional and health needs of the world's poorest people could
be met for an additional $13 billion a year. In 1990, the approximate rev-
enue of the American diet industry was $30 billion.

That's more than tragic irony—it is, in my opinion, disgusting. The
grain we raise to feed the cattle that people are eating by the truckload
on high-protein diets could feed millions of people who will never
look in the mirror and say, "I need to lose weight," because they are
dying of starvation.

I could go on, but I won't. Statistics and facts are sobering, but they
are hard to relate to, hard to bring into our own direct experience.
When you're sitting on your couch trying to decide between a pint of
Ben and Jerry's and a walk in the park, world hunger probably doesn't
enter your mind. When it comes to body image, the only way to understand why you as an individual cringe when you look in the mirror

is to look at the society that is standing behind you, looking over your shoulder, whispering, "Boy, do you need a nose job."

I could very easily lay the blame on the doorstep of the media and the industries that profit from our self-hatred, but there's more to it than that. The pressure to be physically perfect is so deeply ingrained in our society that most people don't even question that fat is unhealthy, that white is best, that wrinkles are ugly.

Why? How did it come to this? How did we go from hunter/gatherer to binge/purge? And how is it that, even knowing how much of our self-image is manufactured and auctioned off, we still have so much trouble believing it, or better yet, living it?

I don't have concrete answers to these questions. I can't point to a moment in history and say, "There, that's it—that's when women became objects and the Goddess became a Barbie doll." The fact is, it doesn't matter when it happened, and it doesn't really matter who's to blame. If anything, it's a vicious cycle—we take in media images, believe what we're spoon-fed, and buy more products and images which support the businesses that profit from our self-hate.

Producers without consumers go bankrupt. The media have no reason to stop putting out starvation imagery, because *we keep buying it.* Drug companies have no reason to focus on AIDS research or cures for cancer, because the real money is in diet pills, which *we continue to buy.* Until we as a country, as women, as priestesses of the Goddess, make the decision to hold up our hands and say, *"Enough,"* to step out of the game and love ourselves in spite of ourselves, our society will remain as shallow, empty, and mindless as it has largely become.

Big business and the media only have the power we give them . . . when we give our own away.

The time has come to call a halt to it all. The Goddess didn't breathe life into the universe and give birth to all its wonder and splendor so that I could throw up my lunch and call myself a big fat cow. I wasn't born

No one can make you feel inferior without your consent.

ELEANOR ROOSEVELT

into this body to treat it like the lowest form of life on Earth. Neither were you.

Uma Thurman is skinny. I'm not. Does that mean she loves herself more than I do? Does that give her greater value as a person, enable her to make a greater contribution to this world? Does being one of *People* magazine's Most Beautiful People mean that Jennifer Aniston will always be happy, or is spiritually fulfilled—or is there a chance that she wakes up looking like complete crap and curses at the mirror, just like us lowly mortals?

Marilyn Monroe, considered one of the most beautiful women in American history (who was, let the record show, not a size four), didn't exactly have a blissful life. Meanwhile, here in Austin there's a high priestess of a local coven, approximately size twenty-four, who never stops smiling—joy and divine energy radiate from her like sunlight, and you'll never once hear her mention "carbs," "fat grams," or even "lite beer." If she wants a piece of cake . . . she *has one*, enjoys it, and that's the end of it, without a single, "This is so bad for me," or "I'll do extra sit-ups tomorrow."

There are people out there who love themselves just the way they are.

No, really.

There are a number of factors that have contributed to the infiltration of body hatred into our lives and minds. The media are, of course, one of them, as is the constant Western need to prove and improve ourselves which leads us into lifestyles that are anything but healthy (even the staunchest anti-diet activist will tell you fast food is the nutritional equivalent of, well, shooting yourself in the face with a bazooka), but in reality their contribution is only a symptom of something much deeper, much simpler . . . and therefore much more sinister.

Oddly enough, body image is something that, for Wiccans, shouldn't even be an issue. We are, however, still products of our culture and our history, and much of that is steeped in the patriarchal and consumerist framework that the modern world seems determined to operate on. It's no surprise, then, that for women who come to the Wiccan path, there's a little more to psychological and spiritual conversion than suddenly deciding to dance around naked without thinking about our jiggling thighs.

Most of us come to Wicca with remarkably heavy baggage. It does not help that, by and large, people who leave the faiths of their childhood are refugees more than seekers. We start by running away from where we were, then realize that we're running toward somewhere, or someone, else. A lot of people who find the Pagan community are survivors of abuse, in recovery, or otherwise injured by the past and often by the religions of the past.

Even those without visible scars are often leaving behind unhappiness or disillusionment; ours is not a path that attracts the complacent or unquestioning. Being satisfied with your religion and your life does not lead you to look for another, and unfortunately by the time we figure out we need to go a-hunting, that dissatisfaction tends to become a deep emotional and spiritual wound.

Therefore, it helps to look at the underlying cause of the Western denigration of the body, particularly the female body, so that we can understand why it simply doesn't fit in with the worldview that Wicca offers us. It is the Great Divide, our fall from grace, and the single greatest hurdle between ourselves and self-acceptance as women and as Wiccans.

The Rift

Maybe it started with Adam and Eve, if the Christian mythos is anything to go by. Maybe one bite of an apple was what messed things up for all womankind—Eve got all spunky and asserted her independence (after all, Lilith did it first), and the rest of us are still paying for it. If so, I'd like to have words with our Foremother about that whole PMS thing—if it's her fault, she owes me a huge bottle of Midol.

Or . . . maybe it was Pandora, come to think of it. Curiosity killed the cat, and it also seems to have given women a bad rap. Women have been the fall guys in a lot of myths and stories the world over. In truth, though, when you strip our body issues to their barest essence, they really have little to do with gender, although that certainly plays a part further out. Denigration of the feminine is an insidious poison in our world, but it stems from another toxin: the false dichotomy of spirit and body.

At some point, for some reason, a shift occurred in human thinking that drove a wedge between the physical world and that of consciousness, thought, and spirit. For our purposes, we'll consider the mind and the spirit as aspects of the same thing: our essential consciousness as human beings. The important thing is that there came a time when the body was relegated to a lesser sphere, deprioritized in favor of mental and spiritual pursuits. That, I believe, is when the trouble started.

It may have been a great idea in the beginning. Imagine yourself back in the fabled Burning Times as a scientist or scholar watching the madness that had gripped Europe over something as vague and impossible to prove or disprove as charges of Witchcraft. Imagine seeing otherwise rational men accuse their neighbors of everything from withering crops to eating babies, and seeing the populace clamor for executions because of what you viewed as superstition, not truth. It was probably pretty disturbing, to say the least.

Enter scientists like René Descartes, who was a renowned philosopher, physicist, and mathematician in the 1600s, right around the time Galileo was condemned by the Inquisition. Descartes theorized that the mind and body were separate substances, which made contact through the pineal gland in the brain. His work formed much of the foundation of modern philosophy, and caused a revolution in thought. Descartes believed everything in nature could be explained through mathematics and science, and was one of the first to describe the workings of the universe with matter and motion. In his view, the universe operated as a giant mathematical machine.

It's understandable given the irrationality of the time that ideas like these would eventually catch on. People were finally growing weary of the Witch hunts and starting to realize the extent of the damage to the European population; they were ready for something that made sense in a world that had apparently lost its collective mind. With the advent of Newtonian physics, which expanded on the idea of the universe as a machine that ran in predictable ways according to systematic laws, the idea of nature as mechanistic and the mind as its own entity became firmly entrenched.

Even before Cartesian philosophy came to dominate the modern mindset, Christian dogma had long contended that the body itself was not as holy as the spirit; the body was dust and would return to dust, but the soul was eternal. The body's urges—to eat, to mate, to protect itself—were behind most of the Church's favorite sins, like adultery, fornication, and gluttony. This worldview made it acceptable to torture suspected Witches and other heretics, as it was the fate of the soul that mattered, not the condition of the body.

Women's bodies in particular were stigmatized, having been the source of the downfall of humankind; part of Eve's punishment for eating the apple, you may remember, was pain in childbirth. Eve was seen as a weaker vessel, unable to resist temptation by the devil yet able to convince the superior and firstborn Adam to join her in her unholy picnic. When the *Malleus Maleficarum* came along in 1486, the underlying misogyny of the Church's leaders came crashing to the forefront. The Witch-hunting guide painted a portrait of woman as a sex-hungry, devious animal. Most Wiccans have heard the infamous quote from the *Malleus*: "All Witchcraft stems from carnal lust, which is in women insatiable."

I find it interesting that, in a very twisted way, they were right. The energy that Witches work with arises from all that lives—there is an inherent eroticism to that energy, the divine interplay between dark and light, masculine and feminine, yin and yang. The magic that it takes to create new life is also the magic we call upon in spellwork and ritual. The woman-hating Dominicans who penned the *Malleus* found a grain of truth and distorted it, as zealots are wont to do.

What could be more insidious than assigning evil intent—intent, of course, being something you cannot defend—to women based on something that was integral to their being, the natural desires of their bodies? If a woman's libido was to blame for all the devil's antics on Earth, there was clear license to treat them as cruelly as one wanted. Rape a woman, it must be her fault, right? She had to have asked for it—she must have been dressed like a whore to arouse a pious man's lust. Sure, you could beat your wife—she was female, she must have brought it on herself.

The problem with believing that women are responsible for the fall of men is that, if a woman had the power to do that, it meant *she had power*. If the female gender could bring down the wrath of God and bring sin into being, or incite men to lust and madness just by showing their ankles, then we must be formidable beings, indeed.

The first thing I usually think when I see a supermodel on television is, "I could snap her in half like a twig." Twigs for arms, knees bigger than her thighs, wobbling about on high heels; the paragon of womanly virtue on the runway is a pitiful sight. The popular image of beauty is, in essence, powerlessness. Skinny little girls who look too weak to lift a spoon, much less climb the corporate ladder, are what we are taught we should be.

The women in our society who opt for liberation and personal power over expected gender roles—feminists, lesbians, Witches, to name a few—are often the ones ridiculed for our rebellion. Being unwilling to conform to what is "normal" marks us as freaks, and we're picked on for everything from not shaving our legs to wearing patchouli. Breaking free from our prescribed role as women is equated with ugliness, and in a materialistic society, ugliness has become a cardinal sin, especially given how many "quick and easy," "thirty days to a brand-new you!" products there are to help us in our quest for perfection. There are so many ways to change ourselves that if you don't fit the prescribed image, you must be a colossal failure as a woman.

Have you ever noticed that a lot of ads feature women only from the neck down, so our heads are cut off?

This world seems to fear our power so much that it wants us to shrink until we disappear. We let those who fear our womanhood control our womanhood.

I refuse to allow it. It's time we all did.

There are a variety of theories on the subject of female power and male terror of that power, reaching all the way back to the day that Og the Caveman first realized his lady fair could bleed for five days and not die, and that baby Ogs grew in her belly and then emerged screaming and naked from between her legs. It is thought that women were the original keepers of the mysteries of life and death, and knew the uses of magic that the menfolk, off hunting mammoths with sticks, weren't privy to. Eventually, the unease that the men felt became out-and-out fear, and from there we get the laws in various societies that keep menstruating women from touching anything a man might touch, or that isolate women from the rest of the tribe when they bleed.

Personally, I would love to have my own moon lodge—I could lie around eating jalapeno potato chips and everyone would leave me the hell alone. But while the women were gathered in the house of the moon, the men were all standing outside wondering (a) what they were up to in there, and (b) why dinner wasn't on the table.

There isn't really a lot of verifiable proof for these theories, but they do make a certain sense. People from Neanderthal to nowadays have always mistrusted what they didn't understand, and it's only in the last couple of centuries that the mysteries of reproduction and the intricacies of the female body have been almost fully understood. It follows, then, that it's only recently that women have made great strides toward being thought of as actual human beings.

With the stigma against the physical firmly entrenched, the rift between body and spirit began to slowly widen. People of faith were supposed to transcend their bodily urges and reach for the state of pure spirit that was Heaven, but meanwhile, despite our lofty goals, it became readily apparent to entrepreneurs that sex sells.

As a result, we in the modern world live in a forced schizophrenia of being, with body on one side of the ravine and spirit/mind on the other, neither complete alone. Priests and ministers say indulgence and vanity are sins, but television and magazines say you can only have a happy life if you have the perfect body.

Well, which is it?

Most Westerners are split down the center, torn between two deep and opposing desires: one, the DNA-deep and natural need to live fully in our bodies; two, the need instilled in us by those in ecclesiastical power, who teach us that listening to the wisdom of the body is a one-way ticket to Hell.

The Greatest Consequence

Unfortunately for the Church fathers, it is impossible to ignore our instincts. We can push them down and push them down, but eventually they will break free, and often by then they have twisted from something natural and beautiful to something disgusting.

Go ask an altar boy who was molested by a Catholic priest if repressing our sexuality has brought us as a society closer to God. Ask a woman in a hospital dying from anorexia if abstaining from physical indulgence has made her a more spiritual being.

One of the questions that Wiccans have to answer for themselves is, "What is evil?" Some people don't even believe that true evil exists, that what we see is simply ignorance and misunderstanding, or a failure of social services. I believe evil exists. What do I think it comes from? Estrangement. Evil is what happens when we are driven so far from the Divine, so far from our own inner sanctity and that of the manifest world, that we can look at everything around us without caring if it gets hurt.

This is different from causing harm—sometimes we do that, despite our best intentions. Sometimes an action that causes harm is the only viable choice. It is not the act of killing, for example, that makes you evil; it's how you feel about it, why you did it, and what happens to your soul afterward. Evil considers its own needs so highly that the desires of others mean nothing, and neither do any consequences.

It has been observed that there is no evil in nature. Violence, yes—survival often means bloodshed when you're a carnivore. But the incidences of violence and cruelty simply for their own sake in nature are few and far between, because evil is the only thing in this world that I think is truly unnatural. (Well, that and low-fat ice cream.) Most of the evil we see in our time comes as a consequence of the rift between the spiritual and the physical, depriving ourselves and our world of their deepest value, rendering the universe a soulless place where killing and causing pain are perfectly acceptable.

My opinion is that what is causing the destruction of the environment, the rise in violence, and the general slide of society is not a decline in "family values" or a lack of moral rectitude. It is allowing ourselves to believe that nature is an object and we are its owners. By convincing ourselves, falsely, that the earth is without spirit—and that our bodies are without spirit—we create a reality in which hatred and violence can run rampant, because if people and the earth have no real value, why not do whatever you want to them?

It is only by healing this rift, by drawing it closed, that we can hope to progress as a people and as individuals. The longer we deny the sacredness of nature, and of ourselves, the wider the rift becomes.

Denying the Feminine, Denying the Earth

While the scholarship of the "peaceful matriarchy" theories has come under fire and been mostly discounted by serious historians and archaeologists, you have only to look at the myths of ancient cultures to see that the natural world has long been equated with the feminine.

In Greece, Demeter was lady of the harvest; Aphrodite was goddess of love, and we're not talking airy heart-chakra love, either, but a very physical and passionate love. Even more elemental was the goddess Gaia, the earth herself. Gaia was born out of Chaos, and born with Eros—that pretty much says it all. There is Mokos, one of the most primal of the Slavic deities; the Celtic Danu; the Aztec Xochiquetzal; and Ninhursag, the Sumerian Queen of the Mountain. Even in nonspiritual discourse, you often hear of "Mother Earth" and "Mother Nature," and the sea is most often referred to as female.

As women give birth to the continuation of the human race, the earth gives life to all her children; it stands to reason that early peoples would have made this intuitive connection. Certainly not every culture agreed with the idea, but it was widespread. The fertility of the earth and the fertility of women were considered by many to be intrinsically linked. Now that we know that sperm is actually important to the whole baby-making process, we understand that men are just as vital to our survival, but even in the modern world, the aura of femininity still surrounds the earth in the collective imagination.

You can understand, then, why the environment is in such a sorry state. Society came to fear and even hate the feminine, and that includes the earth—just like women, the natural world was something to subjugate and control, a wild force that needed to be tamed. In Christian mythology, Adam was given dominion over the animals just as he was over Eve, and the earth has suffered for it ever since.

If a woman's body is sacred, that means it cannot be sold. Something holy cannot be treated like a plaything or like trash. If we think of the body as inherently sacred, using it to sell products or carving it up and pumping it full of chemicals becomes sacrilege.

The same holds true for the planet. If we consider the earth as holy, that means we do not have dominion over it—no one does. Sanctity demands respect, and if we have to respect the earth, strip-mining and slash-and-burn agriculture are no longer acceptable.

Moneymakers and politicians don't like that idea. The businesses and advertisers who make money off tearing down the rainforests and convincing women we need wrinkle cream would really prefer we didn't think of nature or ourselves as divine in essence, because if you are an embodiment of the Goddess from cradle to grave, you probably don't need that tummy tuck. You are, in fact, blessed and perfect as you are—and that whole idea pisses a lot of people off.

AD AWARENESS—EXERCISE #1

By playing on our fears and stereotypes, advertisers lure us into all sorts of crazy gimmicks, products, and even medical procedures.

For instance, somewhere out there right now, a woman is about to have her stomach stapled into a tiny pouch so that she literally cannot eat more than a quarter-cup of food at a time. She will be cut open, and then scarred for life; if she eats even a bite too much, she will be violently ill and risk popping said staples and going in for another surgery. Her caloric intake will be forced below starvation level. The minute the staples are removed and her stomach is returned to normal size, assuming there are no complications (which, incidentally, can include liver failure, brain damage, ulcers, hernias, cardiac arrhythmia, infection, anemia, vitamin deficiency, diarrhea, constipation, vomiting, stomach cancer—oh, and death, let's not forget death), if she eats anywhere close to normally, the weight will pile right back on again at a remarkable rate, because of a simple truth of the universe: bodies don't like to starve.

And why is this woman subjecting herself to all this misery for a temporary reprieve from fatness? She doesn't look like Sandra Bullock. She has to shop in the back of the store among the hugely flowered, billowing clothes that hide every possible curve and negate the sensuality of her flesh. She walks through the grocery store surrounded by low-carb, low-fat, low-calorie everything. When she turns on the TV all she sees are little skinny women who are nothing but elbows and knees. If that's all you see, how else are you supposed to feel but inadequate? The people that others want to look at are skinny, so that must be how women are supposed to look. Right?

Down the street a woman is having Botox treatments. Botox is a waste byproduct of botulinum bacteria, the same bacteria that give you botulism—food poisoning. That chemical is a neurotoxin that paralyzes the nerves in the face, causing it to swell and puff out wrinkles and dents. There are actually people in this world willing to shoot up with poison, a poison that occurs in tainted canned food, to *temporarily* look younger.

Not to be crude, but *what the fuck?*

For the next week, pay attention to your surroundings. Keep a log of every advertisement you see that in some way tells you your body is not good enough like it is. Commercials on TV and the radio, pop-up ads on the Internet, billboards—whenever you see any ad for anything, ask yourself:

What does this company want me to buy?

What are they telling me this product will do?

Why do they say I need it?

What about my life will be better, according to this ad, if I buy it?

What kind of people is this ad aimed at?

How is this product any different from the other dozen just like it on the market?

What assumptions does this ad make about gender, age, and ethnicity?

How do I feel when I see this? Is the advertising working on me?

I find myself having these feelings when I see women on the street or in restaurants, who are eight feet tall and weigh 3.5 pounds—it's unhealthy, and I feel guilty for being so angry with them . . . but I have a problem seeing a woman who, in my opinion, is too weak to buck what's popular and be herself, who'd rather starve and destroy her body to look the way someone else tells her to look.

SIREN

Magazines are my personal favorite. On the same cover of a national woman's magazine you might see "Oprah's Weight Struggle," "100 Ways to Cut 100 Calories," and "Our Favorite Chocolate Desserts!" all superimposed over an airbrushed, retouched photo of Cameron Diaz (who is human and deals with mad hair and pimples just like the rest of us) looking like a walking coat hanger.

As you learn to spot propaganda and attempted manipulation, you will stop falling prey to it. Magazine covers will be funny and a sad commentary on society instead of sending you into a spiral of self-doubt. Most importantly, as you work with the other exercises in this book and begin to reclaim your physical sanctity, you will no longer find it useful or necessary to give these people your money or your time. If the power of the dollar can push us into hating ourselves, we can use our own dollars to push back.

Made in God's Image

Big business isn't the only culprit, however, in continuing the war against women's bodies. I do not believe that there is some vast Judeo-Christian conspiracy to destroy sex, joy, and everything fun about the world, but the fact is, much of how we view the body and the soul comes from the religions of our youth.

I grew up Baptist, or more specifically, Southern Baptist with a little Methodist Bible School thrown in for spice. Until I hit my teens, I never questioned the fact that my father could be a deacon or a minister, but my mother was confined to the kitchen committee. Amid the fire and brimstone was a very clear message: women are meant to be subservient.

Returning to the story of Eve, it is through a woman's body that sin and evil entered the world. God is male, and only male—man was made first, in his image. Woman was made out of man. Thus the precedent was set, and in a few short paragraphs the Book of Genesis sets up the hierarchy of Christianity: men are shaped like God, so they are more like God; women were put together out of spare parts, and caused nothing but havoc from day one. When Adam and Eve were disobedient, what happened? Did they go on a garden killing spree or kick God in the shins? No, they saw their naked bodies and they were *ashamed*.

In the Jewish tradition, baby boys are circumcised as a symbol of the Jew's covenant with God. Women, noticeably lacking a penis and therefore a foreskin, cannot take part in this covenant. From birth, we are that much further away from deity than men—all symbolized in a body part that we can never have, and therefore can never sacrifice.

In Western religious traditions, women are pretty much out of luck, even as infants. We are born with a price on our heads—the price of all the evil in humanity, thanks to the first among us who sought knowledge and then wanted to share it.

There is something fundamentally alienating about having to follow a single God who happens to be male. I never truly felt that God could understand me, despite his supposed omniscience—he was disdainful of girls from the days of Eden. Adam had to toil and work the earth to survive when cast out of Paradise; Eve's punishment was pain in childbirth. Pain. God, it seemed, wanted me to hurt for something I didn't do. Because of my biology, there was a separation that I could never cross—I could not be a man, so I could never look like God, or win his favor the way a boy could.

> The established order had a stake in us not reaching the depths of ourselves. Because if we were completely alive and spontaneous, we'd be impossible to control.
>
> GABRIELLE ROTH

Making God male added another stretch of distance to the Great Divide for women. Our spirits were supposed to be separate from our bodies; our bodies were what made us female, and that made us lesser beings.

It's no wonder, then, that as women reclaim their power and make strides toward equality, we would start to question the dominant paradigm, and to seek spiritual inspiration elsewhere. Seeing that we aren't inferior, finding our way toward equality, we look around at the world and wonder, what else have we been denied because of our biology? If women aren't less than men, but that's what we were taught, we have been lied to. What else have we been lied to about?

As long as women were held down, the Goddess was also banished to the realm of fantasy and myth. For a long time it seemed she was dead, but the memory of a woman's soul is long and deep, and it was only a matter of time before the Lady returned.

This makes religious leaders and conservatives understandably nervous, just as the idea of the earth as sacred gets under the skin of corporate leaders. The feminine is rising, and each time a woman finds her spirit and her self-love, the Goddess takes another step up the road from the Underworld.

Casualties of the Body War

Plastic surgery was created to help reconstruct the faces and bodies of people who had suffered horrible wounds, cancer, and burns. The technology is amazing; doctors may not be able to give you back a perfect re-creation of your face, but if your skin was burned off in a car accident, you don't have to go through life wearing a mask on top of everything else you've suffered. This is a beneficial use of medical progress and has given thousands of people a chance to live fuller lives after incredible ordeals.

More often, though, plastic surgery is not used to reconstruct, but to deconstruct. For about five thousand dollars you can have ten years carved off your face; of course, in five years you'll have aged about twenty, but you can always get another nose job, right?

There was a time when such surgery was considered vain, a waste of money, even a sign of mental disorder. Now it is becoming a badge of affluence, a way to show the world you have so much money you can afford to stay young and thin forever. Being able to throw thousands of dollars away on a temporary fix with risky and possibly deadly side effects is not only normal, it is advertised as "no big deal," like getting a pedicure.

I don't know about you, but the last time I had a pedicure I didn't need anesthesia or pain medication, nor did I have swelling and possible embolisms and infection afterward. Slowly we are being encouraged to forget the "surgery" part of it—having your face cut open and rearranged is *not* a relaxing afternoon at the spa.

Women are heard to say of each other, "She's had work done," as if our bodies are old houses in need of renovation, surrounded by scaffolding with boards over the windows.

What is truly sad to me is that the beauty industry and the weight-loss gurus are promoting homogenization of American bodies; we are all pushed to look pretty much alike—the same size, with the same style, and the same vacant expression.

One of the fastest growing groups of plastic surgery patients are Asian women, who go under the knife *to have their eyes rounded* so they will look more white. African-American women are having their noses and butts reduced, throwing a whitewash over their striking natural beauty. The mere thought makes me want to move to Samoa.

Samoans are fat, by the way. Obese by American standards. Samoans, however, have no stigma placed upon being big, and for some odd reason their incidence of heart disease, high cholesterol, and other "weight-related illnesses" is much lower than ours despite their larger girth . . .

or, at least, it was, until American fast food and attitudes began to cross the ocean to the island countries. Could it be, perhaps, that it isn't so much being fat that kills you as hating yourself for being fat?

Or perhaps it's a combination of that self-hatred and the pace of our lives, ignoring our inner need for rest and silence while we strive, strive, *strive* toward . . . what, exactly? Money. We work our whole lives for money so we can buy the next pill or protein shake, or finance our new breasts.

Building a Bridge

Now that you're good and angry at society for transforming our gender from Goddess to starving supermodel, you may also be incredibly frustrated and wondering, "Well, what can I do about it?"

Knowing the problem is only part of the battle. Watching television for ten minutes, knowing what you know, can be enough to have you on your feet, sword drawn, ready to dismember the patriarchal consumerist machine. Lopping off a few selected organs might be satisfying at the time, but it would be more helpful to opt for what I call the Scorpio approach—sabotage the system from within rather than attacking it from the front.

There are a number of strategies we can utilize to help us, including:

1. Stop body disparagement.
2. Stop blaming men for all of this.
3. Live your life fully, no matter what you look like.
4. Work spiritually and magically to heal your own body/spirit rift.
5. Bring the Goddess and her grace into every aspect of your life.

Stop Body Disparagement

Declare your home, your office, and your life a Body Hatred-Free Zone. Try to clear your environment of negative messages and propaganda. When you see a commercial that is designed to prey on your self-doubt, change the channel. Don't buy fashion magazines. Refuse to allow the outside world to tell you how to think. This will benefit you in far more ways than one.

When a friend or family member starts ragging on herself for being fat or short or having small breasts, speak up. Tell her that you don't want to hear her slander someone you care about, and that if she insists on indulging in such vicious lies, you don't want to talk anymore.

If you catch a young woman or child talking about her body negatively, correct her. We take in these messages at a very young age, and they stick—teach your children and all those you know that bodies come in all shapes, sizes, colors, and textures, and that they are all beautiful.

I've had to deal with a lot of "helpful advice" from total strangers about my body. It's not okay for someone to walk up to a black man in the grocery store and say, "You shouldn't buy that, honey, black people only eat watermelon and fried chicken," but it's perfectly okay for some reason for someone who doesn't know me to suggest I look at the other end of the aisle for the low-fat cookies instead of buying DoubleStuf Oreos.

Out-and-out insults are pretty common for fat girls, too—it's uncouth to make racial jokes or jokes about disabilities, but fat is fair game to comedians, sitcoms, and anyone who feels insecure enough to mock others. There are two ways to combat this: either ignore it, or fight back.

Ignoring it is probably the high road, but there's something very satisfying about having a snappy comeback.

The following is a true story. The names have been changed to protect the moronic. I must preface it by saying that the day this happened, I was having a fat day.

All American women have them—those days where you wake up, toss the blankets aside, and the first thought in your head is, "I'm so fat." Similar thoughts plague you all day, and even the one outfit that you know looks sexy as hell on you is suddenly dowdy, sofa-like. You want to hit people with a nailed bat, and you want to disappear. But most of all you want to be thin; you want it so badly you actually start looking at websites on stomach banding and wonder if you can get a tapeworm on eBay.

Skinny women have fat days, too; in fact, so do a lot of men. But generally the world doesn't help reinforce them quite as handily as it does for fat girls.

Case in point, say you're having a fat day, and for some reason you find yourself at the mall. You want an ice cream cone. You know you'll feel guilty for eating it, having just added another ladleful to the great tub of gelatinous goo you think you are that day, but since nobody's ever going to love you anyway, why the hell not? (No, this is not exaggeration. These thoughts routinely pass through your average fat girl's mind, along with ways to commit suicide that wouldn't involve anyone having to hoist your body onto a gurney and say to the other paramedics, "We got us a big 'un here!")

So you get your ice cream, you sit down, you enjoy the hell out of the first half of it. Then you notice that you're surrounded by skinny white people, and you remember that since they put in a Nordstrom's, this mall has gone to yuppie hell in an Eddie Bauer handbasket. Then you notice people looking at you. Now, given that you spend a lot of your free time surrounded by Pagan men, that's not so unusual—I've had offers of cash at drum circles for a chance to watch me eat a lollipop. But you know immediately by the feel of the look that it's not the same thing, and when you look up you see a bona fide skinny bitch and her bona fide skinny boyfriend across the way. She's picking list-lessly at a salad with dressing on the side, he's having a cheeseburger and fries. (Double standard? What double standard?) She's staring at you with an expression of utter disgust, which continues as you stand up to leave—her cold little eyes sweep you from head to toe, and she curls her lip as if to say, "Thank god I don't look like that."

Suddenly you're thinking back to junior high, when you would walk down the sidewalk and the boys would make vaguely seal-like noises and call you "Shamu." So you're gathering your purse and throwing away your napkin, and she and her boyfriend get up to leave, too. She's still giving you the look, and he seems to notice her atten-tion is on something besides him; he follows her gaze, looks you over, and turns back to the skinny bitch, *laughing*.

This, friends, was my lunch hour on the day this story took place.

You can imagine what a fine mood I was in upon returning to the office from my shopping excursion to find that it was the boss's birth-day, and there was cake. Jennifer, always so attentive, came around to ask if I was going to have any.

"No," I said, my attention still on the stack of reports in my inbox. "Not this time."

"Oh?" she asked. "Are you on low carbs?"

I stared at her a second before the current slang of weight-obsessed America translated. "No."

"Which one are you on?"

"Which one what?"

"Diet. Which diet?"

I gave her the Long Blink and reminded myself that the Goddess loves stupid people, too. "I'm not on a diet, Jennifer."

"Oh? Why aren't you on a diet?"

Obviously if a big girl like me doesn't want cake, it must be because I'm dieting, right? Fat people do nothing but eat, right? But rather than beat her to death with Rupert, the stuffed frog who sat on my monitor,

I just looked at her and said, "My lovers don't want me to lose any weight."

Now she blinked. "How many you got?"

I smiled. "Six."

"Really?" She didn't look like she believed me. "Are they all guys?"

The wickedness began to kick in, in earnest. "Of course not. How boring would that be?"

"Really?" Her voice got higher and higher pitched throughout the conversation. "How'd you get so many?" The emphasis was on "you."

I didn't bat an eye. "I'm double-jointed, I can pick up rolls of quarters with my toes, and I can swallow a banana whole."

"Really?"

"Yep. I've got mad skills."

> Two or three things I know for sure, and one is that I would rather go naked than wear the coat the world has made for me.
> DOROTHY ALLISON

She never looked at me quite the same way again, but Brian in HR started sitting by me at lunch.

The point to this story was that we don't have to sit back and take it when others try to force their stereotypes and stigmas on us. To change the way people think about whatever subculture or minority you might belong to, be fully and unapologetically yourself. Refuse to live someone else's lie.

WORKING FOR WORLD COMPASSION—A SPELL

Buddhists are well-known for praying for peace and love for the whole world. I haven't seen a lot of Wiccans follow the practice. We want good things for the human race, or most of us do, but we take that "regime change begins at home" thing and run with it.

That's certainly not a bad idea. As Gandhi said, "Be the change you want to see in the world." By living our best possible lives, we set an example, and if one other person sees us loving our bodies and celebrating nature, and chooses to do the same, we have made the world a better place just by being ourselves.

Sometimes it does help to think more broadly. To manifest the Goddess in our lives, we have to learn to love all that lives and hold the earth in our minds and hearts in infinite compassion. We may never be able to achieve this absolutely, but it is an admirable goal to work toward.

For this spell, find a seven-day glass votive; it can be whatever color you like. Decorate the outside with pictures of people of all colors, shapes, and sizes, or of the planet itself; you might also spend time cutting words and headlines out of newspapers that reflect the change you want to see, things like "peace," "truth," or "Fat Woman Kills and Eats Aerobics Instructor."

Okay, maybe not that last one. But consecrate this candle to be an ongoing prayer for the world, that all eyes may be opened to the beauty all around us, the beauty in ourselves and each other, and the need to bring the love of deity into every moment of every day. Burn the candle for a few minutes each day, or even once a week, visualizing the Lady holding the earth in her arms, rocking it as her child.

You might chant as you call this image to mind, or recite a prayer like the following, which is a more-or-less Wiccanized version of the Prayer of St. Francis, a personal favorite of mine:

> Lord and Lady, let me be your instrument,
> Let my hands be your hands, lifted in compassion;
> May the Web of Life be woven strand by strand with grace;
> Where there is hatred, may we sow love;
> Where there is intolerance, understanding;
> Where there is violence, peace;
> And where there is sorrow, joy;
> Father and Mother of all things, may our eyes be open;
> May our hearts be open;
> May we see the truth of our holiness;
> May we feel the holiness in each other.
> So mote it be.

Let energy flow out through your heart and bathe the image of the earth in your mind, resonating along the connections that run between and among every human being, leaving the light of acceptance and kindness in its wake.

Keeping all of this in mind, there are times when "May you find peace" doesn't really cut it in the daily struggle against body disparagement. Working for understanding in the whole world is a process that will most likely take years, as the roots of a tree work their way slowly through concrete. When presented with a situation where some fool calls you "Miss Piggy" and oinks at you as you walk past, a different reaction might be called for.

One of the best ways to combat other people's hateful comments is to make them feel stupid—people hate feeling stupid above most other things. Give them disdain, even pity, over their narrow-minded ignorance—my favorite is to laugh out loud, and if I get angry enough, tell them loud enough for everyone to hear, "Sorry about your penis."

Maybe that's not the compassionate, Mother Goddess way to handle the situation, but the Mother knows when to step back and let the Warrior take the wheel. Returning hate for hate is not the answer, but neither is bursting into tears or worse, falling silent, pretending that you aren't offended by people's words.

People will continue to disparage women for their appearance until we stop taking it. We can refuse to remain victims of harassment and violence; we can also refuse to bow before the blatant stupidity of others. As we cast our spells and our prayers for the human race to evolve past its collective adolescence, we must not let ourselves become victims of our own pacifism, smiling blithely at the squirrels while we and those we love become casualties of the body war.

There is, however, one very important thing to remember, one thing we all need to do:

Stop Blaming Men for All of This

None of the men you know created patriarchy. This is a fact. None of the men you know, even the jerks, are responsible for our culture. They may reinforce it, they may benefit from it, but hating all men for the way things are is counterproductive and misplaced energy. It's very easy to create a scapegoat out of the whole male gender, but in the end, it doesn't do us any good—and besides, it's unfair.

Men have body-image issues, too. How many men do you know who are buff, with six-pack abs and perfect hair? How many do you see on television? Bit of a discrepancy there, just like for us.

Granted, there are plenty of men who buy into the beauty myth for women, and belittle and berate their mates for not upholding the standard of models and actresses. A sister Witch of mine was not long ago engaged in conversation with a guy who routinely makes comments about fat women and diligently eggs on his girlfriend's obsession with her appearance. He told my friend that she should consider liposuction for her "saddlebags."

My friend is an attractive, vegetarian, goth-lite Witch with striking brown eyes, facial piercings, and a decided lack of patience with that sort of sexist nonsense. Her response was, appropriately, "Fuck you."

For every man like that, though, there are at least a half dozen who want their female friends and lovers to feel good about themselves, if for no other reason than because hearing women constantly talk about dieting is boring and tedious. It's important for us to remember that we aren't alone in our struggle, and that the prevailing attitude of our culture doesn't necessarily apply to individuals.

I didn't write this book for men, but I have seen a lot of the same problems in our brothers; the messages aren't as blatant, but there's a very definite idea of what a "real man" is like in America, and that idea is just as ridiculous and contradictory as the idea of a "real woman."

A "real man" doesn't cry, but a man in the new millennium is sensitive. A "real man" has lots of muscles and spends half his life in the gym, but isn't vain. Machismo is frowned on by most women, but a "sissy" is just as stigmatized as he always was. Men are supposed to be gourmet cooks, body builders, porn stars, poets, superheroes, and breadwinners all at once.

Compare the average comic book hero's body with that of the guys you see on the street. Not a lot of tights out there (more's the pity). There also aren't a lot of men who are truly comfortable with their sexuality and masculinity, just as there aren't many women who live their womanhood. Every time you see some beer-bellied politician spouting homophobic and sexist rhetoric, remember that beneath that hatefulness is more hate—deep-seated self-hate, and so much fear that the bodies and lives of others become something to dominate.

It's a terrible thing to live in fear, and a great many men do just that in this age. A lot of men are raised in a strange terror of losing their manhood, so that everything that isn't just like them becomes a threat—as if every gay man or liberated woman is secretly hiding in the closet with hedge clippers, waiting to castrate them. The drive to prove oneself, to be a "real man," whatever the hell that is, dogs their steps as much as the narrow definition of feminine beauty dogs women.

This is a hard time for men too; as women are discovering their power and trying to catch hold of it to find equal footing, men are having to relinquish a long-held position at the top of the mountain, or at least move over. Patriarchy went on for hundreds of years. No attitude that deeply rooted in a society can just be shrugged off without effort. Both genders and all sexualities are experiencing growing pains.

Most of the men you know are doing the best they can. The ones who like the old way and won't support your efforts to love yourself are not worth your time. That goes for everyone in your life—anyone that wants you to keep hating your body and denying your worth as a woman of the Goddess is best left to the shallow, vapid "real women" and "real men" they deserve.

Oppression is a two-way street. In this day and age, male dominance isn't so much supported by violence, so what's stopping us from climbing the ladder? Habit, fear, and self-hatred. We buy into the lie that we aren't worthy, and our own delusions of inferiority keep us down. If we keep showing men we don't believe in or respect ourselves, then why should they try any harder than we do?

I've had a number of experiences that might have led me to cast blanket hatred on the whole male gender, but I am fortunate to have some amazing, intelligent, kind, and caring men in my life who continually show me that our God is a loving God, and so are his sons.

Men are not my enemy. Women are not my enemy. Be careful not to slay your allies in your bloodlust for change.

Live Your Life Fully No Matter What You Look Like

They say living well is the best revenge. If you want people to realize that you don't have to look perfect to have a joyful life, you have to show them it's possible. Live like you mean it.

There may be false beliefs holding you back from experiencing life fully. Perhaps you think you can't vacation at the beach until you lose twenty pounds. Perhaps you think you're too old to go for that promotion. Perhaps you think Asian women can't be astronauts—the list goes on and on. The years go by and you don't become a size six; you don't get any younger, or become any whiter. Think of all the time you waste by waiting for the impossible, when the world is full of the possible.

DWELL IN THE POSSIBLE—EXERCISE #2

Make a list of all the things you're putting off until you've achieved a perfect body, or things you think you can't do because of how you look.

Now imagine that you found out there was no way you could ever lose another pound, that plastic surgery suddenly vanished, that everyone in the world would spend the rest of their lives exactly as they look at this moment. Would you still put off taking that trip?

Most Wiccans believe in some form of reincarnation, but we also believe that part of our mission in life is to find our bliss and follow it. Life is a precious and delicate gift. How much of that gift do we squander out of fear?

> I think as Pagans, representing those beliefs to the world, we are called upon to embody our bodies, and to let our bodies embody us . . . if we say that the spirit and the flesh are one, then we need to honor our flesh. If we say our spirituality is Earth-based, we need to honor the vehicle in which we walk the Earth. We need to treat our bodies with respect and sanity.
>
> RAENE

Work to Heal Your Own Rift, and Bring Deity into Your Life

Most of this book is dedicated to this cause. Our lives are a microcosm of the larger life of our people; if we are meant to help and heal others, we have to help ourselves first, or we cut off our own hands and work blind. How can you claim to embody the Goddess on Earth, as one of her perfect children, and still hate yourself? You love the Lady and you are of her essence; therefore, you love yourself—if you remember to.

I'll hammer this point home as many times as it takes: your body is holy. Your life is holy. You are worth kingdoms. There is meaning and purpose to your life, and in order to fulfill that purpose you have to accept and love what you have been given to work with, the little animal your soul inhabits for this walk around the earth.

OBSERVATIONS AND ROLE MODELS—EXERCISE #3

Think of five women you know who hate their bodies. This is probably pretty easy. When you look at them, how do you feel about them?

Chances are, they look just fine to you. I know one woman who is absolutely beautiful, but has been battling the same ten pounds her whole postadolescent life, and she can tell how her whole day is going to go based on the number on the scale. I envied her for her beauty until I realized she didn't appreciate it. No matter how many people tell her she's beautiful, no matter how many surgeries she has or how many miles she jogs, unless she can love those ten pounds along with the other hundred, nothing she does will ever make her happy. I would rather be ugly and fat and love myself than be gorgeous and want to hack off my own thighs.

Unfortunately, that opinion is not very widespread.

Now think of five women you know who seem to have no body image issues whatsoever. (This will probably take a lot longer.) Think of women you have seen, whether celebrities or those in your immediate realm, who walk with their heads high and hips swaying, and who seem to have no fear or doubt. Are they any more attractive by popular standards than the first five on the list? Probably not. In fact, I've noticed a strange trend in that "pretty" women can have the worst body images, perhaps because "unpretty" women have to learn to approach self-love from a different angle than directly into the mirror.

Now picture each of these ten women clearly in your mind and name each of them "Goddess." When you see them, name them "Goddess."

Lastly, try to find pictures of women to be your new role models. Look for those who have survived the body war or simply never engaged in it. Keep their pictures where you will see them often. They may be relatives, friends, authors, singers, actresses—it doesn't matter who they are, whether they're fat or skinny or considered attractive by popular culture, or if you know them personally; it doesn't even matter if they are real. What matters is that they embody the feeling you are trying to cultivate in yourself, and that they radiate the positive energy and confidence you seek. We cannot look outside ourselves to find true acceptance, but we can learn from those who have walked the path before us.

My personal list includes women like Margaret Cho, Melissa Etheridge, Sinéad O'Connor, Katharine Hepburn, author Inga Muscio, Yasmine Galenorn, Queen Latifah, the goddess Artemis, and even fictional characters like Trinity from *The Matrix*, Mirya from the novel *Strands of Starlight*, and Aunt Frances (Stockard Channing's role) from *Practical Magic*. Nobody ever has to know that you want to be Stevie Nicks when you grow up, or that you ask yourself, "What would Joan Jett do?" Your pantheon of inspiring women is your own.

Recommended Reading and Resources for Chapter One

BOOKS

The Invisible Woman: Confronting Weight Prejudice in America by W. Charisse Goodman

Body Outlaws: Young Women Write About Body Image and Identity by Ophira Edut

Body Wars by Margo Maine

Wake Up, I'm Fat! By Camryn Manheim

The Mass-Market Woman: Defining Yourself as a Person in a World that Defines You By Your Appearance by Linda McBryde

No Fat Chicks: How Big Business Profits from Making Women Hate Their Bodies and What You Can Do About It by Terry Poulton

Take it Personally: How to Make Conscious Changes to Change the World by Anita Roddick

God Images and Self-Esteem by Carroll Saussy

The Beauty Myth by Naomi Wolf

DVD/OTHER RESOURCES

I'm the One that I Want and *Notorious C.H.O.* by Margaret Cho

The Truth About Cats and Dogs (movie)

t w o

RETURN

to the altar

We'll begin with a journey:

THE CLOAK—A MEDITATION

We are, each of us, priests and priestesses of the gods. We carry within us a spark of divine wisdom and strength that reaches back through the ages, connecting us to everyone who has ever stood beneath the moon and felt her magic. At heart we are all powerful, beautiful, and capable of changing the world with our bare hands. We, and all creation, are divine love and nurture made manifest.

Sometimes, though, we forget who we are and all that it means. Sometimes the world of dollar signs and willful ignorance batters us from all sides like a storm at sea, and we slowly wear down until we lose touch with our power. Sometimes we need to be reminded.

Think of a time when you felt truly strong, when you knew you were able to face whatever came your way. Think of a moment, however brief, when you could say with surety, "This is who I am." Think of a day when everything seemed perfect, when your thoughts and your words and your actions were aligned, and you felt your essential unity with all that is. If you have never experienced these things, think then of how it might feel in your body and in your heart to be completely yourself and proud of it, to say, "Thou art Goddess," and mean every word.

(pause)

Now imagine that power and strength are gathering in your hands. This energy begins to weave itself into a kind of shimmering cloth. Each thread is a moment in your life, in the past or yet to come, in which you act upon your true will and with your true heart. It shapes itself in your hands into a hooded cloak.

Take a moment to hold the cloak up before your mind's eye. What does it look like? Is it heavy? What is the texture, scent, and color of your power? Get to know this sacred garment, this part of you that is awake and aware and ready for anything.

(pause)

When you are ready, wrap the cloak around your shoulders. Rather than sitting on top of your clothes, the fabric dissolves into your skin, soaking in, infusing every cell of your body with the energy and strength you have held in your hands. This cloak has always been a part of you, but now you can feel and see it. It is the mantle of the God, the wings of the Goddess, and you are its chosen wearer.

If you look closely you can see the energy shimmering on your skin, a soft radiance like that of the moon. Know that this light is your own, that you brought it forth from the shining spirit within you. The confidence and assurance it inspires in you brings your real, unhidden self out of the shadows and into your body.

Do you feel like a priestess, a warrior, a king? What person does the cloak allow you to show the world? This person, who may yet be a familiar stranger, is the core of your being. Take a moment to etch this feeling on your memory so that, from this moment, you will always recognize yourself.

(pause)

When you are ready, come back to the waking world, still wearing the cloak of your power. You need never take it off, but you can put it back on any time it slips from your shoulders. Any time you feel the cold wind of self-doubt and uncertainty, you can call it forth, and it will warm you in the nurturing folds of your own divine self.

Before we go deep into our exploration of the eight archetypes of the body sacred, we should look at the Goddess herself, how we find her, and what she means to us as women and as Wiccans. Understanding the shift in thinking from the old, patriarchal way to the way of the Lord and Lady is essential in understanding both why we have lost our holistic view of the universe and how we can begin to draw body and spirit back into each other's arms.

As I mentioned in the Introduction, at this moment in time only a very small percentage of those who self-identify as Wiccan were raised in any sort of Pagan religion. That means that the vast majority of us converted from other faiths, usually one of the larger mainstream ones, and as a result we have a wide variety of conditioning to unload before we can truly appreciate our new path. Many of us come stumbling into the sanctuary of Wicca scarred, lost, and angry.

It seems from my observation that there are two basic ways that non-family-tradition Wiccans come to the path. In the first, the convert (I hate that word thanks to my own baggage, but it still fits) has never had any particularly negative experiences with the religion of her birth, but was never entirely satisfied either; perhaps quiet disagreements

with church dogma or the conservative mindset of many congrega-
tions gradually drove a wedge between her and the religion.

The second way many come to the path is through spiritual malaise,
one of the many consequences I mentioned of the Great Divide between body and spirit, between earth and the gods. That malaise is
often the breeding ground for conversion, and can lead to overwhelmingly positive experiences (like the ones many people have had with
Wicca), horrible experiences (cults and mind-control groups), or simply
years of aimless wandering and agnosticism. Malaise can unfortunately
become despair after a while, and then morph into a kind of resigna-
tion: "Well, God obviously doesn't give a damn about me, so to hell—
or wherever—with God."

Occasionally, a life-changing experience will draw the person back
into her original faith before she leaves it completely, which often results in the person becoming a vital and devoted member of that religious community. As much as a dark little part of me likes the idea of a
world full of Wiccans, often when people start exploring Wicca they
are simply looking for something different, and haven't really given
their previous faiths a chance. Often when young people start asking
me questions, rather than handing them a book by Scott Cunningham
and saying, "Go to town," I have to ask if they have considered other denominations or organizations within the religions they already know.
Sometimes Wicca is the destination, sometimes it is a stepping stone
toward something else.

(I can't really imagine a world of nothing but Wiccans anyway—
just think of how insane the phonebook would be, with 100,000 en-
tries under "Raven.")

The first method of conversion is a lot less angst-ridden than the second, although the overwhelming joy and relief of "coming home" is
usually pretty amazing to new Wiccans, who have at heart always believed as we do, and were simply looking for others who felt the same
way.

Then there are people like me, who have a more emotionally charged story to tell. I came to Wicca after a period of anger and disillusionment that nearly left me an atheist. For years after I started studying the Craft, I was still very bitter toward Christianity and was one of the many Pagans who indulged in Christian-bashing that today I am rather ashamed of. Nowadays I find that kind of behavior an embarrassment to the community—but at the same time, I totally understand it.

It's human nature to want to distance ourselves from the parts of our lives that we have shed. I liken it to getting a divorce. The process is painful and full of negative emotion; immediately afterward, both parties involved will probably spend a while not speaking, or even actively hating each other. Eventually, with time and healing, there is more of a possibility of friendship, or at least tolerance in public.

The same thing happened to me. I went from outright rage at anyone who was dumb enough to call themselves Christian, to an uneasy truce, to the eventual realization that I have no quarrel whatsoever with real Christians, only those who pervert the message of Christ for their own purposes. I have the good fortune of knowing a number of people who I consider true followers of Christ, and they have allowed me to see that there are angels and assholes in every faith, including my own.

What, you may wonder, does the process of conversion have to do with the body?

It gives us insight into the mindset of people who have come to Wicca from paths that have as part of their doctrine the concept of the Great Divide. We run hard and fast from a worldview that would have us believe our bodies are dirty and sinful—or, at best, simply dust, with no inherent sanctity of their own. Then we find ourselves facing something so radically different that it can take years to fully accept the deeper aspects of Wiccan spirituality.

It's easy to say, "Oh, sure, I'm the Goddess, you're the Goddess, it's all good, the earth is holy, blah blah love and pleasure blah," without really understanding or integrating any of it into our self-concept. A lot of Wiccans run on autopilot for the first few years before it becomes real to us.

Often people describe a "calling," feeling like they were being led away from their old ways, and a series of coincidences and meaningful encounters leads them here. Personally, I feel that this calling comes from the part of us that has refused to accept the Divide, that will not allow spirit and form to be torn asunder; the calling is the voice of the Goddess, but it is also our own authentic spirits crying out not to be stolen from the arms of the manifest world.

Wicca and the Divide

How does Wicca deal with the Great Divide?

By not having one.

Goddess, God, the Universe, and Everything

Yes, that was an oversimplification, but basically it is the truth. In Wicca, we do not view the physical and the spiritual as diametric opposites locked in eternal struggle. The body is not the enemy of the spirit, nor vice versa.

How do we arrive at this conclusion? It comes directly from our view of deity, which is in essence a world apart from what most of us were brought up with. Most of us were raised in traditions in which deity was strictly male, and almost entirely transcendent; God lived somewhere out there, or up there, and our goal was to leave the earth and get to where he was.

Some denominations believe the path to Heaven lies through good works. Others believe it is through God's intermediary and divine child, Jesus. At the heart, though, it is understood that there is a distance to be crossed between the earthly and the heavenly.

This is not true of all Christian, Jewish, or Muslim traditions, but it is a widespread belief, and it has had a lot of influence over how modern Westerners view the world. While some sects take a more mystical approach and describe God as "everywhere," for the most part we learn that he's elsewhere, and that our prayers have to travel a long, long way to be heard.

On one hand, a transcendent God makes a lot of logical sense, as does monotheism; if there are hundreds of gods, where did they come from? Wasn't there something bigger that made them? And what existed before the universe? If there is a great limitless something behind it all, why would you want to worship anything lesser? And how can God create the world if he's part of it? How could he create himself? Transcendent monotheism answers all of these questions, as it is essentially giving a name to the original cause of creation.

On the other hand, it is possible to put a face on deity and not limit it, just as it is possible to believe that the Goddess is real and approachable but also beyond total understanding. Wiccans in particular have found a certain compromise between transcendence and immanence, between the God "out there" and the God "right here." The theological term for this belief is *panentheism*; it's a fairly new word in spiritual circles, but is perfectly in keeping with what many Wiccans believe.

Deity, to us, is both in here and beyond; it is the manifest world, but also everything else. We understand that in its purest essence, deity is not something that can be apprehended by the tiny human mind. It's huge, genderless, and pervades everything that exists and doesn't exist.

At the same time, however, our reverence for the natural world leads us to create faces of deity that tie that nameless and genderless

> One time a friend tried to convince me that God put the earth at our disposal, for our own use, and that someday we would leave this infernal place and go to heaven. I never believed God would exploit the natural world like that. It broke my heart to think I would have to leave this beautiful planet. And as for heaven, the whole "streets made of gold" never appealed to me. Heaven, as Christians described it, sounded so glaringly shiny and cold to the touch. Heaven, to me, was the woods.
>
> AISLIN

force to the reality we know. We feel the awesome power of the Divine in the sunset, and so that we will not forget that feeling, we give it a name: *Goddess*. The many thousands of deities can be seen as how we come to understand our *relationship* with deity, more than describing deity itself. Deity is everything; humans, despite what some of us may think, are not everything. To come as close as possible within the limits of body and spirit, we find symbols to connect us to the greater; the greater, in turn, enters into those symbols, and makes them as real as we allow them to be.

That may not make a lick of sense to you. It's certainly not the only way of looking at Wiccan theology; there are Pagan polytheists and duotheists and all incarnations thereof, and each of us approaches the Divine in her own unique way. What I experience as a Mother, you might experience as a Sister; my Star-Eyed Weaver might be your Demeter. Saying, "All Wiccans believe . . ." would not only be presumptuous in a faith that has little dogma, it would be utterly false—about the only thing that all Wiccans believe is that deity has both feminine and masculine aspects, and even there you find as many approaches as there are Witches. In fact, the wild variety of viewpoints is one of the things that makes Wicca such an appealing religion, as there isn't one right way; we have a lot of room to explore spirituality on our own terms.

As I am not a theologian, I cannot offer you sound evidence or scholarship to back up my ideas—thank the gods for that! Then you might think I was right. You might try to believe the way I do, instead of coming to your own understanding, and that's the last thing either of us needs. Think I'm a fool if you like; then go figure it out for yourself.

At any rate, I feel that the essence of the greater force is a loving one, and that the universe is a nurturing place; deity wants to connect with us as much as we do with it, as a mother seeks out her child. Many people would disagree vehemently with me and argue for an indifferent universe; their loss, I suppose. If I chose to believe in an uncaring universe, I would not have become Wiccan in the first place.

Panentheism is the belief that deity exists both within the world and outside of it at the same time. It takes the logic of transcendence and the comfort of immanence and stirs them together in the cauldron of spiritual synthesis. Maybe my own take on it isn't theologically sound, but religion does not, nor has it ever, made much sense. It doesn't have to, because it doesn't speak to the part of us that needs facts and figures. It speaks to the preverbal, prelogical part of the self that wants pretty pictures and poetry. How you create your pretty pictures and poetry, then, is your religion. If you're lucky, there are other people who use the same box of crayons as you.

The Goddess and God are everything—everything we see, and everything we never can. Wiccans, for the most part, choose to honor the two aspects of deity this way, because we see the importance of the interplay of opposites and the role of erotic energy in creation. The forces of attraction and repulsion, from electrons and protons all the way out to moons and planets, are what drives the universe. We see those equal and opposite forces as Lord and Lady, whose eternal dance turns the Wheel of Life. Others see it quite differently; no way is necessarily better, but our way has proven it works for us.

A God Who Looks Like Us

There is something very comforting, and very alluring, about the idea of the Goddess, even to those who never come to experience her. The thought of the earth as a mother, opening her arms to take us in rather than thundering down at us from above, fires the imagination and sparks a deep longing in the heart.

Women especially find her to be the answer to years of unheard prayers. The minute you open up the possibility that God might be Goddess as well, suddenly the female body is no longer a curse upon man; we no longer feel second best, like God's leftovers. Seeing the Lady as equal to the Lord, we can throw away the false hierarchy in human society that places the feminine far below the masculine in value.

The world as we know it has tried for many decades to push aside the feminine part of the self: the illogical, intuitive, compassionate side, which dreams and feels and listens to the song of the moon. We are taught that ambition, action, and courage are paramount; it's all about "keeping your eyes on the prize," "going for the gold." We are told that logic is better than emotion, that our feelings don't make sense and are therefore invalid. When girls feel and sense things that other people don't, they are informed quite loudly that they are just imagining things, that seeing is believing, and that intuition, hunches, and the wisdom of the body don't matter. "Prove it," they say, but we don't know how. How can "It feels right" stand up to intellectual dissection?

Is it any wonder, then, that we have so much trouble with our bodies as we grow? The messages and rhythms we are born with could be encouraged and our intuition trained to be an amazing positive force in the world, but from day one, we are told that those parts of ourselves—the very traits that distinguish the feminine—are meaningless. When we are emotional they say it must be "that time of the month," and we are then dismissed as slaves to our hormones. When we take time to dream, we are called lazy and selfish.

Each person has within her- or himself both feminine and masculine aspects, as we are all children of both the Goddess and the God. To truly become whole and to evolve spiritually, we must find a balance between sun and moon.

Our culture emphasizes the Hunter traits over the Gatherer, but that doesn't mean that the opposite should be our goal. Without the intellect and instigating power of the masculine, we'd sit around daydreaming and talking to our ovaries and never get anything done. The feminine creates an image or idea, but the masculine is responsible for getting us off our butts to act. Both are absolutely vital.

We have tried to bury the moon, which leaves us in a state where we run, and run, and run, but get nowhere; we strive after money and success, but are essentially empty, because the heart isn't there. If we were to hide the face of the sun, though, we would spend so much time empathizing with the sorrows of the world that those sorrows would never be healed.

As children and priestesses of the Lord and Lady, we must work in our lives to bring both parts of ourselves into harmony. Bringing together spirit and body is an important first step.

Looking on the altar and seeing a goddess brings the feminine spirit rushing back into our bodies and hearts. Knowing that the feminine is as holy as the masculine, that we are as blessed as men in the eyes of deity, is like taking a step back from the cliff and suddenly realizing how close we were to falling.

When I feel the presence of the Lady in circle, I wonder how I ever lived without her.

> My Mother brought me forth, and I am She.
> GAEL BAUDINO

The Goddess is Creatrix, yes, but in my own life she is so much more than that; she has become, to me, the All-Mother, Lady of Darkness and Light, Queen, and Divine Friend. She offers shelter, solace, and peace, as well as strength, courage, and the power to transform worlds. I see her in the women in my circle; I hear her laughing in the wind; I feel her kiss in the spray of the sea. My life without the Goddess was a walking shadow.

That relationship has also revolutionized my connection with the Lord—now that I don't feel like the bastard stepchild of God, we can relate to each other on a different level, one in which I don't feel that God thinks I'm less than a man. When the eyes of deity light upon you as lovingly as on any of his other children, you can finally begin to repair the centuries of patriarchal dogma that have brought our relationship with the Lord to such a sorry state.

I hear a lot about the "fear of God," and wonder why anyone would worship something they feared; the only reason I can think of would be to appease him so he wouldn't screw you over.

I choose otherwise. I choose to revere a Lady and Lord who do not demand my humiliation or terror as a sacrifice to their almighty power. I don't have to throw myself at their feet and beg forgiveness or worthiness; I am expected to find it, and them, in myself.

REVERIE—EXERCISE #1

Think back to a time before you knew there was a Goddess. How has your life changed since then? What has that knowledge given you? If you are truly living the Wiccan path, deity infuses every moment of every day—how have you changed, from the root of your being to your daily life, because of your path?

If you haven't changed at all, well, you're not doing it right.

No one can come to a new spiritual path without becoming someone new. As I said, converting to Wicca shows us a whole new way of looking at the world, in which the Divine is a part of every molecule both inside us and outside. We can no longer walk the world blindly, knowing that the earth is sacred. We lighten our steps.

Knowing that everyone is a face of the Goddess, we make different choices in our interactions with others. Understanding that the universe is made up of cause and effect, and that our actions come back to us one way or another, we find new ways of living in a world that seems to say the ends always justify the means.

A great many people who find Wicca say that it's what they've always believed, they just didn't know there were other people who believed it, too; even so, realizing that there is a whole system of philosophy (or rather, many philosophies that all seem to get along pretty well most of the time), symbolism, and ritual that is a reflection of already-held ideals can be a bit overwhelming. Lucky for us, most of the time that overwhelm is tempered with a heady, breathless joy that carries us through the transition from old ways to new.

Even those who, like me, were genuinely surprised to learn there were other religions out there besides the big three, find a path like Wicca and suddenly feel like the world makes sense when it didn't before. There was always something wrong with what I heard in church on Sundays . . . no, not that the Baptists were wrong, so much as that I was wrong—in the wrong place, a bewildered outsider. There was truth in much of what I was taught, but it was costumed in so much political drag that it was hardly uplifting, and often left me feeling like everything I did was shameful in the eyes of God, no matter how hard I tried to be a good person.

I know now that those years of doubt and boredom were the breeding ground for something new; in a deep, hidden corner of my spirit, forced into the dark by centuries of oppression and denial, the Goddess was fighting her way across the endless distance to take her child's hand. It took a long time for me to name what I was feeling, but when I did, I reached out and didn't look back.

> There was a time when you were not a slave, remember that. You walked alone, full of laughter, you bathed bare-bellied. . . . You say there are no words to describe this time, you say it does not exist. But remember. Make an effort to remember. Or, failing that, invent.
>
> MONIQUE WITTIG

Calling Her Name

It's not enough to know the Goddess exists; to understand your own worth as one of her children, you have to experience her. It often astonishes me when I meet people who have supposedly practiced Wicca for years without ever having felt the presence, either of God or Goddess. Too many work only from the mind, because they're used to belonging to religions that don't inspire them—growing up, I knew intellectually there was a God, because that's what I was taught, but I never had any evidence of his existence except the words of other people. I was expected to take it on faith.

I don't have to go on faith alone anymore, unless you count the faith that I'm not making it all up, which in the final analysis doesn't really matter anyway. There's no way to prove the existence of God, except to yourself. You find a wonderful freedom in knowing without doubt that deity exists, which I do, having hosted the God in my living room and the Goddess in my body. I spent too many years doubting, as I suspect a lot of people have.

Do you remember the first moment you knew—not believed, but knew—that the Goddess was real? How did you arrive at this knowledge? Was there a life-changing ritual, a voice in the wind, a feeling of warmth where there was nothing before? Think back to that time, and that feeling. How often have you felt it since then? Probably not nearly as often as you wish you could, but once you've experienced the power and love of deity, it becomes a part of you.

Indeed there was.

Even once you have that knowledge, however, you can lose it—or rather, forget about it—if you aren't careful. Like any relationship, our connection with the Divine has to be nourished and tended, and allowed to evolve; otherwise it stagnates, or weakens, and the first strong wind that comes along can knock it over. Maintaining a relationship with deity is kind of the point of practicing a religion, after all, so it is well worth the effort to help that relationship develop as strongly and deeply as possible.

Even after you have considered yourself Wiccan for quite some time, you may find your connection to deity wavers in and out, or is stronger at some points than others. There may be months at a stretch in which you can't summon the energy to light a candle, let alone commune; then there will be times you cannot get enough of ritual. This happens to everyone, trust me. Every autumn I suddenly have the urge to do five rituals a day and cast spells all over the place; in the middle of summer I would rather hide under a rock. Our spiritual impulses move in cycles,

So true

like everything else in nature; if you pay attention, you may notice a pattern emerging.

If you come to a place where you feel you've lost it, though, don't panic; the best thing to do, in my observation, is to go back to basics and stop trying so hard. The Lady is as close as your breath, so all you have to do to find her is keep breathing.

PRACTICING THE PRESENCE—EXERCISE #2

There are a number of ways to connect and reconnect with the Goddess. Those who have read my first book already know some of my favorites, but for those who haven't:

As we discuss the aspects of the sacred physical, you will hopefully see that since your body is a holy instrument, its every action is holy as well. That means that you can approach any activity as a ritual and a chance to honor the Lord and Lady. If you can adopt that perspective you will find that you see the gods in all sorts of places that, before, seemed utterly mundane. Adding a spiritual aspect to everyday activities helps you remember that the Goddess is in every part of you and your life, if only you think to look for her.

If you don't already have an altar, build one. You don't need a huge table covered in three colored cloths and a hundred holy relics; a bit of the bathroom counter or the top of a bookshelf will suffice for simple rites. A candle, an incense burner, and a natural object or two are just as effective an altar as a six-foot credenza with two-foot candelabras. Odds are, somewhere in your home is a spot, however tiny, you can make your own.

Another important thing is to set aside time every day to commune with the gods. You may not need to do so more than two or three times a week normally, but during periods when you have trouble staying connected, try to do something every day, such as a short devotional ritual or a few moments of meditation. It doesn't have to be anything elaborate; often the simplest rituals are the ones that become a light in the wilderness to bring us back to the path.

For example, every morning when you rise, stand or sit before your altar and ground and center, then bid good morning to the four elements and to deity. There are also ideas for daily rituals in other parts of this book, such as chapter 7, where we'll talk more about grounding spirit in the body.

Many Wiccans keep a candle on the altar that they light at every ritual, as a sort of signal to the spirit that the circle is cast. I also light mine in the mornings for at least a few minutes as a reminder to look for the sublime in the ordinary.

Another idea is to dedicate a piece of jewelry you wear every day to the Goddess, and then when you put it on in the morning, have a prayer or chant you use to "activate" it. Ritually consecrate the item like any other magical implement, and treat it as such—when you aren't wearing it, you might set it in a special little corner of your altar. You can do the same with a scent you wear, an article of clothing, a stone—anything you can keep with you and see often throughout the day.

We often forget a very useful and effective method of communicating with the gods: divination. Tarot, runes, and other oracles aren't just for unearthing the possible future. They serve as a kind of contact lens for your third eye; when your connection to the unseen is tenuous, an oracle can take up the slack and allow deity to speak to you using symbols and pictures that you are willing to accept and able to understand. In spiritually lean times, you could spend time learning or relearning your favorite deck or other divinatory tool, which can accomplish two things. One, it can keep your mind off the problem, since you are doing something about it rather than just worrying; two, working with an oracle can reopen your awareness without you even realizing it. You may start seeing a symbol or imagery related to a particular tarot card everywhere you go, and that's almost never a coinci-

dence. When I start seeing runes in the tree branches, I know I'm on the right track—and that someone is trying to get my attention.

Finally, of course, is the simplest and perhaps most obvious: go outside. Spend time wandering among the trees, listening to the song of the wind, dipping your toes in the river. The Goddess is in all of these things, and speaks through them more clearly than anywhere else. Go out into the wild, or even a public park, to learn the Mysteries. If we claim to practice an Earth religion, let us do so wholeheartedly. Stick your hands in the dirt, let the rain soak you to the skin. Lay your head against the ground and feel the Mother's heart beating beneath you, around you, and within you.

Weaving the World: Wicca, Magic, and Deity

I have a confession to make. For a long time, nearly a year, I became a Pagan snob.

If you've been around the Pagan community for very long you've encountered the Spellspawn. They're the bright-eyed novices, usually, who want a spell to do everything from changing traffic lights to finding the right cat litter at Wal-Mart. Generally, they take whatever they find in a book or on the Internet, do exactly what the instructions say, and wait for the universe to hand them a shiny new life. Meanwhile, they annoy the crap out of older Witches on message boards and email lists, asking for spells and to be told what to do.

One of two things usually happens. One, the Spellspawn gets her head screwed on straight and realizes how magic actually works; or two, said Spawn realizes how magic actually works, decides it's too *much* work, and says to hell with it.

Having been harassed by a great many Spawn, I finally reached a point where I quit doing magic altogether, on the assumption that a truly spiritual person doesn't need it. After all, if you live your life as a sacred gift, and pray and try to be a good person, everything will just work out, won't it?

Nice idea. Doesn't happen for most of us. And it's not, as I first believed, because our belief isn't strong enough or we're not sufficiently devout. I admit that I looked down on those silly Witches playing with their herbs and candles, when they should have been meditating on the beneficence of the Goddess and letting white light fix all their problems.

I was a really obnoxious snob for a while, until I had a series of epiphanies. The first was that I *like* doing magic. It's fun. I love having my hands in a bowl of herbs, I love carving candles and rubbing them with fragrant oil. This realization led me to comprehend an important truth about Wicca and magic: Wicca is a nature-reverent religion, honoring the manifest world as much as the astral or nonphysical worlds. To embody our gods, we must embody our religion, engaging the whole self in our rites and observances.

Witches take this idea and turn it into an art form. We work with sensual, tactile energies, combining the sacred elements as they are combined in the universe, to create. We immerse ourselves in the scent, the texture, and the taste of magic, and bring ourselves all the more fully into harmony with nature. The thing the Spellspawn miss is that magic isn't some dry, rote process where just saying the right words will do it. True magic is a form of co-creation. We draw upon the power of nature and of ourselves, ask for the assistance and blessing of the gods, and reweave the remotely possible into the highly probable.

This is, to me, an inherently spiritual act. That was my second epiphany—magic without deity is meaningless to me. All the energy used in spellcasting, as in purely celebratory ritual, is divine in origin; therefore I cannot separate my magical life and my spiritual life the way I used to think I could. One informs and completes the other. The religion of Wicca and the art of Witchcraft are lovers entwined. One could live without the other, but together they make something truly beautiful.

When I wrote my first book I was still in the midst of my snobby period, and I didn't truly come to appreciate the elegance and beauty of Witchcraft until long after. I felt like I was above all of that Witchy nonsense, and far too enlightened to bother.

You don't have to tell me I was being a dumbass; I figured that out on my own.

The third epiphany was perhaps the most profound one. Say I am going to build a house, and someone hands me a hammer, nails, and wood. Should I bang the nails in with my palm, or use all the tools given to me for a stronger and more efficient result? Or should I ignore the tools altogether and ask God to build the house for me?

Pretending that the gift of magic is somehow inferior to more sophisticated spiritual pursuits is not only highly irritating to those of us who think otherwise, it is a form of ingratitude. Part of the philosophy of Wicca is that we are each our own clergy, as well as masters of our own lives; we don't hand off our fates to outside authority, we take responsibility for our own happiness. To help us do that, we have been granted all manner of gifts, of which magic is one of the most powerful. Just as we don't have to go by faith alone, we are expected to rely on more than faith to get us through—we are expected to get off our asses and contribute to our bliss.

If you approach magic as a sacred art, you are less likely to use it, true. You learn that such a power is a double-edged sword, and that responsibility goes both ways: we are responsible for our own path as well as the consequences of our actions. When you have experienced magic as a part of the divine life force, you are less inclined to fling it at any minor problem that comes along, and more inclined to consider your options—all your options.

Ethics don't just apply to the "real world." They apply very strongly to magical work as well, perhaps even more so, because oftentimes we can't immediately see the results of magic. Much like the Internet, there is a certain anonymity to magic; people feel like they can be cruel online because no one can see their faces, and sometimes people feel they can do unethical spellwork because no one will ever find out. If you wouldn't be willing or able to walk up to someone and shoot him in the head, how can you be willing to hex him? The consequences will rise up and find you no matter how you accomplish your goals.

NOT TRU [handwritten margin note]

This is doubly true once you begin to treat your body as holy. If I know the Goddess is walking through me, and that my hands are her hands on the earth, what I do with those hands takes on a new significance and a new weight. This does not, however, preclude using her gifts; it simply means that there is more riding on our choices than we can see, and we have to be aware of that and try as much as possible, given our limited knowledge and foresight, to work for the good of all, with harm to none.

> Real magic can never be made by offering up someone else's liver. You must tear out your own, and not expect to get it back. The true witches know that.
>
> PETER S. BEAGLE
> IN *THE LAST UNICORN*

In Wicca, women find new ways to become empowered after spending most of their lives feeling powerless. That is one reason magic is so appealing to us; it works through the feminine side of our being, through intuition and the unseen. To do effective ritual of any kind, magical or otherwise, we have to tone down the aggressive and linear side of the mind and let the gentler side have a turn in the spotlight. Once the ritual is over, though, we have to act in accord, which is where the linear energy really shines.

The Lady's Many Guises

I am not a big fan of the Triple Goddess. I know that makes me a bit of a maverick in Wiccan circles, but it's true; I find that only having three categories and trying to pack all the aspects of the Goddess into them is limiting, as well as vaguely insulting, for it implies that the stages of a woman's life are ruled entirely by biology.

Menarche, childbirth, and menopause are some of the greatest mysteries of womanhood, but they are not the only changes that occur in our lives. Women now have so many more options out in the world— we don't all go straight from our father's house to our husband's anymore. When you leave your parents' house and strike out on your own, not ready to settle down but no longer a child, which of the three do you fit into? What about those of us who don't have any children? Or those who have them, and then they grow and leave home, leaving the woman in a state between Mother and Crone that is neither?

The Triple Goddess paradigm also has a very linear feel to it, as if there is only one order you can go in. It's entirely possible that you never had much of a youth, never felt at all a Maiden; later, though, you find yourself free and embracing the childlike self you never had a chance to enjoy. Can't you be a Maiden then?

Often, people take all the images of the Lady in a category and decide they're all alike, that a Mother is a Mother is a Mother. Not so— you would hardly call Kali Ma a nice mommy figure, though she is known as Mother to many. It's said that the Goddess's three aspects are connected with the phases of the moon, but there are plenty of solar goddesses, and others not concerned with celestial bodies at all. Not all goddesses are lunar, and not all of them are nice; they portray the entire gamut of experience from birth to death, from rage to ecstasy. They portray nature in all its splendor, both moonlight and shadow, green in field and flower and red in tooth and claw.

Womanhood and the Goddess exist in a continuum rather than in distinct stages. They also embody a spiral rather than a straight line. As the years go by, we encounter the same kinds of situations over and over again—loss, joy, success, failure, everything—but each time our bodies are different, our minds are different. There is a wide and glorious variety of roles that women can have, and there is just as great a variety of archetypes that the Goddess can wear.

In this book we'll be discussing a number of those: Healer, Mother, Lover, and so on. There are many more: Warrior, Sorceress, Sister, Midwife, Artisan . . . the list goes on and on. By attempting to put all the Goddesses into such neat little boxes, we diminish their complexity and therefore their reality—nothing in life is so cut-and-dried.

At the age of seventy you may feel called to invoke Artemis, the Virgin Huntress. As a writer I could form a connection to Sarasvati, the Hindu Goddess of the written word. Isis is called a Mother Goddess, but also a Sorceress, for she won the secrets of high magic from the Sun God, as well as bringing her beloved back from the dead. The stories of the goddesses from pantheons the world over reflect what it is to be a woman; it is never-ending change, gathering knowledge and understanding, taking on as many roles as there are stars in the sky.

Therefore, don't hold slavishly to the designations I use—I may speak of Freya in her guise as a Lover, but that is hardly all she is. Each of the archetypes is part of us all; each one symbolizes an aspect of life that is lived through the body. None is more important than the others, as all of them help create and re-create who we are, every day.

The Goddess is not merely an archetype; she is all of them, and none. Her being cannot be contained by human language. We look at the various kinds of goddesses that seem to run in common among different cultures and find similarities, but these are still not the totality of the Goddess—she transforms as the seasons transform, and this, to me, is one of her greatest mysteries; only someone as powerful and loving as the Goddess could take on so many roles, one for each of her daughters, ever-evolving. After all, they say a woman's prerogative is to change her mind.

What About That God Guy, Anyway?

Finding a balance of masculine and feminine qualities is, as I have said, an essential step in spiritual evolution. The problem is, before we can find that balance we have to make peace with the side of creation that has been forced on us for most of our lives. Many Wiccan groups and books, including this one, place a special emphasis on the Goddess because she has been ignored and denigrated for so very long, and because women need to find places they can express their spiritual yearnings among their own gender, to someone of their own gender.

This is understandable, and natural, all the more so because a lot of us were stepped on, devalued, cast aside, or generally pissed off by the representatives of the male divinity who governs a large portion of the world we grew up in. What do we need a God for, anyway? Hasn't he done enough damage?

We forget that humans make their own choices, and the people who have committed atrocities in the name of God were just that—people. Not deities. Human beings have turned the concept of masculine deity into what it is in modern culture. Also, we forget that the God of Wicca is *not* Jehovah, Allah, Yahweh, or any permutation thereof; those particular aspects of the greater masculine force in the universe do not have to be the ones we revere. We have a choice—we can choose someone else, or let someone else choose us.

I said in chapter 1 that the men you know are not to blame for all the ills of the world. The same holds true for the God.

On the other hand, the stereotypical image of the God in a lot of Wiccan literature isn't all that appealing to me, personally—a horned (and horny) little goat fellow who does nothing but shag in the forest until the harvest, when we kill him off with the grain— doesn't inspire me. Part of the reason I took so long to connect with the God was this image; everywhere I looked, it was Pan this and Cernunnos that.

I had experienced the Goddess as a tremendous power—noble, beautiful, and nurturing—a being so awesome that I could barely speak her name without tears of joy; *this* was her consort and equal? No, thank you.

Just as some Wiccans try to box the Lady into a sweet happy Mother figure with no dark side, and try to cram all her faces into limited categories of Maiden, Mother, and Crone, I found myself confining the God into a narrow range of attributes, just because it was what "everyone else" did. (Everyone else meaning, of course, the two or three people who had the loudest voices. I've found that in actuality there aren't nearly as many people devoted to the Pan-like gods as I thought there were ten years ago.)

The God that finally found me was thankfully nothing like anyone I had ever read about. When I finally made the decision to actively cultivate a relationship with the God, I opened myself up to the possibility that there might be just as many hundreds of faces for him to wear as there were for the Lady.

A lot of women have suffered abuse at the hands of men throughout their lives, and they come to Wicca to escape that; what they find, however, is that the things we run away from are the things that eventually outrun us. We can choose to stop running, and transform the pain of the past into something healing for the present. A true, valid spiritual path will not let you escape anything. At some point, all our demons must be slain, and new life invoked in their place.

It may seem that the God himself is irrelevant in a book about women's bodies, but this is not entirely true. Our bodies are feminine, but often we call upon what would be considered masculine energy when we do physical work (and play). The Lord's energy is what moves us, what gets us on our feet; he takes the love of the Goddess, sets it afire, and turns it into passion. The active principle, the thing that helps us break free and run wild, fuels our bodies and puts them in motion. Without it we languish, and our potential remains just that.

(Note: The terms "masculine" and "feminine" translate into male and female in my own practice, but that may not be the case in your own. Your Goddess may in fact be a fierce warrior maid. Gender isn't the issue; finding equilibrium between the two major forces in the universe, however you envision them, is the goal. I come from a fairly traditional God-and-Goddess-as-equals perspective. So if my saying action is a masculine trait offends you, just remember that energy in and of itself does not have genitals.)

[handwritten margin note: and your god be the fem aspect? intriguing]

A RITUAL TO GREET THE GOD *[handwritten: I like the sound of this]*

When I set out to bring balance to my practice, I did a ritual like this one as a way of saying, "Door's open; come on in." Afterward I went about my business as usual and trusted that the Lord would make himself known to me when it was time.

Take a chalice, some sort of beverage (I think I used sparkling apple cider), and some sort of bread or other food with you into a wooded area or park. Find a tree that seems friendly and have a seat beneath it, leaning your back into its bark.

Spend a while meditating on your history with male deity and how you hope your new relationship will be different. If you were to create a God from scratch, what sort of masculine traits would he have? It may be that you've read about or studied someone that is appealing; call that image to mind, if you like. Allow your old conceptions to drain out of your body, down into the earth, leaving room for a powerful but loving energy equal to that of the Goddess.

Pour a chalice of your beverage and imagine you are sharing it with the Lord; do the same with the food. Say out loud that you are ready to meet whoever is watching over you. The forest has eyes, and those eyes belong to the God; open yourself and allow whatever messages, if any, to come to you. Nothing may happen yet, but at least you have put the word out that you're ready. Leave offerings of your bread and drink at the base of the tree.

Altars of the Goddess

Of all the tools and trappings of Wicca, the most basic and, in a way, most important, is the altar. When we create our place of reverence, we fashion something beautiful to dedicate to something beautiful. The altar is the foundation on which we build our circles; it anchors our magic in the physical world, and is the site of everything from celebration to transformation. We cast a larger circle around it, but the circle's heart is the altar, no matter where it is placed.

Our altars are a reservoir for an amazing blend of utility and creativity. We adorn them with things we find symbolic, or pretty; we lay upon them the tools we need to make things happen. They are found on tables, shelves, even the top of the fridge; they are round, square, rectangular; they are grand and impressive, complicated affairs; they are serene, Zen-like in simplicity. Your altar is an expression of your inner goddess.

Just like your body.

We come in all shapes and sizes. We are all colors. We are found everywhere. Some of us are expansive, some introverted. Some of us come draped in bright and glittering raiment; some of us opt for jeans and T-shirts. Our bodies, in all their wondrous variety, are the altars of the Lady; through them we create life and change. Our lives are works of magic, and our bodies are our most fundamental magical tools.

One of the most appealing aspects of Wicca is that rather than going to a building set aside for worship, we create our own temples wherever we are, and then take them down again and leave the place as we found it. This idea of a portable "church" helps to connect us more fully to the natural world, as it shows us that sacred space is everywhere, and that only our perception makes it seem otherwise. Much has been written on the sacred spaces we create, but not so much on the sacred space we embody.

Unlike a circle, however, the altar of the flesh is one you take with you everywhere and never un-cast. Imagine going through your whole life in circle; every action you make would have an air of purpose and importance, just as every gesture made in a temporary circle adds to the ambiance and power of the rite therein. Nothing done before an altar is frivolous or without meaning. Looking at the body as an altar, the same applies; everything you do, no matter how trivial it may seem, has the potential to be very significant indeed.

Being a priestess of the Goddess is more than leading ritual and working magic. When you take up the pentacle, you dedicate yourself to the service of the Lord and Lady; as such, you give yourself and your life over to be remade and molded, through your own free will and choice, as well as their grace, into the very altar that you work upon. You are the first ritual tool, and in truth, the only one that matters. No magic can come into the world through your will without passing over your altar; no magic can be made without the help of your hands, head, and heart.

When you claim the title of Priestess, or Witch, or both, you set yourself apart from the rest of society, but not above. The difference between "sacred" and "mundane" is purely one of perception; all things are inherently sacred, but sometimes we can experience it more readily than others. Your body is as holy as the standing stones and the great redwood forest; you only have to honor it as such, and it is so. The same divine energy that flows down the river also flows through your veins.

There are a number of invocations that evoke this knowledge, variations of, "By the earth that is her body, the air that is her breath, the fire that is her spirit, and the water that is her blood . . ."

It is a strange place to stand in, looking around at other people and wondering what they were doing last night while you were dancing the spiral dance with the wind and the rain. It can be a little lonely, but at the same time, you know at heart you are never alone—not only are you connected to and aware of the blessedness of the world, you are connected by spirit to an endless web of others like you. Every time you light a candle to the full moon, you know that across the planet there are hundreds of others, women and men both, who are sitting or standing at altars much like your own, calling from a place in the heart that we have, at last, remembered.

think on this

You are altar, and circle, athame, and candle; your life is the Great Work, the most important (and longest) ritual you will ever conduct. The invocation began the day you first called to the Lord and Lady, even if you didn't know their names at the time. Each day you cast a new circle of yourself; once you remember that, and see the beauty in every moment, the magic can truly begin.

CONSECRATING THE ALTAR—A DEDICATION RITUAL

There will come a moment when you must decide whether to continue hating your body and allowing others to decide your beauty, or to step up and claim the sacredness that is rightfully yours as a daughter of the Goddess. Perhaps you will find that moment while reading this book; perhaps you won't be ready until after the last page; perhaps you're staring at that moment now. When you reach it, when you choose the path of wholeness and holiness, you may want to mark the passage with a ritual like this one.

Here you will consecrate your body as an altar to the Goddess; like most consecration rituals, this one involves the four elements. Since you are the altar, you don't need to set one up. Gather together a bowl of salt and one of water; incense, preferably the loose kind, which creates more smoke than stick or cone varieties (I recommend frankincense, sandalwood, white sage, or copal, which are typically used in consecrations of all kinds); a candle in some sort of holder that won't be easily knocked over; and a garment of some kind, either a bedsheet or loose robe, that can be easily removed. Perform this ritual somewhere with enough floor space for you to lie down and stretch out.

First, bathe or shower. As you wash each part of your body, visualize all the negative beliefs and feelings you've had toward it dissolving under the soap and into the water. Move your awareness through skin, muscle, and bone, feeling for a moment what your body feels when you malign it or when you treat it with reverence.

When you are done, drape yourself in the sheet or robe, and go to the place you've chosen for your ritual. Set each of the four tools you have gathered in its corresponding quarter in a circle; make sure there is plenty of space inside.

Before you enter the circle, allow the sheet or whatever you were wearing to drop to the floor in a puddle at your feet. You step into the circle fully yourself, unfettered, by your own free will and choice.

You can do this part standing up or sitting in the circle, whichever is easier for you. Face the north, and take up the bowl of salt. Invoke the powers of earth, visualizing the strength of the oak in your bones and the solidity of the mountain standing in you with your head unbowed before those who would deny your worth. Taste the salt; then turn to the east, and invoke air in the same way, focusing on the breath. Waft the incense over your whole body. In the south, call upon the energy that drives your heartbeat, then visualize the candle flame burning in your heart as it burns in the circle; in the west, call upon blood and tears, and let drops of water fall upon your brow.

Use whatever wording you like, or none at all. When you have consecrated yourself with the four elements, lie down on your back in the center of the circle and invoke the Goddess (and the God too, if you wish—it's up to you) as in this example:

Lady of the Radiant Moon
Who sculpted the flesh that I wear in this life
I call you

As my hands are your hands
And my heart is your heart
Bring your love to this temple.
Witness this blessing upon my body
Lend me the courage to accept myself as I am
May your presence here remind me
That I am you
And that my love for you is for myself and all that lives.
Hail and welcome, Star of the Sea
Blessed be.

It would be nice if you could do this ritual outside in view of the moon, but that is very difficult for many of us, so at the very least visualize the moon high above you in a blackened sky. Feel her light flowing down to you, bathing you in acceptance and love; feel the Goddess open her arms to you, and take you in with perfect love. Let the energy of the Goddess infuse every cell of your body, awakening it to its partnership with your spirit. Feel your body become hallowed ground, no longer subject to the vagaries of human greed or the barbs of self-hatred.

Seal this energy inside your body, knowing you will never again forget it is there, and that it was there all along.

Now, anoint each part of your body with the oil. Say aloud an affirmation of that body part's sanctity, such as, "Blessed are my feet." You could also expand the affirmation to include more specific attributes: "Blessed are my feet that walk the path of truth and beauty." (If you have ever attended a ritual involving the Five Fold Kiss, this format should be familiar to you.)

That done, you have further options. You may feel inspired to dance, grounding your awareness in your body even further; you may want to meditate, raise energy to earth into yourself, or share a libation with yourself and the gods. Do whatever you feel moved to do before bidding the Lady farewell and ending the rite. The important thing is, in the following days, become mindful of your body as an instrument of healing and positive change in the world. From this point onward you no longer walk in ignorance—you are a holy instrument, and now you know it—let the world know it, too.

Recommended Reading and Resources for Chapter Two

BOOKS

Practicing the Presence of the Goddess by Barbara Ardinger

The Witches' Goddess: The Feminine Principle of Divinity by Janet and Stewart Farrar

Witch Crafting by Phyllis Curott

Circle of Stones by Judith Duerk

Crafting the Body Divine by Yasmine Galenorn

The Spiral Dance by Starhawk

t h r e e

THE

reflection

Close your eyes.

Listen to the cycle of your breath, the rhythmic pulse of your heart. Feel the air on your skin, the ground or chair beneath you. Take your awareness and let it drift down from your head, feeling each part of your body, greeting it as an old friend. Ask each part how it feels—are your feet cold? Does your head hurt? What about that itch you always get behind your ear when you try to meditate? Become aware of each part of you without assigning any value to its appearance or function. Sometimes a foot is just a foot.

The journey back to the altar begins as simply as that: with awareness. Just being conscious of our bodies is difficult work for most people, as we go through most days stuck in our heads, only vaguely aware of what's happening from the neck down—unless, of course, something goes wrong. To reclaim your physical self, begin by learning what it feels like to really live there.

Now visualize a mirror in front of you—the one in your bathroom, perhaps, or a reflective pool. Gaze into its calm, even surface and let an image come to you. When you look into the mirror, what do you see? What is the first thing that passes through your mind when confronted with your own face? Do you zero in on one part and criticize it, or do you condemn the whole thing with a, "God, I'm ugly," and call it a day? Are you one of those rare and precious people who genuinely knows that you are beautiful? My money is on, "Probably not."

Staring into the mirror, you see that as you criticize yourself, your reflection changes. Suddenly your nose is huge, your breasts sag down to your knees, and you balloon out like a hippo in all directions. If you were right, if all those negative images were the truth, you would be a cartoon. You are not. You are a woman of the Goddess, and you and she are one, each other's own image.

Look again, and see what is really there.

Our first archetype isn't really an archetype per se, it is a mirror of reality: the Reflection.

It is said that we create our own reality. I think this is a dangerous oversimplification of a profound truth. I can believe all I want that I can jump off my apartment roof and fly, but it's not terribly likely; the laws of physics, apparently, create their own reality as well.

Even without conscious magic, we have great power when it comes to the reality we live in; every choice we make changes something, and its echoes reverberate throughout all the worlds. We can affect probability in some amazing, and sometimes tragic, ways. This is one of the first lessons we learn when we first start working magic—be careful what you cast for, and be careful why you cast.

There are, however, limits to our power, and those limits are the choices of others. We all participate in a mutual reality, and can influence each other in both positive and negative ways. A woman who is raped would probably contest the idea that she created that part of her reality; perhaps she chose to walk past that dark alley, but she still didn't choose to be attacked. The attacker made that choice and took hers away. By saying that reality is entirely up to the beholder, we deny the responsibility of others for the consequences of their actions. If I say that I chose to be mugged, I fail to hold the mugger accountable. We are *all* accountable for the state of the world we live in.

The point here is that our own reality is subject to change, both by our own efforts and the often-casual cruelty of others. The things that other people say and do affect us deeply and become part of who we think we are; by becoming passive and letting others form the basis of our self-perception, we surrender our own magic, and lose ourselves in the bargain. Fortunately, just as the power was ours to give away, it is ours to take back.

It may not seem that a reflection is an appropriate symbol for the truth; mirrors show us the world backwards, after all, and the image in the glass can easily be distorted. It is that distortion, however, that makes the Reflection so important—it is your self-concept, your personal truth about your body, and it will always be a product of your perceptions, not some objective standard. The Reflection is how you see yourself, and if you hate what you see, that hatred will show on its surface to anyone who dares to look. As the image in the mirror is reversed, so, too, does our self-concept almost never exactly match what's really there.

The Reflection is both you and your physical shadow self. It is the truth of what you look like, but it is also the monster you create with all the negative images and messages you have absorbed, dressed in the inevitable failure of your attempts to force your body into conformity. We are by and large only accustomed to dealing with the shadow Reflection, seeing through the glass darkly. Its eyes are hard and merciless, able to see only the flaws, the shortcomings, the scars the world has left on you. Anyone who has ever tried on a bathing suit under fluorescent lights knows just how wicked the Reflection can be.

This Reflection makes your graceful neck giraffelike. It makes your skin tone darken from smooth cocoa to drab charcoal. It takes the perfect assemblage of skin and muscle and bone that the Lord and Lady have given you and turns it into Frankenstein.

In our journey, the Reflection is guardian of the gate. Before we can reclaim ourselves, we must first confront the lies we have told ourselves and let others tell us. We must face down that monster, slay it, put its head on a pike and leave it as a warning to the demons of self-hatred and self-degradation that come after: *Caution: Pissed-off Goddess on premises. Enter at your own risk.*

Really, however, the Reflection is not so much an enemy in need of execution as it is a wounded creature in need of transformation. With work and care, we can shift the focus of the mirror, clean its glass, and instead of seeing a distorted image of ourselves, we can see who we really are and who we want to grow into. We can become like Alice and step through the looking glass to find a strange and magical world—a world where how we look has no bearing on our worth as human beings, and where we are loved exactly as we are . . . even by ourselves.

The Reflection can be a powerful tool once we have made peace with it; in addition to offering clarity and truth, it is the source of one of the oldest forms of magic, the glamour—in fact, you have probably constructed a glamour for yourself already, without even realizing it, and wear it every day as it drains your energy and leaves you unsure as to what lies beneath it.

The Trouble with Glamour

For centuries, one of the purported powers of the faery folk has been the ability to appear as something else to mortal eyes—to cast a glamour, to confuse the senses and lure an unsuspecting human into whatever nasty (or enjoyable) fate the Fae had in store. A mischievous pixie could appear to you as your long-lost love and draw you into a nice slimy bog to drown; or he or she could make you think your love was your mortal enemy, and sit giggling behind a tree while you ran your beloved through with a sword.

My own dealings with the Fae have been a lot less dire; mostly they _— Cute_ specialize in stealing my car keys and leaving books open to strategically-themed passages when they think I should know something. However, humans have long sought to harness the Fae power of glamour to make themselves appear more beautiful, more capable, or simply as someone different from who they really are.

That is essentially the purpose of the beauty industry. Have you noticed how the point of wearing makeup is to look like you're not wearing any? To wear a slightly better version of your real face? And, I'm sure you've noticed, when you are expertly made up and wearing your most glamorous outfit, you feel like someone else, someone gorgeous and important (until you spill marinara sauce all over yourself in front of the object of your desires—or maybe that's just me).

There's nothing inherently wrong with this; feeling beautiful never hurt anyone, and when approached from the proper perspective, cosmetics and fashion can help bring out our inner beauty. If we come from a place without self-esteem, however, the things we drape and paint on our skin can make matters much worse.

Spells for glamour abound in the grimoires of antiquity as well as in modern spellbooks.

What we don't realize is that, as modern women, we are already masters of disguise. Every day we don masks to face the "real world" that for most of us feels entirely unreal. We hide our religion, our sexuality, our intelligence, and strap on armor that we hope will be impervious to the slings and arrows of outrageous idiocy and cruelty that we run into day after day. We may have one persona for work, another for our relatives, another for our magical or spiritual group, another for the Pagan community at large, all of which are versions of, but not the totality of, our true selves.

Our fear of the disapproval of the outer world can do deep and lasting damage to our inner world. In my own life, I spent years basing my self-concept on what other people said or thought of me, which meant that my emotions could go from sky-high to hell-low in the course of a single conversation. My Reflection was a cacophony of voices, none of them my own.

The really sad thing is, in all reality, people don't spend nearly as much time thinking about us as we think they do. That guy who called you a freak for having a pierced lip will most likely never think about you again, unless the subject of pierced lips comes up in conversation someday. People forget what they say, and they certainly don't think about the consequences of their words. A remark that hurt you so deeply you cried for hours probably meant nothing at all to the person that said it.

This is especially true when we're teenagers. You may not remember a day of high school, but you remember your nickname, or what the popular girls giggled about behind your back. It's amazing how long we carry our adolescent history; for years, I was still haunted by the haughty face of the girl in gym class who made pig noises when I walked by in those horrible uniform shorts. This was, I might add, the same girl who listened to Vanilla Ice, wore blue eye shadow, and dropped out of senior year to have a baby with a guy who later left her for her fifteen-year-old sister—yet I was willing to let someone with that kind of taste, who was no Angelina Jolie herself, have a say in my worth as a woman. What kind of sense does that make?

The more insidious form of glamour that most of us aren't aware of is the one we create for ourselves out of false perceptions of our appearance. It starts with a moment of doubt—*why did he break up with me? Am I not attractive enough?*—and soon snowballs into a sort of mask we lay over our true selves. This mask is woven of idle comments from others, outright slights and insults, and our own fears of worthlessness and loneliness that are all too easy to exploit for monetary gain. Our first task, then, is to take off that mask, destroy it, and start anew.

NAMING THE GLAMOUR—EXERCISE #1

The first thing I'd like you to do is to sit down with a pen and paper and start writing. Write out everything you can remember anyone ever saying about your body. Write out one comment per line or leave space between each. *No one else says negative - I'm the only one .*

Don't think about what you, yourself, have said or thought privately—focus on specific things that others have actually said to you, both positive and negative. If you had a lover once who thought your breasts were the holy of holies, write it down. If your father told you you were a fat cow, if a construction worker yelled out one of the thousand racial epithets that seem to fall so freely from American tongues, if the dentist said you have remarkably straight teeth, write it down. Search your memory.

Also, write down the nonverbal reactions people have had to you that stand out in your memory. If some skinny clerk at Sears gave you the "What the hell are you shopping in the normal people's sizes for? Shouldn't you be ordering from Austin Tent and Awning?" look, write it down. If a co-worker slapped you on the butt and you slunk red-faced to your desk, too ashamed to call him on his harassment, write it down. If you were attacked, abused, ignored—anything other people have done to you that cut or burned or even made you glow with pride—write it down, too.

This is probably going to make you angry, or sad. That's all right. There is a purpose to this. Don't block out the emotions or think they're childish; honor your feelings and give them a voice if you need to.

When you have as many as you can remember, look at the list. Each entry, each comment, represents a part of yourself you have given away. The fact that you remember these things, that they make you feel angry, means that you haven't let them go and therefore they still have a claw-hold in how you view yourself. How many of these things have since become part of the litany of self-condemnation you automatically recite when you look in the mirror? How much of your self-image has come from the careless and pointless criticism of others? How much of your power have you given these people, who probably don't even remember saying any of this to you?

Now I want you to fold up this list and set it aside. Next, start a new one, but this time write out all the things *you* say about your body, either out loud or in your mind. It doesn't matter if they were originally someone else's words—if you tell yourself the same thing your father did, write it down. Also, pay attention to how thoughts about your body are intimately connected to thoughts about your worth as a person. Have you ever thought, "I'm so ugly, no one will ever love me," or, "I can't even keep from eating donuts—I'm weak, I have no willpower?"

Look over this list as you did the last one. Think about how many of these comments come from what others have said, and how many originated with your own mind. Also think about this—would you ever say any of these things to someone you care about? If you did, you would soon lose all of your friends. Often we are kinder to total strangers than to ourselves.

Next comes the arts and crafts portion of our chapter, which is optional. Find or create a mask form; you can often find these made of plastic at craft stores, but I would strongly recommend a cardboard or paper one instead. The easiest thing to do would be to take a piece of cardboard or paper plate and cut the shape of a mask out of it. It does not have to be a work of art; in fact, the uglier it is the better.

Once you have the shape, start cutting apart the comments you've written down. Glue them to the mask. Overlap them, let some hang off the edges, make it look however you want as long as you can still read whatever lines are on the outermost layer. Decide whether the words of others or yourself should go on the outside. Make sure you use up every single line.

If you don't want to play cut-and-paste, simply keep the lists handy for the ritual that follows.

BANISHING THE GLAMOUR—A RITUAL TO UNCOVER YOUR TRUE REFLECTION

You need to perform this ritual in front a mirror in which you can see your whole face. In fact, you will need to use this mirror for several of the exercises in this chapter, so be sure it is one you have easy access to.

Place a white candle on either side of the sink. You may wish to burn a purifying incense; I'll leave the choice to you, as well as whether you want background music or any other ritual accoutrements. The only necessary tool is the mask you made or the lists themselves, and some sort of fireproof bowl or cauldron. Alternately, you can do the last part of the ritual outside on the patio or elsewhere.

Begin in the dark. This ritual is fairly simple and informal, so use whatever circle casting you prefer, or simply ask the elements for their aid. You may wish to call both the Lord and Lady, or only the Lady; again, use invocations you are comfortable with, or simply call to them silently.

Now light the two white candles, naming one "Truth" and the other "Beauty." Make a statement of your intention, preferably aloud: "I come to the circle this night to do away with the glamour that veils me from myself."

Stare into the mirror at your face for a moment. Then hold up the mask or the lists between your face and the glass, obscuring your reflection from view. Imagine that this paper mask is in fact the false face you have made yourself—the idea that you are ugly, imperfect, somehow unworthy of love and acceptance, even from yourself. Imagine that all the things people have ever said about you have helped to create this mask, and your own power as a Witch has made it even stronger, in effect cursing you to live behind a lie. Imagine that the real you, the absolute truth of your body and self, is waiting behind that glamour, waiting to be uncovered and freed.

Now set the mask on fire; light one spot with the candle of Truth, and the other with Beauty, being careful of your fingers. Immediately drop it into the sink or the fireproof container you had ready. Alternately, take it outside and do the same. If lighting it is impossible (you're afraid of causing too much smoke or setting off alarms, et cetera), then rip the mask to shreds as small as you can tear it or cut it to bits with scissors. If you choose this option, after the ritual is done, take the bits and bury them in the earth somewhere unmarked. The fire option is certainly more dramatic, but be practical (as well as safe).

As you watch the paper burn, know that the perceptions and words of others no longer have any power over you. Neither do the hateful things you have said to yourself in the past. Now is the time to reclaim the face and body that are rightfully yours.

When you look into the mirror now, try to look upon yourself without judgment. See the shape of your face simply as a shape; see your skin as skin; see your nose as a nose. Attach no adjectives to them. They simply are. This is the body you have been given; this is the face that is yours to wear in this life. This is you, in actuality, formed in Truth and Beauty.

An honest self-perception is key to acceptance and self-love. By banishing the glamour, you free yourself to love what is already there and to change the habits and ideas that have kept you from enjoying your body and caring for it as it deserves. You now have a clean slate to write upon.

Behind the Mask

Here, then, is the reality of your body.

Your body has 206 bones, 27 of which are in just one of your hands. Your femur is stronger than granite, and it's hollow. You have 60,000 miles of blood vessels, which would go around the earth twice; you have 45 miles of nerve cells. Your heart beats 100,000 times per day. In the time it takes to read this sentence, 50 million of your cells will have died and been replaced with others. Your liver has over 500 functions. Your brain's storage capacity is currently believed to be over 4 terabytes (1 terabyte is 1,000 gigabytes).

Regardless of its size, its shape, its color, or its age, your body has been with you from your first breath, and you will have the same one at your last gasp. It will have carried you through all the years of your life, quietly going through its millions of processes and changes without any conscious effort on your part. Your muscles and bones will have worked together to help you walk and stretch and have sex. Your brain will have done everything from keeping your heart beating to solving algebra problems to interpreting your favorite poem.

Just turning the page, your nerves sent signals to your muscles and bones to move past one another; your eyes focused and refocused on the new lines of text, and your brain translated them, divined their meaning, and is now supplying extra thoughts that might range from, "I wish I had a bagel," to, "This chick is full of crap." Meanwhile, your lungs fill and empty, your stomach growls, you have an itch on your earlobe—thousands of fantastic things are going on in your skin right now, and you're worried about some extra fat cells?

No matter how you feel about it, your body is the only one you get, and all the surgery and dieting and makeup in the world will not change that. You're not going to get another one in this life. It is one of the most precious gifts the Lord and Lady have handed you—a nifty little animal you can run around in, that lets you taste and touch and smell the world around you. Your body is, in all its gritty, sweaty, messy physicality, an amazing and wonderful thing.

It was your body—you know, the one you complain about and belittle every chance you get—that danced at your first drum circle; it was your body that gave birth to your child; it was your body that got down and dirty in the back seat of your dad's station wagon; it was your body that shivered, sweated, clasped its hands, fell to its knees, wept, and laughed the first time you felt the presence of the Goddess in your life.

MEDITATION ON THE MIRACLE—EXERCISE #2

Sit comfortably in front of your mirror, and breathe deeply for a few minutes. Ground and center in whatever way you usually do.

Now, raise your hands so that you can see them in the glass. (Alternately, if you can't get to a mirror, just look at them directly.) See the actual shape of your hands. Follow their edges and contours with your eyes; look at how the fingers curve, how the lines on your palms intersect and twist around each other. Look at the shape of your fingernails, the taper of your wrists.

Are you wearing any rings or bracelets? What do they symbolize? Why do you wear them on your hands instead of somewhere else, like around your neck?

Which hand do you write with? What else do you do with that hand? I write with my left, but do most everything else with my right, because growing up nobody knew how to teach a left-handed girl how to throw or use scissors. When you write, do you prefer a pen, a pencil, a keyboard? Why?

Now, beginning with the moment you got up this morning, go through your day cataloguing every single action your hands performed. See them picking up a glass, writing a note, opening a door, comforting a child . . . smacking the cat on the rump when he stole your french fry,

You Remember this.
It is Real.

chopping vegetables, drumming on your desk . . . tapping on the steering wheel while you sang "Proud Mary," scratching your neck . . . picking up this book . . . and so on.

Consider the holiness of your hands. They are how you do your work on this earth; they are a microcosm of the hands of the Goddess, and can change the world as easily as hers can. Consider the difference between a caress and a raised fist. Gesture and touch are such a part of our relationships with others that we rarely think about how powerful they are.

Try this: every time you wash your hands, observe the water flowing over them, and let this simple chore consecrate them. You might be surprised how differently you feel about your actions when you think of your hands as holy instruments.

You might say to yourself, *"I dedicate the work of my hands to the Lord and Lady; may my every action be a reflection of their grace."* This can become a part of your daily practice; you could do the same thing before beginning a particular task or starting work for the day.

GRATITUDE—EXERCISE #3

Our culture is not a thankful one, except on that one day a year when we express our thanks by eating ourselves sick. Very few people are thankful for what they have rather than lusting after everything they don't. Rather than berating your body for falling short of the mark, spend a few minutes a day thinking of everything it did for you that you can be grateful for. In fact, it doesn't hurt to literally say, "Thanks," to your body parts as you go along.

In the last day, did your body:

Fight off a headache?

Stop bleeding after you cut yourself shaving?

Carry you up a hill or across a parking lot?

Stay awake long enough for you to get home after a long day?

Fall asleep while you were watching TV so you won't be exhausted in the morning?

Allow you to feel the touch of a lover, or a hug from a child, or your cat rubbing on your legs?

Let you see a gorgeous moon~~rise~~? *Cuz yeah o*

Let you listen to your favorite CD, and sing along?

Keep digesting, moving, growing, and learning despite how you feel about it? *yes*

Think back through the major events of your life, and consider the role your body had in all of them. Could you have painted that picture, gotten that degree, left that insignificant other, or had that baby without your body? I doubt it.

This holds true no matter what level of ability you have. Maybe you're in a wheelchair, and can't walk; what *can* you do? Maybe you have had cancer, and you survived the hell of chemo. Sometimes it's enough just to keep breathing.

Whatever society might have to say about the way you look, it's not your body's fault if you hate it. It goes on doing its thing regardless, as well as it can—perhaps it's time to stop dwelling on its shortcomings and instead do what you can to help it function, feel, and live better.

Acceptance and Love

Admit it: you've gone on a dozen diets, tried this exercise plan and that, worn whatever the magazines said was in fashion, smeared every new anti-aging cream you could find on every square inch you could reach . . . and yet here you are, the same old you again today, staring in the mirror, wondering what went wrong.

As I have discussed at some length, I am against dieting. I am not, however, against making positive and healthy changes—realistic ones—

to enrich our lives as well as prolong them. We'll get more into those kinds of changes in later chapters. The problem most of us face is that until we accept ourselves exactly as we are, warts and all, there's no way we can make lasting changes to our habits.

How many times have you hit Monday running, thinking, "This time it'll be different, I'm going to run five miles and eat nothing but carrots . . ." and by Wednesday you're thinking, "Damn it all, pass the Ben and Jerry's." I've done the same thing time and again, and like you, I chalked it up to a lack of willpower—weakness on my part.

How is it that I could be so weak when it comes to losing weight, but so strong when it comes to, say, surviving abuse, writing books, or not choking the hell out of a hundred people who deserve it on a daily basis?

Fact: I'm not weak, and you're not either. Even if you were, the problem has nothing to do with willpower. The problem is that, if you have already created a self-image with "miserable failure" as one of its main attributes, *you're going to fail.*

Remember how magic works. Intention is everything, but more importantly, underlying motivation is everything. You can tell yourself you're doing a spell to find a lover, but if deep down you're terrified of intimacy or you hate yourself, you're sabotaging your efforts right out of the gate. If you don't believe you deserve success, you can carry a hundred pounds of prosperity charms and nothing whatsoever will come of them.

Along with motivation, belief is vital. You can chant the night away and light enough candles to see from outer space, but if in your dark little heart you really don't believe you have the power to change the fabric of reality, well, you don't. Disbelief is the only true counterspell.

The same principle applies to every aspect of your life. Magic isn't just spells and bells—magic is any time you use energy and your will to weave a new future for yourself or others. The energy of self-loathing,

[handwritten in right margin: I've been more positive about this lately.]

[handwritten at bottom: I Can. I Can do this.]

and undermining your own abilities, can counteract the energy of the strongest cone of power.

Imagine if you were about to have surgery and you heard the anesthesiologist say to one of the techs, "You know, I really hate myself. I'm so dumb and worthless, I just can't do anything right." You'd run screaming, wouldn't you?

You may not want to hear this, but by and large, people do not diet or have plastic surgery because they love themselves. If you love yourself, you do so without condition or question—that means you love yourself fat and funny-looking. The choices you make out of love can make you healthier, but not necessarily prettier by societal standards. If you love yourself, being a size six won't matter to you—certainly not enough to deny yourself all the pleasure of life.

If you love yourself, you will not waste ten seconds every time you pass a reflective surface to bemoan the size of your butt. You will not devote hours and hours to workouts that you hate with every fiber of your being just to lose weight. You will not waste your money on the latest beauty fad, and will not risk your health to follow some idiotic plan or another that expects you to eat nothing but grapefruit. You won't ask a "doctor" to inject botulism into your face to temporarily plump out your wrinkles.

Self-esteem comes from within. It has absolutely nothing to do with the way one looks on the outside. When people realize this, our culture will be much better off.

DEBI

If you love yourself you won't need a number on a scale to tell you you're worthy. You won't need the approval of others. Your own inner light will be all the glamour you need.

That sounds great, you might be thinking. I'd be more than happy to ditch all of this inner criticism and stop wasting time and energy. The burning question is this: how do you learn to love yourself?

I would like more than anything to tell you that all you have to do is (insert quick fix here). Unfortunately, although we live in a world of shortcuts and fast lanes, anything genuinely worth having takes time

[handwritten in margin: Skinny ≠ self love]

and effort. Becoming a priestess, no matter what your tradition, takes months if not years of training, practice, and education . . . or, I hope it does. The same holds true for learning to work effective magic, to cast palpable circles, to become a dentist or a good parent—it takes time, and it takes work. Despite some popular assertions, there are not five easy steps to becoming a Witch, and there are not five easy steps to loving yourself.

Think of it this way: it took you years and years and constant media bombardment, internalization of criticism, and negative emotions to acquire the self-image you have now; that cannot be undone overnight. It could take just as many years to work through it.

It can, however, be done. There are a number of ways to go about it, but you can start with a handful of baby steps that can get you on the right path. The first is an ancient practice borrowed from our spiritual cousins in the East.

CULTIVATING MINDFULNESS—EXERCISE #4

Thich Nhat Hanh, a renowned Vietnamese Buddhist teacher, has a saying: "Washing the dishes is like bathing a baby Buddha." The Zen concept of mindfulness, bringing our full attention to the present moment, is vital to establishing a loving relationship with our bodies; rather than thinking about how great we'll look in the distant future when we've lost twenty pounds or had lipo, we appreciate what our bodies are doing right now. As you wash your hands, brush your teeth, or check your email, remember that—the simplest task can be an act of profound sanctity if you treat it that way.

Most of us live in a very disconnected state; we run our lives purely by mind, and only take notice of what's going on in our skin when we're in pain or uncomfortable. It goes back to the Great Divide; we deem the mind more important than the body, and deny its needs and desires.

text message

For this exercise, think of a sound you hear several times a day, prefer-ably no more than once an hour. You could set the alarm on your phone or watch to go off regularly, or choose an outside source—a local church bell ringing, a favorite song playing on the radio, the chime your com-puter emits when you get an email. I recommend sticking with positive sounds, as opposed to, say, a siren wailing down your street or a baby cry-ing. If you will remember, you could even time the exercise with trips to the restroom to freshen up, or with your coffee break.

In the morning when you get up, take a moment before your altar or mirror (or just sitting up in bed) to set your intent: today, every time you hear your chosen sound, you will "check in" with your body.

When the sound occurs, whatever you're doing, stop. Take a few slow, deep breaths. If possible, close your eyes. Now simply become aware of your body. Feel the edges of your skin, the temperature of the room; feel your back in contact with your chair; feel your bones, your posture. Take note of places that are tense or hurting. Each thing you notice, say to yourself silently: "My head hurts. My feet are cold. My butt is falling asleep." If you feel great, say so—in fact, say so twice for good measure. Also notice how your level of stress or whatever emotion you are experiencing at the moment affects your body. Are there butterflies in your stomach? Are your shoulders slumped? Are you contorted in the back seat of a Volkswagen?

Don't try to change anything, necessarily, though if you're in pain I highly recommend doing something about it. Just become aware of your physical self, of exactly what you are doing and exactly how it feels. Make no judgments.

You might be surprised how this simple exercise can connect you more fully with your life. We tend to rush through the day in a fog; I've driven home from work a hundred times without remembering a sec-ond of the trip. Becoming mindful is one of the most profound prac-tices of Buddhism, and in and of itself can revolutionize your spiritual

[handwritten, top margin: Be 'in your body' not disconnected from!]

[handwritten, right margin: try to be mindful! days,]

practice. It doesn't require long hours of the lotus position or candles in six different colors; it is a tribute to beauty in simplicity.

Try checking in while you're eating, bathing, playing. You may find yourself enjoying some activities more than you thought you did, because now you are fully engaged in what you are doing—and you may find that there are some things you've been doing by rote that you can eliminate from your day. For example, if you grit your teeth and curse under your breath every second you're on the Stairmaster, you might consider finding a new form of exercise.

You can also pair mindfulness with the next essential practice.

> I can feel so
> unsexy for
> someone so
> beautiful
>
> So unloved for
> someone so fine
>
> I can feel so
> boring for
> someone so
> interesting
>
> So ignorant
> for someone of
> sound mind . . .
>
> ALANIS
> MORISSETTE

[handwritten: Stopped here. for the next few]

Affirmations and the Evil Auctioneer

All day long, every day, there is a voice in your head—sometimes a murmur, sometimes a roar, but almost always annoying. It's the voice that tells you you're not good enough, not beautiful enough, not white or young or thin or tall enough. This voice takes all of those things people said, which you burned away earlier in this chapter, and runs them over and over in an endless monologue of criticism.

Some people think of the voice as a series of tapes. Each tape is labeled: "You're the ugliest thing that ever lived," "Nobody will ever love you," "Men don't make passes at girls with fat asses." Depending on the situation, your ego puts in the appropriate tape to make you feel as horrible about yourself as possible.

Still others hear the voices of people who have hurt them—an abusive father, a sworn enemy from grade school. You don't consciously choose this voice; it's a minion of the shadow Reflection, made up of your fears and doubts about your own worth.

This voice is often referred to as the inner critic, the judge, and so on; mine is more like an evil auctioneer. He talks a hundred miles per hour, and the words don't really matter so much as the fact that he's trying to sell me a load of snake oil.

You can never be rid of your internal monologue. It's how your brain processes what's going on around you and relates it to the knowledge and experience you already have. What you can do, though, is choose to banish the evil auctioneer and hire someone with a gentler voice. You can reprogram your mind to serve up affirmations instead of criticism.

Affirmations are a powerful tool, but they often end up lumped into the category of New Age Crystal Granola Nonsense. For some reason, every time I read a list of affirmations in a book, in my mind's eye I see a hippie woman in tie-dye sitting cross-legged, thumbs and forefingers in circles, swaying back and forth and intoning in a vague, airy voice, "I am a being of pure, healing light . . ." Like working with quartz crystals and aromatherapy, affirmations get a bad rap among "serious" Pagans. I've been guilty of a bit of snobbery myself. That's a shame, because positive messages can become just as deeply embedded in your brain as negative ones, and if the evil auctioneer can have his say, so can my inner flower child.

A RITUAL TO CHANGE YOUR INNER VOICE

Again, perform this ritual in front of your mirror; it's important that, as you say the words that follow, you can look yourself in the face and know who you're talking to. You might feel a little self-conscious at first, so you may need to do this ritual several times, or even regularly, to feel the effect.

Part of this ritual is a guided meditation, so you should have a way to sit down in front of the mirror. If you still have your candles of Truth and Beauty, light them; you will also need a list of affirmations, which we'll discuss in a moment. Again, you can dress this rite up as much or as little as you like.

Beforehand, choose one or two of the affirmations listed below, or if there's another one you prefer, use it instead.

I am a child of the God and Goddess, and I am beautiful.

I am strong, creative, and wise (or insert three positive attributes of your own).

My body is a holy instrument of the Lord and Lady.

I accept and love myself fully, just as I am at this moment.

I am born of earth, water, fire, and air, essentially perfect and one of a kind.

I have the power to make healthy choices.

I am a Witch, a woman of the Goddess, and I am blessed.

I recommend using positive language, "I am" statements rather than "I am not" statements, although the "not" can have a power of its own, like a banishing spell. Generally, though, it's best to think in positives, because the second you include a negative like "not," "never," or "won't," your mind latches onto the tone before it even interprets the words, and the negativity is what stays with you. But if you really feel like you need to say, "I am not a hideous waste of carbon atoms," go for it.

Cast circle in your usual way, as before. Light the Truth and Beauty candles, and state your intention: "I come to the circle this night to change my inner voice" (or similar).

Call to the Lord and Lady as you did in the last ritual, or however you feel moved to.

Now, look your Reflection in the eyes. Remember that you banished the false impression of yourself and burned it to ashes, so what you are looking at is the absolute truth as you perceive it. Before your inner critic can open its mouth, begin by saying your name aloud three times. (Use your legal, Craft, or whatever name you feel is the one most connected to your true self.) As you speak, extend your senses and feel the entirety of your body around you, checking in briefly as you have learned to do. The repetition is important, because as you feel your body and say your name, you anchor your glamour-free Reflection in your identity. Who you are looking at, without the mask, is the essence of who you are as a physical being.

Next, speak each of your affirmations aloud once or twice, just to get a feel for them. You'll be using them a lot from here on out, so be sure they are right for you. As I said before, you might feel a bit silly, but do it anyway. The heart of any good ritual is removing the constraints of the "adult" world and returning to a simpler, sillier way of seeing.

Then sit back, get comfortable, and close your eyes. In your mind's eye, imagine that the voice in your head that denigrates you is an actual person or being. Create an image of that person—hopefully it isn't someone you know, but if the voice of your inner critic is your mother, try not to connect the image too strongly with the real person. Change its appearance if at all possible. Visualize the critic as a nasty, cruel little creature like a goblin or troll, if that feels more appropriate.

Now, imagine silencing it. You could squash it or set it on fire, but a less deadly method might be more believable as well as more ethical—we can't have you gathering imaginary-creature-death karma. Visualize it packing its bags and moving out, or with a big strip of duct tape over its mouth, or trapped in a mason jar; if its fate is ridiculous, that's fine, because the inner critic is, at heart, ridiculous. It tells you lies, it distorts the truth, it makes a cartoon and a mockery of your natural Goddess-given beauty. Kick it to the curb.

You can't stop here, however. Without the judge, there is now a void in your mind, just waiting for another wicked voice to take advantage of your vulnerability. Like any pest, after you banish the existing critters, you have to make sure the environment is inhospitable for any others that come along.

Silently or aloud, say, "Lady of the starlit night, I ask that you lend me your voice, so that the words I hear inside will be a true reflection of the beauty you have created in me."

Feel the energy of the Goddess gently washing through your mind, cleansing you of the negative programming and any remaining traces of the judge. Open your eyes so that you can read your affirmations again, but this time, imagine you can hear the voice of the Mother speaking with you; let her voice replace the old one. Remember that the voice of the Lady will speak only the truth, which means that your affirmations are the truth. You are beautiful, and blessed, and filled with spirit just as you are.

You can close the ritual at this point, or meditate on your affirmations; one of my favorite ways to end a circle like this is with the following traditional chant:

Woman am I

Spirit am I

I am the infinite within my soul

I have no beginning and I have no end

All this I am

Blessed am I

Spirit am I

I am the infinite within my soul

I have no beginning and I have no end

All this I am . . .

(See the end of the chapter for places you can find recordings of this chant.)

You may think that this ritual is similar in function to the one before, but the first ritual was the first step in enabling yourself to see clearly; the second builds on that clarity. You must be able to see your true Reflection before affirmations like the above can really take root—if you still look at yourself through the glamour of false perception, you will never believe anything positive about your body or your value to the world. Think of it as taking off your sunglasses and then putting in a new pair of contacts.

To take the ritual into your daily life, combine it with the mindfulness practice. Every time you check in, in addition to becoming mindful of your body, pay attention to your mental state. If you are having negative thoughts toward yourself, repeat your affirmations, hearing them echo with the Goddess's voice.

The Glamour that Matters

You may have noticed that in the Pagan community there are several subcultures, each with its own fashion. At any large gathering, you will probably see a hundred variations on Standard Wiccan Outfit #1, which usually involves a sarong and not much else. Aside from that, though, there may also be a hippie chick in an embroidered tunic with flowers in her hair; a goth all in black, who come to think of it probably won't be at the gathering because she doesn't go out in daylight; the S&M maven in leather with what looks like a swing set in her tent; the feminist in solid hiking boots and an "A Woman Needs a Man Like a Fish Needs a Bicycle" T-shirt; the newer class, Indie Witch, often seen in an Avril Lavigne-esque combination of all of the above. Oh, and let's not forget the skyclad crowd, who are often sunburned.

Then at rituals, we all put on our Pagan finery—velvet, hooded cloaks, all sorts of gear that would terrify the Renaissance re-enactors with its mad, anachronistic variety.

Are we creating and adhering to stereotypes by dressing a part? We try very hard to be individuals, but you don't see a lot of business suits in circle, and there usually seems to be a common theme: any time period but now. Have we set up a whole new kind of fashion fascism in our own community even as we distance ourselves from the Gap-shopping, polo-shirt-wearing population?

I don't think it matters what you wear, either in circle or out of it. If you want to put on full makeup to go check the mail, if you want to wear short shorts or ball gowns, I say, knock yourself out. What is important isn't what you put on, but *why* you put it on.

Subcultures, both within Paganism and in society in general, often adopt a standard of appearance as a way of dealing with the Reflection. They feel different from the rest of the world, and so they dress to reflect the inside on the outside. This creates its own sort of glamour, as showing your inner self to the world is a very empowering feeling. Not to mention that there is an even greater sense of rightness when you know that there are others who feel as you do; even the bohemian rebels that tend to wind up in the Pagan community have a very human need to belong. When you don your goth chic and go to the club to be surrounded by those whose tastes match your own, you evoke a kind of magic of unity—as there is safety in numbers, there is also power, and the incredible relief of, as they say, letting your freak flag fly, and no longer denying who you are.

This only becomes a problem when we lose sight of why we choose to dress and look the way we do. When it becomes purely an issue of fitting in instead of a combination of solidarity and self-expression, we find ourselves in the same kind of bondage we were in in mainstream culture, going along with what is considered "normal" even if that's a skewed normal indeed.

WHAT THE HELL ARE YOU WEARING?— EXERCISE #5

Look down at yourself. What are you wearing?

Why are you wearing it? Does what you have on at this moment express something about yourself—a favorite color, an era, a texture that you like feeling on your skin? Or did you put it on as Muggle drag for your day job or to avoid drawing too much attention to yourself?

Think about the times you've felt genuinely sexy, totally confident, or completely and utterly yourself. How did you look on the outside at the time?

What do you base your wardrobe, makeup, and jewelry choices on—how you feel that morning, what you're expected to look like, what will shock people, what makes you feel like a true badass? Do you strap yourself into uncomfortable clothes, and with them an uncomfortable role?

Now that you have shed the glamour of the distorted Reflection, how can you begin to express your inner beauty on the outside, so that anyone who meets you can immediately tell they're dealing with an amazing human being?

When you are comfortable in your own skin, you will find that assuming the uniform of conformity chafes a lot more than it used to. The outside is only skin deep, but the inside can't be seen at all unless you let it out to play.

For many years I dressed in Wal-Mart plus-sized hideousness; nothing colorful, nothing form-fitting, and for the love of Goddess, nothing that would show my upper arms. The more I grew to appreciate my body and its inherent fabulousness, and the more I came to know myself, the less acceptable it was to be a shapeless grey blob. The turning point, I think, was a birthday present from my mother, my black leather "What is the Matrix?" trench coat. When I put it on, it was like the real Sylvan suddenly came sauntering out of the shadows, and damn, but I like the way she walks.

I found that I still didn't like bright colors—given my choice, every article of clothing I own would be black, dark red, or possibly brown. I chucked the elastic-waist "fat girl pants" and invested in jeans that let the world know that yes, I have a butt, and it's a fine and mighty one. I go for shirts that show off my breasts; being looked at isn't the horror it once was, now that I am not afraid to look at myself. Next stop: corsets.

What have you been avoiding, clothes-wise, because you were told people your size/coloring/shape/age didn't wear that? Who are they to tell you what to do? Calvin Klein doesn't have breasts, and neither do his models. Fashion shows often boast marvels like a toothpick girl wearing what looks like a live ocelot on her head. Does somebody with that kind of taste in women and clothes get to dictate how you look?

AWARENESS—EXERCISE #6

The last thing I'd like to mention as integral to your quest toward self-acceptance is awareness—not of yourself this time, but of the women all around you.

First, become aware of how you react to bodies that are different from your own. Judging each other on appearance is almost a reflex in Western women; despite all the progress we've made in society, we continue to sabotage ourselves and each other by treating our sisters as the enemy. We are forced into competition over jobs, mates, status; this is worsened when our own self-esteem is damaged, and we often run others down in a desperate bid to feel superior.

When you're out wandering the world, take notice of the thoughts that fly through your head when you see a person with a different skin color. Consider those thoughts—are they from your authentic self, or from societal prejudices that have been pounded into your head? Put yourself into the life of the person you are looking at, and imagine what they face.

I have had to fight racism my entire life—not towards me, but from me. I grew up in the Southern United States, where skin color is still a sharp dividing line in how people are treated. Most of the people in my hometown are decent folk, but they are a product of their culture and their time; it's very common to hear things like, "She's black, but she's such a good person" or "Chinese people are so good at math."

These are thought of as compliments, believe it or not. In my family, overt racism is almost unheard of, but latent racism is as traditional as Sunday barbecue. From a very young age I have had to teach myself not to internalize those messages, and I'll be the first to admit that it's very hard to get past what I've been taught. I feel fortunate to live in such a diverse city as Austin, where I am constantly exposed to new cultures and creeds that keep my mind open and ready to learn.

In addition, pay attention to how you think of those with "disabilities." Do you remind yourself of the challenges they face, or are you just ticked that you can't park in the designated spot? The first impulse most of us have is pity, which is frankly an insult to most disabled people, who are just as capable of leading full and happy lives as anyone else. Who is more disabled—a woman with no legs who competes in wheelchair races, or a woman with two fully functioning legs who never leaves the house in summer because she hates how she looks in shorts?

All women of all shapes and sizes face the onslaught of the body wars. We have all suffered the same wound, though it is expressed differently for all of us. We are warriors in a common struggle, and if we turn our swords on each other, we'll never storm the castle.

Though the fight to reclaim our personal sanctity may feel like a very lonely one at times, I can assure you, you are not alone. Chances are most of the women you know have faced some kind of difficulty, discrimination, or just plain disrespect because of their appearance. Even "beautiful" women can be victims—most people with anorexia don't weigh 260 pounds; they reach 100 and keep starving, because "you can never be too rich or too thin." Not to mention that the few women (all five of them) who were born fitting into our current societal standard are almost universally hated by the other 99 percent of us.

When you meet other women, or even see them on the street, try to think of a mythological or legendary figure that they remind you of. Remember the vast and wondrous diversity of the Goddess's faces, and see them in the faces of the women you encounter, as you see her in yourself.

Goddesses of the Reflection

Since the Reflection isn't an archetype in the way, say, the Mother is, there just aren't a lot of associated myths. Mirrors are a common motif in faery tales and folklore, however, and almost always relate somehow to concepts of beauty.

There is Snow White's wicked stepmother, of course, and her "Mirror, mirror, on the wall . . ." The story of Snow White, in fact, is an interesting look at what makes an ideal princess. The stepmother is insanely jealous of her young, attractive stepchild, and does everything she possibly can to make Snow's life difficult, up to trying to kill her. When the Prince comes to wake sleeping Snow, he is drawn to her beauty—you'll notice that after she wakes up he whisks her off to wed without even asking if she's read any good books lately.

When it comes to the Reflection, however, it is more important to look for those who embody what the mirror symbolizes: comfort in one's own skin.

While most Wiccans are used to seeing the Goddess as a lunar deity, in Shintoism, the principal female figure was the sun goddess Amaterasu, whose name in Japanese means "she who shines in the heavens." Amaterasu was unbelievably brilliant and beautiful, so much so that her parents sent her up the celestial ladder to the heavens, where she ruled ever afterward. Up until modern times, members of the imperial family were considered her descendants.

There came a day, however, when Amaterasu took her light from the world; her brother, Susanowo the storm god, got a bit carried away and ravaged the earth, and Amaterasu grew so angry at his depredations that she closed herself in her cave, hauling a heavy rock over the entrance. The sun no longer shone, and the earth began to die for lack of her warmth; day and night were confused with one another, the crops could not grow, and demons threatened to take over the world. The gods banded together to try and coax Amaterasu out of hiding, but all failed.

Then, Uzume, the dancing goddess of joy, decided to give it a try. She got up in front of the gods and performed bawdy songs and dances until they were laughing uproariously. Amaterasu was intrigued by the sound of such merriment, and peeked out of the cave just a bit—luckily for the world, Uzume had hung a mirror from a nearby tree angled perfectly to catch the tiny sliver of light that slipped through the entrance.

Amaterasu had never seen her own reflection before, and the sight of her own incredible radiance hypnotized her. She drew closer to the mirror, amazed, and the gods closed the cave behind her and sealed it so the sun could never again leave the world.

Much like Amaterasu, women often need to be reminded of our own innate beauty. We get used to seeing ourselves a certain way—beneath the glamour, in the darkness of the cave—until something makes us look again, shaking up our perceptions, and suddenly we are enchanted by our own light. It is only when we emerge and truly see ourselves that we can shine for the whole world.

In addition to Amaterasu, Warrior women and goddesses seem especially appropriate for learning to step up and be fully yourself. I'll bet you money that Xena never asked Gabrielle, "Does this tunic make me look fat?" Joan of Arc probably didn't spend much time contemplating a boob job, either.

One of my favorite goddesses in this respect is Artemis, the Greek goddess of the wilds and the hunt, often associated with the waxing crescent moon. She was later known to the Romans as Diana, who absorbed most of Artemis' attributes; even today Wiccans often refer to the waxing crescent as "Diana's Bow."

At an early age, Artemis implored her father, Zeus, to allow her eternal virginity. It is thought, in current interpretations of Greek myth, that "virgin" originally had nothing to do with one's level of sexual experience; to say you were virgin meant you were pure, whole unto yourself.

Artemis had no use for the influence of men, and in fact lived apart from most of the rest of the Olympians, roaming the woodlands with her nymphs, also virgins.

Woe to any man who dared look upon the goddess as she bathed; a hunter named Actaeon made that mistake, and she turned him into a stag and set his own hounds upon him. In another story, Orion attempted to rape her, and she conjured up a scorpion that killed him and his dog, who later became the constellations Sirius and Orion.

Like Artemis, we as women can choose not to be swayed by the will of others. Her strength and self-assurance were as natural to her as the deer of the wood; she valued herself highly enough that she exacted immediate vengeance on anyone who tried to disparage her. She can help us see ourselves as valuable, worthy of respect and honor, especially from ourselves. She never questions her place in the world and never hesitates to defend it; everyone knows you don't screw around with the Divine Huntress.

A MEDITATION ON ARTEMIS

Artemis is an intensely physical goddess; I often envision her very differently from the traditional Greek image of a woman in a white toga. By all means, adjust the imagery in the meditation to the traditional, if you prefer. If you wish to bring her energy into your life, start by learning her myths and history, as well as something of the culture that named her. Then call to her, ritually speaking; if the two of you get along, she may stay with you until you have learned all she has to teach.

For this meditation, find a comfortable place to sit for a while where you won't be disturbed. You might want to have quiet music or recorded forest or stream sounds playing in the background, if it won't skew your focus. Burn a woodsy incense like pine, cedar, or patchouli; though Artemis is a lunar goddess, we'll be talking more about her earthy aspects here.

Ground and center, and relax your body in whatever way you generally do for meditations. Allow the images to grow around you.

You are standing in the forest, and it is night. High above, a thin crescent moon cups a scattering of stars. The night is calm and peaceful, with the sounds of owls and animals in the trees and thicket around you. This wood is unknown to you, yet something about it is familiar, as if you remember it from another life.

You wander along the paths of the wood a while, taking in the serenity of the evening as it deepens and the circle of time turns in its ageless waltz in the sky. Eventually you come upon a well-worn track through the underbrush, too wide to have been made by deer alone; curious, you follow it into the heart of the forest.

(pause)

The track opens out into a small clearing, where a fire has been built in a hollow in the ground. There is no one here except for you, but you have nothing to fear. The sense of familiarity has grown, and you are almost sure you have seen this place before.

On the far side of the fire pit, you catch sight of a shining object leaning back against a massive dark oak. You approach it, stepping around the fire, and see that it is a mirror in an old, worn frame. It looks almost as if it has grown out of the tree, whose roots surround it protectively. On the ground before the mirror is a polished antler, perhaps left as an offering.

You look into the mirror, but it is not your face that stares out at you. It is the face of a woman in green and grey, watching you with a mischievous smile. She wears a quiver full of white-feathered arrows, and holds a longbow in her hands.

You know her as you know your own name: Artemis, Lady of the Wild. She is protectress of this wood, the Divine Huntress whose hands deal both life and death. The crescent moon above you is reflected in her eyes, which look you over, evaluating you keenly.

"Take my hand," she says.

You reach out and touch the mirror, and find that her hand is real—it is your hand. The image in the mirror blurs like a stone dropped into a still pond, and when it clears again, the Goddess reflected has your face, your eyes, your hair. You look down and see a bow in your hands.

You know your own name as you knew her: Artemis, Lady of the Wild. You leave the mirror and the clearing, for you have work to do this night; the forest is your home and your child, and you have a sacred charge to protect it from the vagaries of humankind.

As you walk, you find you are not alone on the path. A silver-white hound slips gracefully out of the thicket to your side, followed by another, and another. You may find that other young women come to your hunt; they, too, have heard the call from beyond the borders of the city, and seek to fulfill a longing in their blood for freedom.

You run through the forest, jumping fallen logs, swinging joyfully from low-hanging limbs; your muscles are strong, your limbs lithe and quick, and you exult in the kiss of the night air on your skin. Your feet are purposeful on the path, curving through lands where no one has ever walked but you and the beasts of the wood. You splash through a shallow creek, laughing at the freezing water that hits your legs.

You run to the top of a rise that gives you an unobstructed view of your home, and stand with your shoulders back, arms crossed, a satisfied smile playing about your lips. You are mistress of all that is wild and free, untamed, unchallenged in your power. No man would dare approach you without your leave; no man would dare kill one of your beasts, and risk the wrath of the Huntress.

(pause)

Alone, you bring down an animal for meat. You track it silently for an hour or more, moving so carefully not a leaf stirs in your wake. Your arms are steady as you aim and loose the arrow, a single shot to the heart; you kneel beside the creature, thanking it for its sacrifice, knowing your place on the Wheel of Life means that life must end so that life may continue.

Your companions emerge from the wood to escort you to the clearing where the fire pit is burning, where you will feast and pass the rest of the night far from the world of civilized folk, safe and imprisoned in their beds. Your women laugh and tell stories, their voices unrestrained; they have learned from you to hold their heads high and to be unashamed.

(pause)

As dawn approaches, you rise from the fireside and stretch, feeling muscle and bone lengthen as you breathe. All around you is quiet, the moon has long set. Your eyes fall upon the mirror once more.

You return to its polished surface, see the face of the Goddess looking back. You touch a hand to the glass, and the hand in the mirror is the Lady's again, and you are yourself as before.

But the strength of Artemis is still in your veins, and you bid her farewell, leaving an offering of the creature whose flesh fed your hunting party; and you walk back into the forest, the way you came, feeling the energy of the Wild One singing through you, infusing your whole being with appreciation for the legs that walk you, the skin that holds you, the fiery heart that beats its tribal rhythm as you walk out into the sunrise.

SUGGESTIONS FOR EXPLORING THE REFLECTION

1. Find a copy of Maya Angelou's poem, "Phenomenal Woman." Tape it to your mirror.

2. Walk around your house naked. Nothing will get you used to your body faster than having to see it all the time instead of hiding it under a floral-print tent. Be careful when answering the door, however, or you'll have the UPS guy winking at you for years to come.

3. Designate a special candle that you keep in the bathroom or in front of whatever mirror you've been using for the exercises in this chapter. Consecrate the candle as a reminder of your true, Goddess-given beauty, and burn it whenever you are getting

dressed, bathing, or attending to any other beauty and hygiene pursuits. When you light it, say a brief invocation such as, "By the grace of the Lady, whose face mirrors my own, may I ever remember I am made in her image, blessed and beautiful."

Recommended Reading and Resources for Chapter Three

BOOKS

Phenomenal Woman by Maya Angelou

Bountiful Women by Bonnie Bernell

Kiss My Tiara: How to Rule the World as a Smart-Mouthed Goddess by Susan J. Gilman

200 Ways to Love the Body You Have by Marcia G. Hutchinson

Women's Bodies, Women's Wisdom by Christiane Northrup

Peace is Every Step by Thich Nhat Hanh

Fat! So? Because You Don't Have to Apologize for Your Size by Marilyn Wann

CDS

"Woman am I, Blessed am I" can be found on the CD *Circle of Women*, which you may have a hard time finding; if you can locate it, however, it's worth its weight in gold.

THE

mother

I have prepared a place for you, child
Within the circle of my arms
Sit with me at the table, yield up your hurry
Shed the noise and the haste
And hold out your hands.
I bring you the grain that has grown
On my skin,
I bring you the wind that blows
Through my hair,
I bring you the water that flows
Through my veins,
I bring you the light that flashes
In my eyes.
I bring you the song of birds,
The rustle of leaves,

The scent of rain,
The hundred butterfly colors of sunset.
Hold out your hands
Open your heart:
May you never hunger
May you never thirst
But first, close your mouth
And be still.

As a face of the Goddess, the Mother doesn't really need a lot of explanation. Even if you grew up without one, you probably know what a mother is, what she does, and why—at least, ideally.

For our purposes, we'll define the Mother as that part of ourselves that nurtures, whether ourselves or others. While it's the most well-known feminine archetype, it also carries the most baggage for modern women.

Today women are expected to want it all, and to have it all—career, house, husband, kids. Somehow we are supposed to fit all possible roles into one life, preferably all at the same time; if we can't figure out a way to balance on the tightrope of society's expectations with a child in one hand, a briefcase in the other, and a bridal veil on our heads, we are looked on as failures. Essentially, our place in society is still wavering between Housewife/Mother and Breadwinner. If we opt for one over the other, we're in for trouble.

Stay-at-home moms come under fire from career women, who often accuse them of succumbing to sex stereotypes. Career women are criticized by a wide variety of people, particularly if (gasp!) a career gal doesn't want children, or (double gasp!) a husband.

I don't want children. I never have. I am perfectly content to be an aunt, and a cousin, and to shower gifts and hugs on certain kids and then hand them back to mom. Just try telling that to people, though, and you'll hear:

"Oh, you'll change your mind someday."

"It's different when it's your children."

"Of course you do, honey, all women want babies."

Don't even get me started on not wanting a husband. I'm what you might call a semitypical-looking Southern woman with a fairly typical American background; I grew up in a small town, raised by good Protestant parents, I'm white—when people meet me they make a set of assumptions that include words like "Christian," "straight," and, "looking for Prince Charming."

Imagine their surprise when they find out I'm a heteroflexible Wiccan who has been known to have multiple lovers (some at the same time) and has very little interest in babies, white picket fences, and the PTA.

A woman without a husband and family in the Western world is considered less of a woman, as if there is only one way to be creative and to contribute to the world. We have as a culture taken the Mother archetype and turned her into a repository for all of the negative gender bias that we strive so hard to overcome: the image of woman as caring, loving helpmeet, staying at home, barefoot and pregnant, making meatloaf and keeping a spotless house, doting on her man . . . pardon me while I gag.

I know plenty of women who are stay-at-home moms and are perfectly happy and fulfilled in that role and not at all subjugated or stereotypical—more power to them. It's not as if a mom dealing with a screaming wee beast isn't work. Just because that's not really in the cards for me doesn't mean I have the right to look down on them, which I wish I could say about everyone who takes a different path. If stay-at-home moms can raise children who are smarter and kinder than the majority of those out there nowadays, I salute them. Good, responsible parents seem to be in short supply these days. Child rearing is not for the faint of heart—but it's also not for everyone.

We've got to learn to stop living *for* other people— to listen to our own will and our own hearts, and be who we are—and stop trying to con- form to what the media/the church/the hus- band/whoever wants us to be. We cannot be whole in our own power until we stop trying to be what we're not.

SIREN

The Mother archetype is mistakenly equated with giving birth to human children and taking care of a household. This drastic oversimplification is a disservice to all women, including those who do take that route. There are a thousand ways to be a woman, and there are as many ways to be a Mother.

Any time you create something, from an art project to a poem to a casserole to a business merger, you are working with the strength of the Mother. She is the Great Creatrix who births the universe every day and then sits down with the morning paper and a cup of tea. She is the part of us that cares, and loves deeply, and tends to the wounds and ailments of friends, fam- ily, and society. She is the center of our compassion.

Although the archetype has a lot of negative connota- tions in modern life, the Mother is still the most widely called-upon image of the Goddess, both for Wiccans and for many an- cient cultures. Why? There is no relationship more instinctive, no call more primal than that of a child for its mother. It is the call heard most often, and the call most often betrayed; whether we have been deprived of her love in human form or not, when life becomes difficult, we want our Mother.

Not even Church dogma could destroy this need; the Virgin Mary is invoked as the Mother of God, but also as Mother to all, even if she is never named so. Perhaps we look to a masculine God for protection, deliverance, and guidance, but when we need to be held, rocked, and sheltered, our hearts cry for the Lady's arms.

When it comes to our bodies, the Mother is our caretaker there, as well. Her manifestation in our physical lives is in how we nurture ourselves.

What do I mean by nurture? The Mother's domain includes those things we do that feed us, whether literally speaking or figuratively. She makes sure we have breakfast and sends us sighing into a hot bath at the end of the day. She helps us make healthy choices that prolong our lives and improve our quality of life—things as basic as what to have for dinner, what to wear in winter, and how often we sit and breathe, are her specialties.

As much as the Mother gives her compassion and kindness to others, she will also give it to us, if we allow her to. That is, however, easier said than done.

Women are taught from a young age to act as Mother to the world, but almost never to ourselves. From the time our first doll is thrust into our hands, we learn that girls take care of other people. We learn that it's okay to give and give until we have nothing left, but to take time and space for ourselves . . . well, that's just selfish.

Selfish is one of the words the Mother has to face on a regular basis. Though self-help books and yoga classes and aromatherapy bath salts proliferate, we are still made to feel guilty for taking care of ourselves. Lying in bed early on a weeknight, we think of a dozen things we should be doing, useful things, like laundry and leveraged buyouts. Surely, we say, there are more important things than naps.

We are terrified of wasting time. Think of it—we have all these labor-saving devices, from palm pilots to self-cleaning ovens, but do you really have more time now than you did ten years ago? Does having a cell phone make your life easier? At the end of the week do you suddenly find yourself in a stretch of hours with nothing to do, because you saved so much time all week long with our wondrous modern technology?

Not likely. If anything, you're busier. The ability to do business anywhere doesn't mean you'll get it done faster; it means you'll do more business. We live in a constant state of stress, usually over work, which most of us don't even enjoy. The prevailing lifestyle in America seems to be working at a job you don't like to buy junk you don't need. Is it any wonder that heart attacks and depression are creeping their way into our lives?

The major side effect of our fast-paced rat race is that we forget the essential practice of self-nurture. We cram fast food into our mouths while driving, drink gallons of coffee, stay up way too late, and barely even notice the passage of seasons or even the passage of days. That, to me, isn't living, it's existing. For beings who have been given the divine gifts of intellect, imagination, and passion, mere existence isn't much of a goal.

SOMETHING TO THINK ABOUT—EXERCISE #1

When was the last time you took an entire day just for yourself? What did you do? Did you feel guilty the whole time, or were you able to let go and enjoy it?

Chances are you haven't had a whole day in years, so what about an evening? An hour? When was the last time you got a massage, or a decent haircut, or spent a Sunday in your pajamas watching reruns of *I Love Lucy*?

Do you keep your cell phone on you, and turned on, at all times? Why? Is it more necessary now for people to be able to track you down anywhere, anytime, than it was before you had the phone? How did you live, then, when all phones were confined to the indoors?

Do you have an altar or shrine of some kind in your home? When was the last time you took twenty minutes to simply sit in front of it and talk to the Lord and Lady? If you make time on a daily basis to commune and meditate, you're doing splendidly; even twice a week is really something, given how insane most people's lives have become.

Women and Food

Eating is a loaded subject for most women. We spend an inordinate amount of time worrying over what to eat, how much to eat, how often to eat . . . we probably think about food more than the people who are starving in Third World countries.

Only in a civilization as materialistic and wealthy as the modern West could some people be dying of hunger in the streets while other people eat perfectly good meals and then vomit them up afterward. If we're not denying ourselves the simple pleasure of an occasional candy bar, we're sneaking a whole bag of chocolate kisses in the middle of the night and hiding them under the mattress like common criminals.

Strange, really, that we have developed a separate set of morals to apply only to food. Cake is bad, carrots are good. Cookies are naughty, plain grilled chicken is virtuous. We applaud ourselves for abstaining from "bad" foods, things that taste sinful—which of course means that those foods are the ones we want more than anything else in the world.

Remember being a teenager, when your parents said you couldn't have something? Didn't that make you want it that much more? That guy in the leather jacket who smoked and listened to Metallica was your parents' worst nightmare, and the one you snuck off to make out with. We do the same thing to ourselves at every meal. "I can't have dessert, I'm on a diet." Meanwhile, in the back of your mind you're planning a late-night trip to the Quickie Mart for a pint of Ben and Jerry's and all the candy you can buy with the change under the couch cushions.

It's said that eating disorders are about control. Young women and girls especially feel powerless in their lives for one reason or another. Their hormones are wreaking havoc, their families might not get along, they may have problems at school with feeling "different" or being made fun of, but food is the one thing they feel they can have power

> My only problem with food is that there never seems to be enough cake in my pantry.
> ANISE

over . . . for a time. They can say no to a meal, they can do the exact number of sit-ups it takes to work off a sandwich . . . but what they don't realize is that food is controlling them just as strongly as if they ate nonstop.

In reality, we have all given food too much power in our lives. When you're on a diet it's all you think about—what you're going to eat at the next meal, how many calories/carbs/grams of fat it has, what you wish you could eat instead, what other people are eating that you can't . . . every bite becomes a matter of life and death, as if a single suck off a lollipop will turn you into Elephant Woman and one "meal replacement shake" makes you a saint.

Think of all the foods you avoid because they're "bad." Are they really? Did that donut hold up a convenience store? Do those french fries moonlight as child molesters? It sounds pretty stupid from that perspective—well, there is an inherent stupidity in assigning a moral value to something that by its nature cannot have morals. That's like saying a chair is evil because you leaned too far back and fell out of it.

> No food is bad food, except maybe beets.
>
> TERRI

Despite all the crazy, useless, and sometimes dangerous fad diets and recommendations of various quacks throughout the centuries, we all know pretty much what nutrients our bodies need and what foods, eaten in overabundance, are detrimental to our health. We're not stupid, despite what advertisers want us to think. The majority of people, even those who fall prey to the idiocy of the trends, know deep down that any eating plan that claims five hamburgers with bacon is a better lunch than soup and a salad is, if not completely ridiculous, at least suspect.

Bah, you say. Eating like that isn't bad for you if you only do it for a little while. And it's worth it to lose weight.

Sure. You only need one kidney to live, anyway. And added cholesterol is like ankle weights for your heart—makes it stronger, you know.

In case you can't smell it from where you are, that was sarcasm.

But I'm not here to tell you what to eat—like I said, you already know that. Any kid who's taken grade-school health class knows that. The basics of good nutrition have not changed, despite all the diet industry's efforts to the contrary. What matters to me is our relationship with food, and therefore our relationship with the Mother, who is our provider and our sustenance.

What you put in your mouth matters very little if you put it there for the wrong reasons. (That applies to so many areas of life . . . but I digress.) We eat to fuel our bodies, yes, but just as often we eat to celebrate, to escape, to anesthetize ourselves, to grieve, to sublimate our rage, to fit in . . . the list goes on and on.

For most of my adult life, I've had problems with food. I might even go so far as to call myself a compulsive eater, though in my mind almost everyone is a compulsive eater these days. There was a time when I ate to fill a great aching void in myself as well as to hide from the world that had hurt me. Some part of me decided that if I was fat enough, nobody would ever want to look at me, let alone lay a hand on me.

It's flawed logic, but it's very widespread; so is the idea that ice cream will never insult you, will never leave you, will never forget to call, will never sleep with your sister. Eventually I reached the point where I never knew the difference between genuine hunger and just wanting to eat, and the habit remained even though the issues behind it weren't so pressing. I ate whether I was hungry or not, and ate things that I didn't even like, just to have something to eat. I lived off mouth hunger rather than belly hunger.

Mouth hunger is what you feel when you stand in front of the fridge an hour after dinner pondering whether to suck on the can of whipped cream or make a batch of cookie dough with no intention of baking cookies. Mouth hunger is what seizes you when you have a hard day at work and come home to slip into a nice tub of fried chicken. It has no connection to your stomach or your body's needs for nutrition; it is emotional, compulsive, and rarely thought out. Cravings are a form of mouth hunger, because if you can wait a craving out, it usually fades, unless it's for chocolate, which has an agenda of its own.

Belly hunger is the real deal, and even there we have trouble—in our frantic pace of life we eat too much too quickly, short-circuiting our natural feelings of satiety. It takes about twenty minutes for your stomach to register it's full, and in that time you can eat a lot of Twinkies. Between our pacing and our seeming inability to sit down for a meal, our bodies get confused as to when they're really hungry—not that we would listen anyway.

MOUTH HUNGER—EXERCISE #2

For the next few days, write down everything you eat. This is not one of those diet diaries where you tally up calories or carbs or fat grams; make no judgments on what you ate, just write it down, and include the time. We're not looking to cut out all your desserts, just to examine the whys and wherefores of your eating habits. Also write down how you were feeling when you ate whatever it was. Was your body really hungry, or were you eating to feed something else? Did you sit down, or were you standing over the sink eating cake with your fingers?

I'm not here to tell you that emotional eating is some forbidden, disgusting thing you should avoid at all cost. Throughout human history, we have celebrated over food; in the Southern U.S., no death in the family would be complete without at least a dozen friends and neighbors bringing over casseroles. Eating is so deeply bound to our well-being that there is simply no way to separate it from our emotions, and I don't think we should anyway. I like eating. You do, too. There's no reason to reduce one of the greatest pleasures of life to nothing more than a chemical reaction that produces energy.

The important distinction is to know that you're eating emotionally, to evaluate the situation and make a conscious choice about it, rather than running on autopilot and barely even tasting your food.

In the last chapter we discussed mindfulness, which is just as relevant to eating as to anything else. Becoming mindful of the reasons we treat our bodies the way we do, and paying attention, will lead us to make better choices.

I'm of the opinion that chocolate is good for women. An entire pan of brownies, not so much.

MINDFULNESS AT THE TABLE—EXERCISE #3

Now that you have looked at your eating habits, you can become aware of them as they're happening, and decide with intent how to nurture yourself. So many of our food choices are based on routine and compulsion that we don't even think about them anymore; we have a giant latte and a Powerbar every morning because that's what we've had every day for a year, or because some expert has told us it's healthy—not because of how it makes us feel.

When you begin to eat something, whether a full-out meal or a handful of movie popcorn, ask yourself the following questions:

Is my body hungry right now? How does my stomach feel?

Am I upset and eating because I don't know what else to do about the situation?

Am I eating this because I'm bored?

Is this really what I want to eat, or is it just convenient? Would something else satisfy me more?

If I eat this, how will my body feel afterward? How will I feel about myself?

Is my choice to eat this nourishing to my body, mind, and spirit?

When you have answered these questions, if you consider that pie in front of you and decide consciously that you do indeed plan to eat the whole damn thing, at least you will understand why you're doing it and the effect it will have on how you feel about yourself and how your body feels.

Afterward, ask yourself the questions again: How do you feel? Are you going to carry around guilt over that pie for the rest of the day? Will it make you sick? I can almost guarantee that you knew that before you ate it, so why do you think you chose to anyway? If you really enjoyed it, and are satisfied, that's excellent. If you knew you were having a snack because you were grouchy after work, and now you feel better and can move on to something else, great. But even if you tore through a half-gallon of mint chocolate chip and still want to eat the fridge, do it with knowledge and forethought. Don't beat yourself up over your choices, but know yourself and why you make them.

You will find that when you make conscious choices, your unhealthy ones will diminish. Knowing what you're doing to yourself is often all it takes to spark a change in habit. I may look down at the package of Oreos and think, "I don't really want these. I'm frustrated and irritated because it's been so long since I had sex I'm worried that they've changed it." At that point, rather than continuing with a behavior that will only make me feel worse about myself, I put the cookies away and go find a nice lad or lass to drag off to my tent. I don't waste time berating myself for emotional eating; instead, I try to get to the roots of the problem and change the situation so that next time I'll opt for the direct approach to my problems, rather than smothering them with gravy. To quote Janet Greeson: "It's not what you're eating, it's what's eating you."

A Ritual Goddess Feast

Another way to help heal our relationship with food is to truly appreciate what we eat. The planet Earth has grown thousands of wonderful, colorful, aromatic, tasty things for us to nourish our bodies with; we should celebrate that bounty, especially since we live in a time and place where that bounty is available to us and we don't go to bed hungry because there is no food.

There are countries in the world where people eat one thing every day, because that's all that will grow there or all they can afford. At least in America, even if you're living off ramen noodles, you have your choice of flavors. That variety and abundance is something we take for granted.

Gather together a half-dozen or so of the most fabulous, gorgeous, and divinely badass women you know (and men, too, if you like—boys like to eat as much as we do, though by and large if a man wants a sandwich he just has one, then gets on with the rest of the day without angsting over it, a lesson we could learn well from our brothers). Tell them to bring foods that they truly enjoy. Have all the participants lounge on the floor on cushions, or drape themselves over the furniture like courtesans. Lay a blanket out on the floor or cover a coffee table with all the foods your guests bring; arrange them as artfully as you can, so that you have a feast for the eyes as well as the tastebuds.

There are a lot of things you can do with a feast. Cast circle if you like, calling upon the Goddess as Mother. Let each participant talk about what she brought, its history in her life. Feed each other. Pass the items around in a prolonged version of Cakes and Ale, blessing each dish, blessing each other with abundance and joy. Let every bite be a sacrament—offer up your thanks to the gods for living in a world where we are surrounded with such gifts. Pass around wine, mead, or juice, and toast one another.

Feasting is an ages-old practice that brings together the people we love and the foods we enjoy; back in the days of yore, sweets and rich foods were only really enjoyed by the wealthy or at weddings and holidays. Now we live in a constant holiday mentality, where every day is Cake Day, so these special foods cease to be special. Adopt the practice of holding dinner parties, potlucks, seasonal feasts in honor of the sabbats; make meals an event. Have themed feasts—people can bring foods that are traditional to their ancestors, or that evoke a specific event or emotion; you could feast on aphrodisiacs (careful with that one), or have

Vegetarian Night, or bring the things you enjoyed as a child (watch five people bring macaroni and cheese).

Even if you live and practice alone, there's no reason to eat like a college student for the rest of your life. You are worth a little effort, aren't you? Sit down for dinner and actually taste every bite. Cook for yourself, or at least spend your money on restaurants that don't require shouting into a clown's mouth. Find dishes and glassware that you love, and treat them like altar tools—any glass can be a chalice.

One of the most important things we can do to begin to heal our relationship with food is to pray over our meals. Give thanks for the glory of the earth, for the labor of the people and the lives of the plants and animals who went into what's on your plate. After a few weeks of "saying grace," it will grow harder and harder to follow your old eat-and-run habits. It will also be harder to justify living on mass-produced, factory-farmed cheeseburgers.

A MEALTIME PRAYER

Mother Earth,
I give thanks for your thousand blessings
For the creatures, hoofed and leafed
Who yielded up their lives to mine,
And for the bounty you give freely to all.
May we never hunger,
May we never thirst,
May we know we are loved and love each other
Blessed be.

Animal Rites

From an ethical standpoint, it would do us well to consider the sources of our food. Even if you are a vegan, something had to die so you could eat, but shouldn't we draw the line between that sacrifice and the suffering that most animals endure before slaughter? If you ever want to get angry at the human race, do some research on how veal calves live.

It's commonly known that Americans eat a lot of cows. Most of the farming done where I grew up was for feed corn; acres and acres of arable land grew food for our food. What if instead, we used that land just for food for us, and let the cows be? In Brazil every year hundreds of square miles of rainforest are mowed down for pastureland. There are people starving in our streets, but the cows are well fed, up until we shoot them in the head with a bolt gun and start cutting them up while they're still alive.

Whether the suffering of animals moves you or not, you have to admit that, as a worker of magic, it's probably a bad idea to take in the energy of a creature in pain or in terror. Our own energy is purer and stronger when we fuel it with "cleaner" resources—a great many Pagans I know choose free-range and organic foods whenever possible for just that reason. All the hormones and chemicals pumped into cows these days—and that's before you even consider mad cow disease—contribute as much to our collective poor health as cholesterol does, if only from a metaphysical perspective.

As I write this, I am not a vegetarian. I have been off and on since I was a teenager, and I know that eventually I'll end up there again. My days as a guilt-free meatasaurus ended when I made the catastrophic mistake of looking a cow in the eyes. After that, and to this day, I can't eat a hamburger without thinking about the gentleness and dignity I have seen in the faces of the animals we slaughter, needlessly, every day. Humans can't live without plants, but we can live without meat. We choose not to because we like it, and because we're told we need to, much the same way we buy makeup and go on diets because we're told we must, *must* be beautiful.

My problem of course is that I live in Texas, I love barbecue, and hate most soy products. These excuses are just that—excuses—but changing your entire way of eating and behaving isn't an overnight transformation, and it's an intensely personal path to take. Rather than beating myself up over it, I try to make smarter and more ethical choices when it comes to the animal products I buy. There are free-range and organic options that are endlessly more humane than commercial meat products. Whatever choices you make, keep in mind that you do have choices.

I also give thanks to whatever creatures gave themselves (or were taken) so that I can live another day. Gratitude is the least I can offer the Mother for her generosity, and one of these days I fully intend to make the switch to vegetarianism permanently . . . well, maybe when they manage to make a soy hot dog that actually tastes like a Hebrew National beef frank. I can't stand here and tell you, "Stop eating meat, damn your cruel, cruel heart," when I myself had chicken for dinner; I can, however, point out that as we practice a nature-devoted religion, we cannot ignore the parts of nature that become part of us.

> The animals of the world exist for their own reasons. They were not made for humans any more than black people were made for white, or women created for men.
>
> ALICE WALKER

While we're on the subject of eating and ethics, a great many of us can trace our food problems to the "clean plate club," hearing our parents say, "Eat all your lima beans. There are children starving in China who have no lima beans." (I always thought, lucky them!) We learned from this that eating everything in front of us, even if we weren't hungry, was morally good; stopping when we were full was wasteful and somehow deprived youth in Asia.

In case you haven't figured it out by now, that half-cup of beans isn't going to save the world. If you want to help the hungry there are much more efficient ways right here in your own city—volunteer at a food bank or soup kitchen, or get politically involved in legislation and programs that help those in need. Start by making more ethical choices before you pick up your fork. Don't force yourself to eat what you don't want just because it's there in some mistaken belief that you could pack up your last bite of mashed potato and mail it to Bosnia. Try not to be wasteful, for the sake of the planet if for no other reason, but start by taking a smaller portion, then translate your concern for others into direct action rather than indirect guilt.

A VEGGIESAURUS CHARM

If you decide to make the transition to a meat-free diet or to reduce the amount of animal products you consume in whatever way you can, you'll find you face a lot of opposition both from society and from those you spend time with, some of whom will roll their eyes when you ask not to eat at Crazy Hank's House of Fried Critter Parts. I've found that here in Texas even Pagans tend to look down their noses at vegetarians, and I know several people whose attempts have been actively sabotaged by well-meaning friends and family. "Here," they say, "have some bacon . . . aw, come on, you love bacon! You didn't climb to the top of the food chain to eat broccoli, did you?"

To aid in sticking to your guns, try this spell:

Find a figurine of a farm animal of some kind; the variety you eat most often is preferable. The best kind in fact would be hollow, perhaps ceramic or glass, with a hole in the bottom.

On a piece of paper write down all the reasons you are changing the way you eat, whether they're environmental, humane, health-related, or political. Roll the list up and tuck it inside the figurine. If you can't, tie the paper to it somehow.

Charge the figure, along with a tiger eye stone, which I often work with to lend strength of conviction, courage, and emotional balance.

Keep the figure in your kitchen somewhere you will see it every time you cook; carry the stone with you, and whatever your choices, know that you are making them with full knowledge and forethought, and don't let anyone dissuade you. You alone are entitled to make decisions for you.

The Kitchen Goddess

You are worth making an effort for your meals, and you are also worth the best ingredients you can afford and the occasional extravagance. Even people who hate to cook have more options than ever, as most supermarkets have ready-made fresh dishes, salad bars, and deli foods galore. Sometimes I splurge and go to Central Market, our local gourmet store, which has organic produce and every vegetable you can think of, grains in bulk, and foods from around the world. One of my favorite meals is a few slices of handmade bread, a tub of chipotle pesto, and a hunk of farm-raised cheese, followed with passion fruit sorbet. You're an adult—if every once in a while you want to make a meal off peach cobbler, just do it, enjoy the hell out of it, and get on with your life. If we could get over our fixation on eating and let it be one of the many wonderful things we get to experience every day rather than the one thing our lives revolve around, many of our food issues will disappear.

Kitchen Witchery is very popular among Pagans, partly because it's fun, and partly because it's one of the most ancient and effective forms of magic. Cooking is a form of alchemy, and is already magical in and of itself: you put dry ingredients in a bowl, add some eggs, and apply heat—suddenly you have cake out of practically nowhere. Chemistry, physics, and art all combine in the kitchen. It's only natural to add religion to the mix.

Many Witches keep a kitchen altar and develop rituals for cooking and baking; even if you don't Witch up your food for specific magical purposes, treating meal preparation as a sacred art is yet another way to bring holiness to your body, as the sacred plants and animals of the Mother are taken in to become the body of a Wiccan priestess who has the power to transform worlds.

I am an avid baker; one of my favorite ways to show my love for my friends and family is to create fabulous desserts for special occasions. I choose recipes with care, reflecting over who has what food allergy and who hates what, and hearing people go into raptures over my cookies is one of the best feelings I get. It's an offering of my time, my effort, and my artistry; baking then becomes a ritual, and I usually light a candle before beginning and tap my wooden spoon on the counter like a conductor at the podium. I ask the Goddess to guide my hands, to help me nurture my chosen tribe, and to bring sweet feelings and harmony wherever the food is consumed.

Bring that same care to what you cook for yourself, and you're on your way to valuing your body and its needs the way they deserve to be valued.

A RITUAL TO INVOKE THE MOTHER

Fittingly, this ritual involves eating. For this you will have to cook something—even if you hate cooking, buy some refrigerated bread dough or cookies to bake. It's best if what you choose involves getting your hands dirty, but I'd hardly ask you to become a pastry chef when a typical meal at your house is a frozen dinner and a margarita. Try to go above and beyond your usual cooking habits, though, since this is a special occasion.

Feasting is not the only way that we can ritualize with food. Another ancient practice is to bake bread kneaded with specific herbs to bring about magical results, most often love, harmony, and health. Bread is a perfect choice for this sort of ritual, but I've done something very similar with soup, cake, and even teriyaki stir-fry. The important thing is the coming together, the blending, and the addition of energy and at least one symbolic ingredient.

So, gather in your kitchen all the ingredients you need for whatever food it is you choose to prepare. Depending on what you are making, choose one additive that you will charge with the Mother's energy, preferably something that is already in the recipe or that would complement its flavors. Here are some suggestions:

Rosemary

Cinnamon

Pecans, walnuts, almonds, or sesame seeds

Pepper

Salt

Milk

Honey

I don't recommend adding rosemary to cookies, for example, but cinnamon might do. Likewise, go easy on the pepper if you are a spice wimp like me. Salt is almost always a good suggestion, as it's used in both sweet and savory dishes and is deeply symbolic of the earth, grounding, prosperity, and purification.

Create sacred space in your kitchen in whatever way you like. You might call on the elements in a way tailored to the rite: the grain for earth, the oven for fire, the water or other liquid for water, the scent of cooking for air, and so on. Your kitchen is your sacred circle, and your counter is your altar. Ask a blessing over your assembled tools and ingredients.

Now invoke the Mother, in whatever words you prefer, or these:

I call upon the Great Mother,
She whose love is poured out upon the earth
She whose body yields up the harvest

She whose hair is the golden grain
Lady of abundance,
Lend your love and care to this meal/bread/etc.
So mote it be.

Prepare your food, all the while letting the energy of love and nurturing flow from your heart into your hands, into the bowl or pan. Visualize the Mother working through you. You might wish to chant or sing while you work. When you come to the ingredient you chose as your symbol, hold it aloft and ask a blessing on it, for example:

May this honey be filled and blessed with the strength of the Mother;
may it bring to my life the sweetness of her love.

Once the food is ready, sit down to eat it with reverence. Take in the Mother's energy with each bite.

You can do this same sort of thing when cooking for others, but take care to be sure they know about it beforehand, as it is generally looked upon as ethically questionable to mojo someone's food without their consent. I typically charge things I bake with love and peace, for the good of all—if anyone out there is fool enough to reject love and peace, they won't receive it from my hand. It's a grey area, one you must choose your own path through.

Fat Girls are Goddesses, Too

We've already talked about the diet and beauty industries' insatiable hunger for our self-hatred (and our money), so I won't belabor that particular point any further, but one thing bears repeating: thou art Goddess. Mini-size, Average-size, Plus-size, Super-size . . . we are all divine, and all beautiful.

Would you believe in a rail-thin goddess of abundance? Few of our ancestors-of-faith did either. Throughout the ancient cultures you see figures of goddesses with hips, full bellies, heavy breasts. Those are the images of the feminine that have the capacity to feed and nurture us—a goddess who is all hipbones and ribs is an image of starvation, just like a supermodel on a billboard. Prehistoric cultures didn't think the earth was anorexic, and they certainly wouldn't have wanted to celebrate without enough to eat. They saw the earth's bounty, her beauty, her generosity raining down from the trees and rising from the fields, and knew she was a loving goddess, who gave as a mother gives.

Our modern beauty standard is hardly universal, and hardly immortal. Back in the Middle Ages, a bony woman wasn't seen as a terribly good marriage prospect. A voluptuous body meant that, for one thing, your family could afford to eat well, and for another thing, it meant you weren't a field laborer who had to use her muscles and work off every pound. Classist it may be—but how much less elitist is it to consider women who can afford plastic surgery and gym memberships more attractive?

I want to share a secret with you that I only learned very recently. Being fat is not disgusting. It's not gross. It's not a sign of laziness or gluttony. It's not a disease, despite what "doctors" want us to think. It is a state of being, but moreover it has become a state of mind. Being fat in our culture means you aren't good enough.

You are good enough.

Fat is not disgusting. Rape is disgusting. Fat is not gross. Liposuction is gross.

The idea that fat women are lacking in willpower is a load of crap. I've seen more discipline in dieters than any athlete, and perhaps more so, because athletes aren't fighting nature. If your body carries more fat than someone else's, it just does. If it's true that being fat makes you weak, how do you explain all the voluptuous images of the Goddess who created the universe in her big, fat belly? Sometimes the Goddess is fat. Is she weak? Is she gross? Is she lazy?

Hell, no.

I have learned the hard way, over many years of struggle, that there is a reason for everything that happens to me, and that while many of the events of my life are out of my control, my reaction to them all is under my control. I don't say that lightly, and I know what a hard lesson it is to accept when you're in the middle of a dark night of the soul or a personal tragedy, but looking back, I can pinpoint all the things I learned from adversity and how my spirit was better off having come through it.

That in mind, look at the current state of your body—fat, thin, black, Asian, old, paraplegic, scarred, all of it—and ask yourself what you could learn from it right now. Could being fat be a chance to learn to accept yourself as you are? Could dealing with chronic illness be a way for your body to make you slow down and value its gifts?

Don't think for a moment this is in any way related to punishment. The universe does not punish; things happen because of a complex web of choice and interaction between you, other people, and the environment, and the choices of others affect your life as much as your own decisions do.

By the same token, I am fat. I am fat because I spent years eating to suffocate my emotions and push people away. I am fat because I chose to eat fast food and about five metric assloads of pastry. This does not make me weak, or morally suspect, or lazy; it makes me fat. I choose to see it as an opportunity to learn to love myself as I am so that I can make more positive choices from here on out and come to value my body no matter what. It is, after all, the only one I have this time around.

There came a day, and I'm sad to say it was only recently, that I suddenly stopped hating my body for being fat. I had been working on it for a very long time, struggling as we all do, but it seemed an uphill battle I was destined to lose. I remember it very clearly: I was on the elevator at my day job, which is mirrored in back from floor to ceiling, and I was scowling at how huge and disgusting my belly was and how, ten years ago, I was a size ten.

That anger at myself stayed with me all day, coloring my perception of everything that happened; I wanted a soda, but even as I drank it I berated myself for the calories; it was ninety-seven degrees outside (welcome to summer in Texas), but I judged myself harshly for not being outside exercising even in the blistering heat. Everything that was wrong with the day and my life was a direct consequence of being a lazy cow. Chances are you've had a similar experience with obsessing over your breast size, skin color, skinny legs, or any of a hundred other imagined inadequacies that we allow to dominate and erode our self-esteem.

That was the same day, as it happens, that I got the contract for this book.

I remember sitting there reading the email, and like a cosmic two by four from the Goddess, the thought occurred to me: I was tired of it all. I was tired of denying all my gifts, my magic, my talent, my beauty, because of one little thing, my big fat body. I had spent years allowing one flaw—a flaw of perception created by other people's expectations—to negate all the accomplishments and good work I had done. Because I was fat, because I didn't fit someone else's standard for how I should look, everything else I had ever achieved was worthless.

At that moment, something seemed to fall off my shoulders, and out of the clear blue nowhere I started to cry, not something I like to do at the office, as a general rule. It was so *unfair*, and so *stupid*, that I would do this to myself, that I would be a good friend to everyone but me, and treat total strangers better than the Goddess-given body that was currently enabling me to write, to dance, to breathe.

And as strange as it may sound, that was the end of it. Oh, I'm sure I'll have fat days in the future, but it's as if someone had hit the "mute" button on my evil auctioneer and all those derisive voices in my head no longer had any power over me. There was more freedom in that single realization than I had felt in years.

Once these realizations start to come, there's no stopping them. Once you have even a moment of love for your body and appreciation for its divinity, your heart will remember that feeling, and seek it out again and again, if you are willing to let it. Like the return of the Goddess to her children from centuries of exile, our memory of sanctity can only be denied for so long before it breaks free . . . and when it does, the world will never be the same.

Self-Mothering

Food is definitely not the only problem that arises from a dysfunctional relationship to the Mother archetype. As I have mentioned, our time and society are overly focused on masculine values—action, determination, will—and take little time for feminine ones—intuition, compassion, nurturing. The result is that no matter how great our birth or adoptive mothers were, we become adults and have no idea how to mother ourselves.

You always need a Mother, even as a supposed grownup, but once you get out into the world, it becomes your responsibility to be your own source of nourishment, even if you still spend time with the mother you grew up with. Many of us didn't have the gift of a good, loving mother our whole lives; perhaps she died, or left, or we never knew her, or she was too drunk or preoccupied or abusive to be the Mother we needed. Self-mothering becomes all the more important when we don't know what it's like to be taken care of.

I realized years ago how fortunate I've been. I was adopted at a very early age by parents who absolutely wanted me, and never let me forget it; they weren't perfect, but they were close to it, and if they made mistakes they were made out of love. I know this is rare, especially nowadays; I am one of the few women I know who didn't grow up with divorced parents and wasn't raised by crazy people.

Even so, when it came to taking care of myself in the "real" world, I was at a loss. I had a good example set before me, but never had to apply it to my own life before. When I moved out, I didn't even know how to do my own laundry, if that tells you anything. I had to learn everything from the fundamentals of appliance-wrangling to how to put myself to bed at a decent hour and remember to eat more than once a day.

On the other hand, a friend of mine lost her mother at an early age and became an emancipated minor as a teen; she had to mother herself, with very little example to go on, even when she was still mostly a child. Whatever your situation, at some point in your life you have to step up and be your own parent—you have to set rules and standards for your everyday life, because once you're grown, nobody is going to do it for you. If you want to live off Cheez Doodles and wear the same jeans for three weeks, no one will stop you, though you may become very unpopular.

The Mother archetype is the part of us that knows better, and if we listen to her, she will point us toward the right action, right livelihood, and clean underwear.

NOT ENOUGH HOURS IN THE DAY—EXERCISE #4

This activity can help you see where in your life you are denying the Mother the chance to express herself.

Sit down with some paper and think about the last twenty-four hours. Now break them down according to how long you did each of the following:

Sleeping

Eating

Cooking

Working

Waiting in line

Having sex

Playing

Worrying/Stressing out

Moving your body

Bathing/grooming

Talking on the phone

Watching television

Praying, meditating, or doing ritual

Driving

Surfing the Internet

Doing housework like laundry, cleaning, and so on

If you can remember what you did yesterday, do the same for it, and then carry the exercise forward for the next few days. You can probably figure out just by glancing at the list which of these activities are nurturing and which aren't—does it surprise you how little time you spend on these things, and how much you spend doing things you don't want to do?

Now, go into your imagination and dream up the ideal day for yourself. By this I don't mean if you were to win the lottery or not have to work anymore; I mean a day that fits into your life as it is now, but that flows perfectly, in which you accomplish everything you need to and get to do what you want to as well. How would that day be divided up? Write it out in terms of hours, too.

Most likely, the two do not match up. Notice where the largest discrepancies are. How can you change them? Look at the week as a whole rather than a single day, if that makes it easier to think about. How can you expand the amount of time you spend sleeping, playing, shagging, or meditating? What is the one thing you hate doing most, and how can you make that activity more pleasant or at least shorter? Do you have to be the one to vacuum, or can someone else in the household do it while you work on something else?

Now imagine your mother is standing over your shoulder. If you didn't have one or yours wasn't all that stellar, picture the Goddess herself looking over your lists. If you were your mother, or the Lady, and your child was constantly forgetting to eat three meals a day, you would put your foot down, wouldn't you?

The Goddess is as much a part of you as you were or are still a part of your earthly mother. Your hands are her hands. How are you to nurture your family, your creativity, your life, without nurturing yourself?

Sacred Pampering

In my reading I ran across the concept of sacred pampering and was instantly drawn to the idea, which brought to mind Cleopatra or a priestess of Aphrodite lounging in a milk bath, fanned by loincloth-clad servants with palm fronds.

Really, pampering isn't as decadent a practice as it sounds. It is simply the art of treating your body as the holy of holies, using tools and techniques that may seem self-indulgent unless you remember the importance of nourishment for your body and soul.

The image of a priestess or queen is an excellent one for this purpose. You are a priestess because of the fact that you are Wiccan; you may not be as public as other priestesses, and your temple may only be your home, but you are the clergy in your own religious life. You are also queen of your own country, though your only subject may be the dog.

Pampering can take place with others who are undergoing the same treatment, but pampering is not getting your hair cut while the kids are running around screaming underfoot—pampering is about you, not your family, or friends, or anyone else. You might engage a loved one's help in creating the environment, but ultimately, pampering is how you become a better expression of the Mother's energy by reserving some of that energy for yourself, and it is a solitary art.

PAMPERING RITUAL—THE QUEEN'S BATH

Bathing has been a sacred art for years beyond counting. In Wiccan practice it's used for cleansing and grounding before ritual, as well as being a ritual in and of itself; depending on your intent, different salts and herbs can be added to the water, and by absorbing their essences into your skin, you take in the magical changes you seek.

The kind of bath I'm talking about now is not for preparation, and accomplishes nothing as far as discrete magical goals are concerned. It has no point at all except to make you feel good, relaxed, and in touch with your inner self.

First of all, make sure the bathroom is clean, or at least that the tub is livable. The last thing you need is to get settled in your bathing rite and have a pile of dirty clothes catch your eye and skew your attention.

Then gather your ritual implements: bath salts, bubbles, oil, or an herbal sachet (some scent ideas follow); bath mitts or washcloths; plush and fluffy towels (clean ones, and preferably at least one in a special color that you use for nothing else); a bathrobe or comfy clothes to put on after; something to hold up your hair if you don't want it wet; music, if you like; candles; a glass of wine and plate of chocolates is a nice touch, just be sure you don't drop either into the tub, because, yuck. You might want a book, or not, depending on how relaxed you want to get—for some of us a chance to spend an hour alone reading is such a luxury it goes hand in hand with a bath.

Important advice if you have other people living with you: lock the bathroom door.

Set up all of your tools in whatever arrangement makes them convenient to reach from the tub. You don't want to have to get out until you're ready.

You might wish to have a salt scrub before you run the bath; stand in the tub and wet a handful of salt, then rub it all over your body (gently, please). This helps remove dead skin and is also a natural purifier; as you wash the salt down the drain, visualize all of your stress flowing out of you as well.

Run your bathwater, adding in your smelly goodness toward the end so it doesn't lose all its power before you get in. I recommend you avoid using straight essential oils unless you know they are very mild, like lavender or rose; many essentials are irritating to the skin, or poisonous, or can have ill effects on your body if used in too great a concentration. If you use herbs rather than salts, bind them up in a cheesecloth bag or coffee filter so you don't spend the next three days picking rosemary out of strange places.

Scents I like for pampering baths include lavender, vanilla, honey and almond, rose, jasmine, and deeper scents such as sandalwood. Don't use anything that has a specific magical association in your mind to its scent—I think of patchouli as a money herb, for example, and in this case I'm not looking for money, so I'd leave it out. You can also add oatmeal to an herbal sachet, which is very nourishing for the skin; milk, particularly whole milk, is also a wonderful softener and leaves you feeling silky and comforted.

Your ritual instructions are: get in the water and soak. Not too complicated. As you lower yourself into the tub, remember that you are cleansing and soothing the body of a priestess and an embodiment of the Goddess; you can visualize your bathroom as a scene from Rome, or Egypt, with marble columns and tile, and the music issuing from your CD player is coming from a group of musicians who were hired just for the purpose of playing during the Queen's bath. When you rise, robe yourself as if you are putting on the finest imported silks, even if all you have is ratty terrycloth and bunny slippers.

You can continue this pampering ritual into other areas of your personal grooming if you like; after a long hot bath you might want to do some sort of facial treatment like an oatmeal or cucumber masque, for example. Find products or make your own that speak to your spirit, and keep them set aside for your private, self-nurturing use.

If you aren't used to taking care of your body this way, all of this may seem ridiculous, but I say again, you are worth a little indulgence. Surely a long bath once a week is not asking too much of the world.

My mother came from a long line of old-school Southern women, and as such she had a definite skin-care routine she followed whenever possible. (A lot of women call it a "regime," but I'd prefer not to think of my face as a war zone.) I remember sitting at her knee watching her apply masques and cold cream, pluck stray hairs, and smooth on one of a wide variety of lotions and creams that she kept on a mirrored tray. She always told me that it was vitally important to use lotion on my elbows, knees, and feet.

I didn't listen. Now you could sand a table with my elbows and my knees throw off sparks.

One habit I did learn from her was toenail painting. Even in the winter, my toenails are painted—nobody may see it, but I will. It's the same reason I refuse to wear white underwear; whatever stress someone is giving me, I can still think to myself, "Oh yeah? Well, I'm wearing bright red Hello Kitty panties, and you'll sure as hell never see them."

I prefer the term "eccentric," thank you.

At any rate, you may be wondering how all of this pampering differs from the beauty obsession I've been ranting about up to this point. There is a very important distinction—pampering is done for *you*. It may have zero effect on how you look on the outside, but it makes you feel beautiful inside, and helps you to find peace with your body. There is absolutely nothing wrong with things like makeup, clothing, and the like; again, it's the motivation behind it that matters.

Also, the rituals you develop for pampering should not compromise your health or make you feel inadequate in any way—if instead of luxuriating in the feel of a homemade facial, you stare at the mirror critiquing every bump and line, you need to find another way to pamper yourself until you can let go of your negative feelings. You are not trying to change your appearance in these rituals; you are allowing your appearance to be what it is, and loving it through your actions.

If you decide you want to include other people occasionally in your rites, you could start a spa club of sorts with your fellow Witches; there are even kits sold nowadays with everything you need to do manicures, pedicures, facials, and such in a slumber party kind of atmosphere. Just be sure that you save some of your pampering time to be alone with yourself.

Perchance to Dream

I don't get enough sleep. As I write this it is after midnight and I have to be up for work in seven hours, but I am a night owl by nature, and given the choice I would be completely nocturnal. "Not a morning person" doesn't even begin to cover it for me. Before eleven I communicate mostly in Neanderthal grunts.

Sleep, however, is one of the major ingredients in self-care. Nocturnal or not, almost nobody I know gets enough sleep on a regular basis. Sleep deprivation is much more detrimental to our health, both physical and mental, than we realize. Sleep is our body's time to recharge; our brain tissues and organs regenerate while we sleep, since they aren't busy like they are when we are awake and active. Different stages of sleep are important for the regeneration of neurons, memory, and other useful functions. Lack of sleep can compromise our immune system, leaving us open to increased illness (as well as accidents and general grouchiness). There is evidence that chronic sleep deprivation results in insulin resistance, becoming a risk factor for diabetes and high blood pressure.

Sleep is also the time when we dream, and our dreams are a fertile playground for the gods and our subconscious to speak to us. By cutting out opportunities for sleep, we lose dreamtime, and every Witch knows the importance of her dreams, even if all they ever are to her is entertainment.

Having dealt with years of periodic insomnia, I have discovered a few tricks that can help you achieve better quality rest:

First of all, if at all possible, reserve your bedroom for sleep alone. (Okay, for sleep and sex, but the same basic rules apply.) No TV, no computer, as few electronic devices to buzz and whine in your ear or distract you. All that is in my bedroom, besides my bed, is my altar, herb cabinet, and bookshelves; reading and meditation are both very restful activities, and can help relax me enough to sleep. Being able to see my altar from the bed is also a great comfort to me.

Second, employ your Witchy arts to help you fall and stay asleep, and to ward off nightmares and other interruptions. Chamomile tea is a very popular bedtime beverage, and is especially effective if you charge it with magical energy to help bolster its innate qualities. Some authors swear by valerian tea, but I have yet to meet a person in real life who can drink it of her own free will and not make horrible faces and gag. Valerian is a very powerful sleep inducer, and works remarkably well, but I recommend capsules unless you have a cast-iron tongue. Skullcap is also often used for its sedative properties; consult a medicinal herbal book to find recipes and proportions, or ask someone at the store where you buy your herbs what they recommend.

Dream pillows can be used to protect you during sleep and foster sweet dreams; usually a mixture of lavender, rose petals, chamomile, hops, and other herbs are sewn or tied up and left beneath your regular pillow. One word of caution, however, with regard to mugwort: many dream pillow formulas list it as an ingredient, neglecting to mention that mugwort induces visions and psychic dreams, which are very rarely restful. If you are looking for peaceful sleep I suggest leaving it out.

Lastly, spend half an hour before you go to bed unwinding, preferably in bed; read, meditate, listen to music, or do something else that will disengage your mind from the fast pace of daytime. Watching television doesn't count, because it is simply bringing the waking world inside, and though it doesn't encourage much independent thought, it does keep your brain running at a higher speed than you want for trying to sleep.

Allowing your body time to recharge and renew is a vital key to self-nurturing, and to bringing the Mother's blessing into your life. Don't be surprised if, after finding ways to get more and better sleep, she comes to visit you in your dreams.

Goddesses of the Mother Archetype

There is no shortage of Mother goddesses in the world's pantheons. Wiccans are most familiar with ladies like Demeter and Isis, whose stories have become metaphors for the Wheel of the Year and for our own lives.

Beyond specific deities, however, there lies the Great Mother, whom many Wiccans seem to call upon, particularly those like myself who do not subscribe to a particular tradition or pantheon. The image of the Great Mother is a strange and beautiful combination of immanence and transcendence; she is Mother of each of us, and Creatrix of the entire universe. Her story is that of the Big Bang, and our own birth, and the life cycle of every plant and animal upon her skin. Choosing one symbol for her is problematic, as everything alive is her symbol.

Each of us sees her a little differently, and yet we often find ourselves drawn to others who see her in a way akin to our own; not long ago some sister Witches and I decided to start working together magically, and sat down to discuss our own practices—in the course of our conversation we realized that we all worked with startlingly similar symbolism when it came to the Goddess. For whatever reason, to whatever end, we had all been called by a celestial lady whose primary energy could only be described as *starlight*. One of us had bonded with Nuit; I had started my path with Isis, the Star of the Sea; our third worked primarily with faery energy, but when the Goddess began to show her face, she was stellar and lunar as well as Fae. As much as I would like to dismiss it as coincidence due to our having read the same books, the fact remained that the Mother had come to each of us in a way that brought us together.

The Great Mother is the most primal of all Goddesses because she is the originator of all things, the alpha and omega. In my own practice, she has a very particular form and role: she is the Bright Weaver, the Woman who spins the stars into their patterns, who creates—and embodies—the Web of Life in all its form and splendor. In the time before time, she and the Lord built the Sky Loom, and it was her task to choose the color and weave of all that would come to be; her hands dance over the threads that connect us all to one another, and to her. The spiral of the galaxy turns in its endless waltz in her eyes.

I think Doreen Valiente, in the *Charge of the Goddess,* said it best: "I am the Mother of all things, and my love is poured out upon the earth." I remember the first time I read those words; my heart constricted with a sudden feeling of recognition, and the poetry of it settled into a niche in my heart that had gone unfulfilled for my whole life.

A MEDITATION ON THE MOTHER AND CHILD

This meditation is designed for those of us whose childhoods were not idyllic, regardless of the sort of earthly mothers we had. If you grew up without any sort of pain in your youth, you can still use this; just skip the parts that do not apply to you.

Imagine yourself as a child.

Imagine yourself as the child you wish you had been—take the shadows from your eyes, the burden of loss and memory from your young shoulders. Brighten your smile, straighten your spine; imagine yourself with the innocence and wonder that should be every child's birthright.

You are playing somewhere in nature, perhaps a meadow, or a wood; search your memory for a place you always loved to sneak off to, or create one from scratch. This place is safe, and you know you are safe in it. Here you can have your tea party, or get good and dirty climbing trees, or whatever your heart desires.

Whatever the events of your past, this place you create holds no fear or judgment. Let your child self run along the hills, find shapes in the clouds, turn brown as a squirrel in the sunlight. Let her have adventures with the animals and the land.

You are alone, but never alone; all around you you can sense the spirits of the earth and other elements, and you know with a child's knowing how to speak the language of trees and stones, deer and sparrows. You wander the woods and plains as a sibling and friend.

Then, as the sun dips toward its farewell bow for the day, you hear someone call your name.

Her voice echoes over the hills, calling you homeward. You may never have heard this voice in your childhood, or you may have heard her whisper in the wind and the rustle of leaves. It is not the voice of any woman you have seen, but you know her and come without hesitation.

Where do you go? A house? The edge of a shining lake? A grove of trees? The sea? Where does her voice call from?

You come around a curve, or through a stand of tall grass, and at the edge of the field or the river, there she is, waiting for you, smiling.

You call her name back to her, and she opens her arms.

Joyfully, you run into her embrace, and she lifts you up and spins you around, laughing, the warmth of her arms and her smile like no other love you have ever felt—it is given without reservation or demand, and you return it with all your heart. Your whole being is cared for, nourished, and this is the feeling you will carry with you when you return to the waking world, to recreate the Mother's love for you in your love for yourself. Let the bright-eyed maiden child within you lead the way.

SUGGESTIONS FOR EXPLORING THE MOTHER

1. Play. Part of self-nurture is finding and encouraging that little girl who is hiding around the corner of your memory, waiting to come out and have a tickle fight. Most of the women I know who have learned to cultivate the Mother's grace, weird as it may seem, have toys of their own, or at least know how to let go of the stern adult face they have to wear most of the time and be completely, utterly silly on occasion. If your whole childhood you longed for a Cabbage Patch Kid or a Snoopy Snow-cone Machine, find one.

2. Declare one night a week your night for sacred pampering, and defend it like an Amazon if necessary. Even if all you can manage is an hour, manage it. If your family and friends don't think you are worth an hour of private time, they aren't worth that hour either. Harsh, but true.

3. Dedicate the items you use for self care to the Goddess and your spiritual practice. Create an altar, if you like, in your bathroom or on your vanity.

4. At least once a week, try a new food or recipe, preferably a healthier one. Variety is good for you, and exploring new cuisines can help you appreciate both the abundance of the Lady and the experience of eating as a sacred art. You could take the opportunity to start a goddess feasting club of sorts in conjunction with your culinary experiments.

5. Look at the clock. Should you be in bed right now? I thought so—put this book down and go to sleep.

Recommended Reading and Resources for Chapter Four

BOOKS

Sacred Pampering Principles: An African-American Woman's Guide to Self-Care and Inner Renewal by Debrena J. Gandy

A Witch in the Kitchen: Magical Cooking for All Seasons by Cait Johnson

Eating in the Light of the Moon: How Women Can Transform Their Relationship with Food Through Myths, Metaphors and Storytelling by Anita A. Johnston, PhD

The Woman's Comfort Book by Jennifer Louden

Change Your Life Without Getting out of Bed: The Ultimate Nap Book by Sark

Intuitive Eating by Evelyn Tribole

f i v e

THE
healer

The Lady known as Airmid awaits you deep within the forest, at the side of the holy well. You have walked many a weary night to reach her, won your way over water and stone to her side. It is she who holds the secrets of herb lore, the knowledge of healing both magical and mundane; it is to her you have come to bargain for your life.

You find her sitting cross-legged beneath a tree, the wind of an early morning catching her abundant hair, which is woven through with blossoms of chamomile. All around her grow the sacred herbs; you recognize many of these plants, but Airmid alone knows their use. If you are lucky, she will show you.

As you approach, she looks up at you through calm green eyes that shine with reflected sunlight, and a slight smile plays about her lips.

"You come seeking wisdom," she says. "You come seeking healing. But I cannot heal you."

Your heart sinks. The village doctors have no answers for you; the priests say it is the will of God that you suffer and die. Women have been put to the flame for seeking out Airmid's help; a woman with too much knowledge is a heretic among your people . . . but still they come, by the shadows of night, and return with magic and medicine that they work in secret, passing it among their daughters. Airmid was your last hope.

She sees your grief, and her smile broadens a hair. "I said I cannot heal you," she adds, "but I did not say you cannot be healed. Tell me, child, which of these plants is the most powerful in curing disease?"

You stare at the herbs that have grown in a circle around where she sits, and you frown. You have heard that the one to her left can still bleeding; you have heard that the one at her feet is both sedative and poison. Which would be more powerful, one that could stave off death, or one that could cause it? Or both? You finally admit you do not know.

"Honesty," she says. "I like that in my students. I will tell you this: the bark of this tree behind me is just that, bark. It is a part of a plant with no power to take away pain, until it is harvested, blessed, and pre- pared. The flowers around me are flowers; they are beautiful, and sa- cred living things in my sight, but still are not medicine until taken from the ground and administered to one in need. And even then, if a patient does not truly wish to be healed, all the willow in the world will not kill her pain. I cannot heal you; a plant alone cannot heal you. Only you have that power, if you have the courage to learn its ways." She smiles again, and relief courses through you like sweet spring rain. "Now sit with me, child, upon my cloak, and I will show you."

Witches, when not demonized in popular culture, have long been imag- ined as healers and wise women. Legend has it that many of the women killed by the Inquisition were in fact midwives and herbalists, easy tar- gets in a world that was swiftly becoming dominated by misogyny and fear of female power. Most of these women were probably no more

Witches than your average doctor, but whatever their creed, they kept the spirit of the Healer alive.

It makes sense that in our early history as humans, healing became the province of women. The menfolk were often called away from home to protect or to hunt, leaving the tribe's women to care for the aged, the young, and the sick. Women were, it seems, first to discover healing methods both sacred and mundane, from herb lore to energy work. For many centuries, healing was women's work, particularly as our role became more and more confined to the hearth. It wasn't until the Middle Ages that men started to take even that power from us. But that theft could not last; women are healing again, traditionally and otherwise, this time acknowledging that men have considerable wisdom and skill to offer the art, as well.

The Healer archetype is an outgrowth, of sorts, of the Mother— both are caretakers, but the Healer, for our purposes, can be defined as one who uses magic, medicine, and knowledge of the body and spirit to create and maintain wellness.

What Is Wellness?

Health in our culture is often derived from a set of numbers: weight, body mass index, measurements, blood pressure, cholesterol, and others. While these can at times be a good indicator of possible problems in the body, they do not define how we feel in our bodies. We are taught to chase after health, after a specific gamut of numbers on a chart established by some outside authority, but what we really need is *wellness*.

Wellness, for our purposes, is a state of balance. It is a place of ease, in which our bodies function at the best level they can, and our habits support that level. In a state of wellness we are living in harmony with our bodies. There are no percentages or ratio charts to measure wellness; it is entirely self-determined and largely dependent on attitude.

You might weigh 120 pounds, work out an hour every day, not have an ounce of spare body fat, and still be incredibly unhealthy—particularly if you eat nothing but Twinkies, drink your weight in beer every night, and smoke like a chimney. Wellness can be a 98-pound black belt, a 250-pound accountant; it can be found among any race, religion, or age. Whatever size or shape your body, if you take care of it, it will eventually reach a place where it tells you, "It's all good," every time you stop to check in.

Western medicine treats every "abnormality" in the body as a disease, a problem to be overcome. Thanks to its philosophy, we view childbirth as a medical procedure, menstruation as a "condition," and the inevitable physical changes that come with aging as "symptoms."

Often doctors prescribe the equivalent of napalm to combat illness, and hit the body with chemicals that throw off our goddess-given ability to heal ourselves; anyone who has ever gotten a yeast infection thanks to antibiotics knows what I mean.

> It's bizarre that the produce manager is more important to my children's health than the pediatrician.
> MERYL STREEP

When I say the word *healer*, what images come to your mind? Oddly enough, a doctor of Western medicine is the last thing I think of. A quick poll of my friends reveals the same trend: we think of Witches, of herbalists, Reiki masters, and shamans, but not surgeons. Sad, really, that the people we trust our health to don't even register as Healers to the imagination.

In my experience, Western medical practitioners do not heal. They attack. They suppress. They want to make you "normal," and your own definition of "normal" doesn't matter; they want you to conform to the numbers of health rather than the feeling of wellness. If you see and hear things other people don't, you are labeled crazy; if you trust your body's instinct rather than a bottle of pills, you are ignorant. Like the beauty industry, the medical field wants to homogenize people, not simply to deal with pain and illness, but to fit into a narrow range of what they consider healthy.

It wasn't all that long ago that PMS was considered a myth, labeled "hysteria," and men were encouraged not to take it seriously, because everything from mood swings to cramps was "all in her head." Kick a guy in the crotch and tell him the pain is all in his head, and he'll probably kick you back. Women, however, swallowed the prejudices of doctors for a long time, believing them to be wise and authoritative over female bodies that they didn't even have themselves. Male doctors were supposed to be more knowledgeable about female life than we were.

This has begun to change. The cynic in me wants to attribute these changes as the response of drug companies and healthcare product producers to the increased disposable income that women have, but I have also seen many doctors beginning to work with "alternative" methods and accept that the largest part of healing from any illness is, indeed, all in our heads. Studies have been done showing the beneficial effect of prayer on cancer patients—whether an act of God or the placebo effect, belief in healing creates healing.

The Healer has far more than drugs and scalpels at her disposal. She works with the power of herbs, stones, scent, food, and magic as much as with brews and capsules; moreover, she sees the body and spirit as partners, and her sacred task as bringing the two into balance. The Healer does not view this task as warfare or the triumph of science over nature; she understands that even illness has its place, and that wellness is something more than simply not being sick.

The Healer is that part of us who listens to the body, and who works to keep it in a state of equilibrium. Healing and wellness are more than physical; the Healer works with energy, with spirit, understanding that both physical and nonphysical reality make up our being, and that harmony between the two is the only way to truly heal.

In this chapter we will talk about several important facets of the Healer's magic, including breathwork, energy work, meditation, and healing magic; all of these are vital aspects of achieving wellness. We will also look at how the Healer archetype approaches disease, disability, and other physical challenges we face in daily life.

Magic to Make Healthier Choices

At heart, you know what's beneficial for your body and what isn't. As I mentioned earlier, we're not stupid; between health class and the dozens of diet and beauty regimens we've been on over the years, women tend to know a ridiculous amount about nutrition and metabolism, for starters. If you ask the average American female who the tenth President was, she'll probably blink at you, but if you ask how many calories are in a Powerbar, she'll rattle off a number without even thinking.

That in mind, when it comes to your body, you already have a deep instinctive wisdom of what will bring you to a state of wellness and what will throw you off-kilter. The difficulty lies in trusting that wisdom rather than the facts and figures that "experts" like to throw at us to convince us to buy this or swallow that.

To help you make more sound decisions for your body, you might work with affirmations like we did in chapter 3:

I trust the divine wisdom of my body.
I make healthy choices toward my own wellness.
I am a priestess of the Goddess, and today I will do better than yesterday.

Try to identify small, measurable steps you can take to promote wellness. Don't tackle your whole life at once; if you do, you'll get overwhelmed and frustrated and probably quit. Could you drink one more glass of water a day? Go to sleep half an hour earlier? Meditate ten minutes twice a week to start with? Set small goals for yourself and work on them from one cycle of the moon to the next, to give your body time to decide how it feels about the change. From there, consider making another alteration, but don't rush things; it took you a long time to develop the habits you have now, and it may take a long time to undo them.

You could also keep a charged blue candle (a color often associated with healing) in your bathroom by the mirror, to burn while you get dressed in the morning and remind you to be mindful of your body and its needs. Hold the flame in your mind when presented with either a candy bar and Coke or soup and sandwich for lunch; say your affirmations silently each time you drink a glass of water, imagining your body's gratitude for the smarter choices you make.

> Learning why I make choices, and finding that I can make a different choice, has absolutely revolutionized my relationship to my body, and my beliefs about my power.
> RAENE

Healing with Air: The Breath

You would think that there is no wrong way to breathe, as long as you're still alive. Breathing is the most basic thing humans do, and we do it every minute of every day from our first second out of the womb to our last moment of life. It's a no-brainer, on the surface: inhale, exhale. Repeat.

Westerners, however, do not breathe as we should. Pause a moment and lay your hand over your chest—does it move when you breathe? Lower your hand to your belly. Does it move? I'll bet not. We breathe high in our chests, usually, and have a fairly short breath cycle, never allowing air to reach deep into the body.

Why is this bad? Shallow, chest-high breathing is typical of a condition that you generally don't want to invoke on a daily basis: panic. We breathe as if we are constantly in terror of our lives, and as if the only parts of our bodies worth keeping alive are from the chest up. The way most of us usually breathe leaves us in a state of high anxiety much of the time. The body's energy moves with the pulse and the breath; you have to breathe all the way down to your feet to fill your body with energy.

THE MOON'S LOOP—EXERCISE #1

Wherever you are, bring your attention to your breath. Follow it as it ebbs and flows in and out of your chest, bringing life-giving air to your trillions of cells.

Put your hand on your belly and close your eyes. Now, as you inhale, push your diaphragm gently outward, allowing the air to fill the bottom of your lungs first. Your hand will move in and out as you breathe this way—the goal is to always breathe deep from the belly, letting the chest be the last thing that inhales and the first thing that exhales. Just stopping to breathe deeply like this can ground you almost instantly; you move out of the panicked state of chest-high breathing, and your whole body calms down. Any time you start to get frazzled by stress or fear, take the time to breathe from your diaphragm at least ten cycles, and notice how you feel afterward.

For now, continue to breathe deeply; as you do so, visualize the life energy that you breathe in as a loop in your body, rising up your back on the inhale, falling down your front on the exhale. Breathe in, and draw the energy upward; breathe out, and let it flow downward. Each breath moves effortlessly into the next, as the tide moves in and out from the shore. Your breath waxes and wanes like the moon. Imagine that you are in fact breathing in the moon's light, the light of the Goddess, and it runs through its cycle in your body, bathing you on the inside with her radiance.

Every part of your being can benefit from deeper breathing; using the rhythm of your breath, you can move energy through your body from foot to head and head to foot, healing and cleansing as it flows.

Going to Ground

Most Pagans of any stripe are familiar with grounding and centering. If you weren't taught how to do it, or haven't read at least a half-dozen methods in various books, your training is woefully incomplete. Grounding and centering, often simply called "grounding," is probably the most basic and essential energy/meditation exercise we have at our disposal, and its benefits are myriad. Chances are you ground even if you don't know what it's called.

It is in fact a dual process, though many people do the whole thing at once for expediency. To ground, you connect yourself to the environment; to center, you connect yourself to yourself, and to the divinity within. Not only is it a useful practice before any sort of ritual or magical action, it is an excellent way to help you get through the day, and can help remind you of your own holiness and that of the world around you.

Like any form of meditation, grounding has definite physical benefits—it slows down the pulse and breath, lowers your blood pressure, and gives an all-over sense of well-being that can mean the difference between just surviving and really living.

The majority of us start our Wiccan careers with some variation of the Tree of Life grounding: you visualize yourself as a tree, or as having roots that extend into the earth and branches that reach into the sky. This is an excellent way to go about it, as it connects you to both Goddess and God, and the energy that you draw into your body from above and below can achieve the centering aspect. The problem with this method is that it takes a while, and sometimes you're lucky to get two minutes in a bathroom stall at the office to ground; it is a good idea, therefore, to have a variety of methods to work with.

The Dancer's Devotion in chapter 7 is another way to ground, and can be much shorter, though it does require at least enough room to move your arms.

INSTA-GROUNDING—EXERCISE #2

Here are several ideas for very quick grounding methods.

1. For a week or two, ground using a longer format, and when you reach the grounded state, say a word or phrase to yourself that you will use as a trigger, something as simple as "I am grounded." Eventually, you will be able to take a few deep breaths, repeat the phrase to yourself, and almost immediately return to ground with very little effort. You'll be surprised how well this works.

2. Another variation of this practice is to hold a stone or charm of some kind in your hands when you do a long grounding, and allow the feeling to sink into the object each time. That way all you will have to do is take the object out of your pocket and hold it a moment. Hematite is an excellent grounding stone. I do something very similar with rainbow fluorite, as its colors represent the chakras to me, and when I work with a certain piece of fluorite I can feel my chakras, one by one, coming into balance. Alternately, choose a stone that you feel represents your inner essence, as this will help you center as well as ground; you may feel a special connection to amethyst, for example, and find that it resonates with your personal energy. What you choose is less important than how it makes you feel.

3. If you are lucky enough to have a friendly tree nearby and quick access to it, very often just walking up and putting your palms and forehead on its bark will ground you faster than any human method yet devised. Trees are the Great Converters, and are almost always willing to take excess stress energy from your body and draw it into the earth, where it can be transformed into something positive.

Meditation

Aside from grounding and centering, other forms of meditation are important to both your physical health and spiritual health.

One thing that I have noticed, however, is that most forms of meditation practiced today are derived from Eastern paths, Buddhism in particular. There's nothing wrong with this whatsoever, but Eastern meditation places its emphasis on stilling the mind and letting go of thoughts.

I don't know about you, but I can't do that. Maybe if I were a monk living on a mountaintop, without a day job, a book to finish, a yowling cat, noisy neighbors, war, sexism, and Republicans to worry about, I would have an easier time just sitting down and blanking out my mind, but the harder I try, the less successful I am. My conscious mind does not respond to absolute silence, though my body certainly enjoys it.

One way some people get around this is instead of trying to get rid of thoughts, they simply let them drift in and out without paying any attention to them. This is a little easier for me, but still problematic, as my inner peace tends to run off and have wild affairs with my drifting thoughts.

I finally had to admit to myself that I am not a Buddhist monk. Most meditation practices used today were created hundreds of years ago, mostly by men, who had a lot less on their minds than we are forced to have today. If you have trouble with "sitting" meditation, don't consider yourself a failure—there are other ways.

A meditative state is simply a state in which you are receptive, and can move past mundane concerns to hear what whispers deep within (and from without as well). There is no law saying the only way to get there is to sit on your butt and not think about anything.

At least a few Eastern mystics have had the same problem, and so have developed techniques that might work better for modern women. A much more effective (in my experience, which may vary wildly from yours) idea is chanting, or the use of mantras, simple words or sentences repeated over and over. If you give your conscious mind something to latch onto, like a chant or music, it will be so busy playing that it will step out of the way, allowing your subconscious to come to the fore. It's a technique of distraction rather than suppression, and I have found that it is often easier for women. Why? It may be that, like in ritual, such activity bypasses the linear side of the mind and allows the intuitive, more feminine side to arise.

There are of course a wide variety of chants available, both from Pagan traditions and others. Even singing can achieve the same goal. Another thing I have found is that using mantras in Sanskrit (or other languages, such as Latin chants borrowed from the older Catholic traditions, particularly those dedicated to Mary) is amazingly powerful, because when I work with them my conscious mind has no idea what I'm chanting and has to focus on the feeling behind the words. I do always find translations into English so that I know what I'm saying, of course, but I've found that if I use chants in English I tend to pay too much attention to the words themselves and can't get past them to a meditative frame of mind.

One mantra I have worked with for quite some time is known as the Gayatri Mantra; it is said to be the oldest mantra in existence, and its basic purpose is to invoke divine wisdom. The words of the mantra have layers and layers of meaning, which you can study and learn from for years, but even without a deeper dissection of its translation, chanting or singing it is like shooting deity into a vein.

If you prefer a more distinctly Wiccan technique I suggest something like the "Earth My Body" chant:

Earth my body
Water my blood
Air my breath and
Fire my spirit . . .

Or, choose any chant or song that you know very well and find meaningful, and sing it slowly, timing the words to your breath and letting the vibration lead you. Let your mind move deeper than the words, into the rise and fall of the sound itself, reaching for the true essence of the chant which is beyond language. You can do much the same with recorded music; some of my most powerful trance experiences, even when I'm not up and dancing, have been with headphones on my ears and the volume cranked up high.

Meditation in any form releases stress from the body and allows your energy to flow more freely from chakra to chakra and through your entire being. Even if you can only manage five minutes a day, try; it is a simple, and important, way of healing yourself.

The Chakras: The Healer's Toolkit

It has always been very interesting to me that, for all that Wicca is supposed to be a Western, European-based religion, one of our most well-known tools is the chakra system, a purely Eastern form of wisdom. I have been told that similar systems existed in pre-Christian Celtic and other Pagan societies, but evidence for this is fairly sketchy, and may, in fact, be mostly wishful thinking. Luckily, even in the East chakra work is not confined to a single belief system, and people of myriad religions have found ways to incorporate this knowledge into their own paths.

The chakras are a vital part of the Healer's discipline, as they represent the places where spiritual energy enters the body (both the physical body and the energy body, sometimes labeled the aura) and is transformed into aspects of our being. Most Wiccans have at least some background in chakra work, but there are a variety of approaches, and divergent opinions as to what each chakra does, where it is located, and so on. Many of the ideas and exercises in this chapter will be based on the chakras, so we'll review them briefly.

For our purposes we'll discuss the seven-chakra system, which is the most widely utilized; I usually work also with the minor energy centers in the hands and feet, as I have twin disciplines of writing and dance in my spiritual path. The major seven are generally described as follows:

The Root Chakra—Survival

The root chakra is located at the base of the spine, and it is the foundation upon which the entire column rests. The root governs physical existence and survival. It is the chakra of earth—manifestation of health and material needs. The root is a very dense and solid chakra, and its desires are difficult, if not impossible, to ignore; we cannot progress up the column until our physical needs are met.

The root is the chakra of grounding; it maintains our deep, instinctive connection to the earth and to the whole of nature. It is connected also to sexuality, or rather to procreation; all our animal instincts are a part of the root, from the fight-or-flight response to the eat-mate-kill impulse. The root also governs our body image and how we perceive our physical selves. If that image is distorted, the energy of the root can become cloudy, and our self-nurturing behavior (what we eat, how we treat ourselves) suffers. The sense of self-worth, of being worthy of material success and abundance, is deeply bound in the root chakra.

The Sacral Chakra—Connection

The second chakra lies within the womb and genitals, and as expected, it governs sexuality and desire. It is the chakra of water, and therefore is deeply connected to the moon (especially in women); as water, its essence is fluid and changeable. In the first chakra we are only aware of ourselves; in the second, we become aware of our connection to others and our need to be connected. The sacral chakra is the home of most of our emotions, as emotion is primarily born out of our interaction with others.

The sacral chakra governs pleasure, and as such is easy to knock out of balance in today's world. People often live fixated on the second chakra, seeking sexual gratification and pleasure through food, alcohol, drugs, and risky behavior of all kinds.

The Solar Plexus Chakra—Will

The solar plexus is all about fire—power, will, drive, energy. Its purpose is transformation and the achievement of our true will, our sacred purpose on the earth. It is the chakra that overcomes inertia and breaks through outmoded habits. It is also the chakra that, if not healthy and stable, is most easily threatened by the energy of other people. The solar plexus is territorial; it is our sense of place and purpose, knowing who we are and where we belong, and feeling sure of ourselves. This is where we get "butterflies" when we feel nervous or uncertain.

Power is directed energy, and this is the essential function of the third chakra: it takes our personal energy and sends it outward toward our goals. A dysfunctional third chakra leaves us feeling useless, pointless, and indecisive, as if the universe is conspiring against us. We rely upon the solar plexus to "fire us up," get us moving, and overcome obstacles between us and our chosen path.

The Heart Chakra—Love

This is the center point of the whole system, the "heart of the matter." The heart chakra naturally governs love, but not the codependent romantic "love" we are taught to want by popular music and media; the heart chakra is the center of divine love, and of compassion. Sacral-chakra love is the love of a person for a person or a thing; heart-chakra love needs no object. It emanates from our divine essence.

The heart is the chakra of wholeness and acceptance; it balances the self-centeredness of the lower three chakras with the lofty spirituality of the upper three, and integrates all the various aspects of our being. The heart chakra shows us our inherent connection to all that lives, and removes the boundaries between us and the rest of creation. It is the sense of being deeply spiritually connected. The heart chakra is also the center of healing, as it receives healing energy and lets it flow to where it is most needed by the body, heart, or spirit.

The Throat Chakra—Expression

The fifth chakra governs the word, whether spoken or thought; moreover, it governs all forms of expression, how we represent ourselves to the world and how we communicate with others. It is the chakra of creativity, music, and humor.

In addition, the throat chakra reminds us of the importance of what we say and what we mean; it is in many ways a chakra of integrity, expressing the will of the solar plexus with creativity and then living up to that expression. It is overall the chakra of truth, both personal and universal. The throat is responsible for naming—putting a word or a symbol to a concept so that we can relate our thoughts and ideas to the rest of the world.

Often the throat is the site of a lot of blocked energy in women, who are by nature more emotional, but face a world where we are expected to "keep it together" and repress our feelings. Such repression is toxic to the throat chakra, and before long we find it hard to speak at all, our energy is so clogged with the things we didn't say.

The Brow Chakra—Perception

The sixth chakra gives us sight, both inner and outer. Also called the Third Eye chakra, its domain is perception and intuition: the things we know because we see them, and the things we know because we simply *know*. Its talents are primarily visual, such as clairvoyance, formed out of images rather than sounds or other sensation.

The brow chakra's world is the world of knowledge, taking in information through both kinds of sight. It also is the seat of our innate intelligence and the intelligence we have gathered from year to year, building upon the lessons we have already learned. All functions of the mind are part of the brow chakra.

The Crown Chakra—Understanding

The crown is actually located a few inches above the top of the head, within the etheric (or energy) body rather than the physical body. It is the doorway through which cosmic consciousness and divine connection can occur. The crown is the center of our spiritual growth, and of enlightenment.

The crown takes the knowledge we have gained in the brow chakra and applies divine wisdom, giving us true understanding of a subject, person, or the universe itself. It gives us an appreciation of divinity, both inside ourselves and all around, and shows us true beauty and peace.

There is a tendency in some spiritual circles to emphasize the upper chakras over the lower, as the upper chakras are considered less physical and more spiritual. The problem with this approach is that, for one thing, avoiding work with the lower chakras tends to leave you a space cadet, completely ungrounded in reality. In Wicca, with our understanding that the body is just as important as the mind, we understand that all seven chakras must be balanced and spinning equally in order for the energy of deity to flow through us strongly.

Energy flows both from the crown downward and from the root upward; the two currents produced by this flow are known as the Manifesting and Liberating currents. The Manifesting current, which moves downward, is how we take an idea and turn it into reality; the Liberating current is how we move through our bodies and outward to reach beyond the physical. Both are vital to our physical, mental, and spiritual health.

As my own path is devoted to a celestial goddess and a god of Earth, I often think of the Liberating current as the Goddess current, and the Manifesting as the God current. When both are flowing through the seven chakras, they turn around each other like the two helixes of DNA, an endless spiral moving from the heavens to the earth and back again. In ritual, to raise energy I work with both—I draw energy up from the earth and down from the moon, channel them into my body and out through my hands, or through whichever chakra my magic is most closely bound to.

For instance, say I was doing a spell for love (which I almost never do, but it makes a good example). I would draw energy through both currents, then concentrate it in the belly or heart chakra or both, allowing the energy to take on the "flavor" and color of that chakra; then I would push it out through my hands into a charm, candle, Cone of Power, or whatever the particular spell called for, to do its work.

Though the chakras are excellent to work with for magic, their essential purpose is more in keeping with the Healer's task.

HEALING WITH FIRE: THE SEVEN SUNS— EXERCISE #3

I'll warn you: this meditation is very powerful and can cause a variety of side effects. Any kind of intense chakra work will start your energy moving very quickly, and suddenly removing blockages can cause a sort of spiritual flash flood. Most people go through life with one or more of their chakras clogged, or too open, or totally blocked off; releasing the stuck energy will also release whatever emotions and memories that chakra was holding onto. If your sacral chakra has been blocked, and is cleansed, all the pent-up emotional issues you have been pushing down and denying can overwhelm you; this process is often necessary to release the stuck energy and attain balance, but can be painful in the short term.

Be patient and gentle with yourself if this occurs. The only way out is through; the only way to get rid of the side effects is to keep working with your chakras, cleansing and balancing them regularly (once a week is usually enough, though if you are in an especially negative environment all day, doing an abbreviated and less-intense version every day might be a good idea), and trying to keep both your body and mind healthy to keep the energy flowing. After doing this exercise be sure to ground and center, and remember to do the same frequently when you are doing regular energy work of this kind.

Close your eyes and bring your attention to your breath. As we did before, allow your breath to deepen, originating with the diaphragm and slowly filling the lungs, waking and invigorating your whole body.

Now bring your awareness to the lowest point of your body, where you meet the floor. Focus on the area at the base of your spine, and see a faint red glow forming there. Each time you breathe in and out, it glows a little brighter, until it becomes a visible sphere of light that turns slowly. Examine it with your senses. Is its light bright, or cloudy? Is it spinning freely, or sluggishly? The sphere may pulse in time to your breath or heartbeat, or it may simply shine; alternately, you might see a closed flower or a flame.

With each breath, let energy from the circuit of your breath flow into the chakra, and see it beginning to glow brighter, to expand, to spin a little faster. Don't rush this process; let it build naturally. If there were any dark spots on the sphere, see them being thrown off as the spin increases, growing and spinning faster, brighter, until the chakra is a healthy red color and shines clearly. If you are visualizing flowers, see them open and glow; if you see flame, see it brighten and dance.

When the base chakra is as full of energy and as open as it can be, draw the flow of energy up, breath by breath, into your belly, just behind your navel. Repeat the process of the base chakra with the belly chakra— see it glowing faintly, a fiery orange, then see its light strengthen; then speed it up and brighten it until it is clear and strong.

When the belly chakra is open and bright, draw the energy upward to your solar plexus, where the light glows a sunlit yellow.

Repeat the opening and cleansing process, then move up again to your heart. The heart chakra glows a vibrant, spring green. After the heart, draw the energy up to your throat, where the light is a pure sky blue.

When the heart is open and spinning, move up to your third eye, just above and between your eyebrows. The third eye is a deep indigo; some people see it as purple instead. Neither of these is wrong. Everyone's chakras are slightly different, in different places and in different shades of the color. Only you can know when they are healthy and energized.

After the third eye, move up to the crown chakra, at the top of your head. It may hover just above your head, in your aura. The crown chakra is a crystalline violet, almost white, sparkling like a jewel. Open it and cleanse it, just like the others.

Now all of your chakras are open, all glowing brightly and spinning rapidly. Feel the energy of your breath as it flows in its endless circle, and feel the seven chakras spreading their light throughout your body. Let the energy flow through and around the chakras, helping bring them into balance, clearing out any blockages and soothing any rough edges.

Spend a few minutes here, just breathing, experiencing. There are also secondary chakras in your palms and feet, and if you like you can let the energy cleanse them as well, while you're at it. (Whatever you do, do not stop at this point and skip closing the chakras—going out into the world with your chakras wide open is a recipe for overload and all manner of disasters.)

Eventually, return your awareness to your crown chakra. Gently pull its energy inward, shrinking it, dulling the glow just a little. Do not shut it down entirely; simply bring it down to a more manageable level. Slow its spin, draw it in, and then move down to your third eye. Pull in the energy, slow it down, still moving with the circle of your breath.

Gradually work downward, through your throat, then your heart, then your solar plexus, your belly, and the root. If you brightened your hand and foot chakras, do the same with them, pulling in their edges, damping the light. During all of this your aura will most likely have ballooned out quite a bit, so draw it in as well, visualizing your personal energy grounding, any excess flowing down into the earth where it will be put to good use by the environment. When you have returned to your original state, open your eyes. Eating and drinking something afterward will help you fully ground.

Illness and the Chakras

Aside from cleansing and balancing your chakras regularly, another important practice is to work with them when you have problems with your body. Each chakra is traditionally linked to kinds of wellness issues that are located in the same general area, or with the same kind of function as the chakra itself.

The root chakra is most often connected to problems with the legs and feet (as well as the bones in general), digestive imbalances, and most chronic illness; as it is the most physical chakra, if you are having pain or dis-ease and don't know exactly what the problem is, you may want to start off by looking at the root. The sacral chakra is associated with reproductive disorders, problems with the bladder and urinary tract, menstrual issues, back pain, and problems with the hips and hip joints; the solar plexus out of balance can lead to imbalance in the metabolic system, in particular the liver, pancreas, and blood sugar levels, and can also bring on chronic fatigue. The heart, as you might expect, is connected to circulatory and respiratory illness as well as immune function; the throat chakra can fall prey to excess or deficiency in the thyroid gland, and also to tooth, gum, and tonsil infection. Headaches are the primary demon of the brow chakra, especially migraines or any pain exacerbated by bright light. Difficulties with eyesight are also the brow's domain. The crown, while a very metaphysical rather than physical energy center, can show an imbalance through upset in brain chemistry, which can lead to psychological and emotional problems.

Of course, if you are having a new and unexpected problem in your body, my first suggestion is to go to a doctor; Western medicine, for all its faults, is still a good first line of defense, and you can take what you learn and consult other wellness practitioners as well. If you already know your diagnosis, however, working to help the associated chakra run smoothly can bolster your other healing efforts.

Witch, Heal Thyself

The important thing to remember with energy healing is to walk softly. As we'll discuss shortly, sending a tsunami of energy into an injured or ailing body can achieve the opposite effect of what you desire, throwing the whole system off kilter. My recommendation is rather than zapping a chakra with an overabundance of energy, use a gentler, less powerful current, in small doses.

There are many methods of energy healing, but most require that you have someone else do it for you by the laying on of hands or similar procedure. Working on yourself can be a bit problematic when it comes to this technique—it's hard to hold your hands on your own upper back, for example, without making the problem worse. If you are lying down you can't really reach your feet.

The same technique that I spoke of for doing magic through the chakras is useful for healing work; draw the two currents into your body, then channel the energy through your hands and into another person, focusing on the area of the body that is affected or, if it's not a specific part, on the chakra related to the issue at hand. To work on yourself, rather than using your hands, draw the energy and then concentrate it in the chakra in question; you can do this in any position and focus on any area. Just be sure to allow excess energy to drain back into the environment to avoid overloading the chakra and turning it into a puffer fish.

Stress and the Healer's Work

A few hundred years ago, matters of life and death were a much bigger worry than they are nowadays—influenza could easily kill you, starvation in winter was a distinct possibility, and because we were more dependent on the seasons and the earth, her whims and rhythms were much more important to our lives. Perhaps we don't have to be so concerned anymore with whether or not the plague will kill off our entire country, but our disconnection from the land beneath our feet combined with the mad pace of our lives has created another life-and-death struggle for us, one that is much more subtle: stress.

The more affluent our society becomes, the harder it is to avoid problems like depression, anxiety, and other emotional and mental disturbances that arise from squeezing too much activity and expectation into a life that has already denied its own natural patterns. The crown and brow chakras, in particular, are adversely affected by the unnatural state of our lives; we cut ourselves off from the sacred source, and take in toxic energy and messages, confusing and bewildering our senses and our spirits.

In the past, in winter people were homebound—they couldn't get out and work in the fields, so they confined their activities to those that could be accomplished indoors, including the many crafts that could help supplement their incomes. Work was timed with the rising and setting of the sun, not with a number on a clock. Candles were expensive, so staying up late wasn't very common.

Though humans don't hibernate the way animals do, in winter we once rested and drew inward. In the current century we run, run, run all year, all day and night, heedless of the pull of the seasons and the movements of sun and moon. It's common to find people at the office until midnight, and we work just as hard in December as we do in June.

Add to that the constant noise and rush of our world—electronic devices constantly buzzing and humming, cars honking, people in a hurry to get somewhere, anywhere, as fast as possible—and the influence of advertising, which convinces us we need more things, more money, which takes more work—and it's no wonder we're dropping like flies from heart attacks and stress. Stress is a greater killer than any of our other diseases of affluence, because it often underlies those diseases and speeds us toward an early grave, cheerfully helping our other health problems to grow worse. People eat crap food, drink, smoke, and treat their bodies like trash very often because they "don't have time" to do better, or are trying to numb their anxiety with drugs.

The rise of "trendy" Eastern practices like yoga and meditation, and the growing popularity of earth-based religions, reflects what our bodies already know deep down—we can't go on like this.

The Healer has her work cut out for her. Usually, her first task is to step out onto the six-lane freeway of our lives, hold up her hand, and yell, "STOP!"

I have observed the same problem affecting our stress levels that affects women's ability to take care of themselves in other areas of life—we don't feel worthy of silence. If we aren't constantly filling our days with activity, if we spend even a little time sitting and "doing nothing," we feel guilty for not doing something useful.

Unfortunately, it's hard to climb the corporate ladder if you're so exhausted you fall off.

We need silence in our lives. We need stillness. This is not wishful thinking, it's absolute truth—our bodies need down time, our minds need freedom to drift and daydream. Our spirits need to ground and center. It is impossible to grow spiritually if you're running too fast to be watered.

> For fast-acting relief, try slow-ing down.
> LILY TOMLIN

Many of us seem afraid of quiet, as if to stop drowning out the voice of deity means we'll hear things we'd rather not. Sometimes it does. You can put your hand over a screaming soul's mouth, but it's still screaming, and not likely to stop until you listen.

Wiccans are fortunate in that the basis of our religion is connection to nature and to the inner self, which flies in the face of what we are expected to do by society at large. "Sorry," you say, "I can't stay late at work tonight. I have to go howl at the moon." Aside from its obvious spiritual benefits, at the very least, ritual is a great stress reliever. When we step into circle, we let the world fall from our shoulders and clothe ourselves in what really matters—moonlight, sanctity, and truth.

To begin to undo all the damage that stress has wreaked on just about every adult in the West, we can start with the absolute basics, the breathing exercises we've already discussed. Cleansing and balancing the chakras is another important tool, but because of its complexity—and intensity—it isn't entirely practical to do every day unless you can either condense it into a few minutes or have a lot of free time. Meditation, of course, accomplishes a good deal of balancing on its own. In addition to all of this, however, as Wiccans we have even more tools at our disposal.

Magical Healing

The Healer understands that our will and intention are the strongest medicine we have, but she also knows that the Goddess has given us the knowledge to work in partnership with many of her other children to heal ourselves. From our earliest history as thinking animals, we have used herbs and other natural substances to reach and keep wellness in body and mind.

I am not a medicinal herbalist, but I do work extensively with herbs in a magical context. The two are easily joined together, in fact; you can charge herbal remedies just like you can charms. The main difference is that in magical herbalism you work with a lot of plants that you would never dream of using on or in your body. Mandrake may be useful for drawing love, but taken internally it's more useful for drawing paramedics.

As tempting as it is, when we fall ill or receive a difficult diagnosis, to do a ritual to zap ourselves with white light, this sometimes has about the same effect as antibiotics—it comes roaring in with guns blazing and can overload your body, which is already in a delicate state. Sometimes a wiser course of action, particularly for long-term illness or chronic problems, is to work gently on the chakras as I already mentioned; another is to work magic that is more subtle and won't throw off your already-precarious balance.

Think of how you feel after a hardcore ritual that involves channeling a lot of energy, and imagine how much worse that would feel when you're already sick, which often impairs our ability to ground and release excess magical power. I've discovered that a softer way to work healing magic is through the use of enchantment—you charge up a charm to wear, a stone to carry, or fill an herbal or other remedy with energy so that it can be absorbed into your body slowly as needed rather than hitting you all at once like lightning. This, too, can be linked to the chakras; you can envision the object's stored energy flowing into the chakra and being dispersed through the body by its spinning.

For immediate and dire situations, the zap method can be your best (or only) course of action. Most of our physical ailments, however, respond better to slower work—again, we need to let go of the need to get things done *right now*, and listen to what our bodies are really asking for. Sometimes we fall ill because of stress, as our body's way of getting our attention; your body might say, "You won't take a break? Fine. It's a slipped disc for you, missy!" and a part of your body that never bothered you before may simply give out.

Emotions, especially negative ones, tend to stay in our bodies and build and build until they drag us down. Where do you carry stress? Some people keep it in their heads, and get migraines; some, like me, keep it in their digestive systems. My stomach is the first thing to go south when I'm not taking proper care of myself, holding onto worry and anger, or becoming overly anxious about anything. Other people have back trouble, neck trouble, heart problems—the body can be very creative in its warning systems. As you learn to listen to your body, you will learn its cues, and pay attention to the little red flags that mean an explosion is imminent.

Western medicine tends to be violent; doctors cut us open, hit us with a drug arsenal, and then duck. Magical medicine seems to work best when it takes a gentler path.

A HEALING CHARM

Healing spells are some of the most widely used, after love and money spells. This one is simple, powerful, and has the added advantage of smelling good. (I've always subscribed to the philosophy that magic shouldn't stink, but that's just me, and that doesn't apply to banishing.) It also combines the magical and medicinal properties of herbs.

Find or make a small pouch you can wear around your neck or carry somewhere on your body; you want this to touch you, so its energy can seep into you more easily.

Gather together the following:

A clove of garlic

A pinch of eucalyptus

A pinch of cinnamon

A pinch of sage

A pinch of orange peel

A small piece of rose quartz

Then, depending on what kind of illness you have, add:

Ginger for digestive problems

Catnip for emotional problems like depression

Mint for lung ailments

Lavender for problems with the head

Red raspberry leaf for menstrual pain or irregularity

Chamomile for difficulty sleeping

Eyebright for eye problems . . .

. . . and so on. If you are working with herbal medicine to help you with your illness, add some of whatever you are using; even a capsule from your bottle will do.

Mix the herbs together with your hands (you can crush them in a mortar, but I don't recommend crushing the garlic unless you want to smell like it), and as you do so, visualize healing energy rising up from the earth and falling from the sky, running through your chakras, and centering in the chakra that is physically closest to whatever part of your body is affected. Visualize the energy becoming the color of that chakra, then let it flow out through your hands and into the herbs.

See the energy waking up the latent potential of each plant. An herb, after all, can't heal just by sitting there; your own energy merges with its own properties in order for it to help you. You might wish to chant the names of the herbs and perhaps what each one does as you work, for example, "Garlic . . . protection . . . eucalyptus . . . cleansing . . ." and so on.

Fill the pouch with the herbs and the stone. Add a bit of salt, as salt absorbs negative energy and, with the garlic, will draw illness out of your body to be replaced with the healing energy of the other herbs in the pouch. Wear the pouch continuously until you are completely well; if you have a more lasting illness, you might want to replace the herbs in the pouch every month or so to give fresh energy to the spell.

HEALING WITH EARTH—EXERCISE #4

If making charms isn't to your liking, there are other ways the Healer can work with the energy of the element earth. Find a place in nature where you can lie down upon the earth, in as much contact with the ground as possible; if you have privacy and the weather permits, you might even do so skyclad. Ask the earth to help you cleanse yourself of your illness.

Visualize yourself sinking partway into the ground, and the world around you taking you in as a part of itself. The grass grows over you, the wind blows through you, the rain soaks you and carries disease and negative energy out of your body, into the earth, where it is cleansed and transformed. Then allow the earth's energy to fill you slowly, breathing it in, replenishing your strength and renewing your spirit.

You can do the same thing floating on your back in the water, standing on a hillside where the wind can move through you, or lying in the sunlight and letting its fire burn the illness away. These methods are very subtle, and you may not feel terribly different the first time, but do it regularly for several days and the effects can be astounding.

Healing with Water

Very few people really drink enough water. I freely admit I'm one of them. Every year science discovers a dozen new benefits of getting your sixty-four ounces a day, but it doesn't take a scientist to know water is good for you. It cleanses the body of toxins, replenishes our cells, and gives life energy to all the chakras; many of our minor physical complaints, from fatigue to generalized aches, can be traced to mild dehydration. You get all the water you *need* from what you drink regardless, but this is only the bare minimum.

Pretty much everyone knows that, in most situations, a little lubrication makes life a lot more enjoyable. My problem is I don't like drinking water—I hate the way it tastes. I have to make myself drink it, most of the time, and I've even tried to trick myself by adding lemon or lime slices. I am told that if I were to drink my eight glasses a day for a few weeks, I'd start liking it; this has yet to happen to me, but I try my best regardless, because not liking water is like not liking breathing or watching daytime TV; maybe you hate it, but you still can't stop doing it.

Water on the outside of the body is as beneficial as water inside. We've discussed the benefits of bathing as a pampering tool, but aside from the mental and emotional perks of a long hot bath, keeping your body clean is one of those things that we take for granted. You forget how valuable cleansing can be until you have to go without a shower— or until you run into someone else that obviously has trouble with the whole "soap" concept.

The atmosphere in most cities is toxic—smog, pesticides, and a fun mix of other chemicals get on our skin every day, not to mention the cosmetics, perfumes, and body care products we slather on ourselves. Add sweat, and you have the recipe for a dirty, dirty little Witch.

Even the products we use to clean ourselves can do more harm than good. Most soaps made these days are actually detergents and are full of harsh chemicals. Many are produced by companies that perform unnecessary animal testing or use ingredients obtained from critters in all sorts of unpleasant ways. I find I feel a lot cleaner using cruelty-free soap and shampoo, and even more so if I know who made it. You don't have to make your own soap, though, in the age of the Internet, where homemade body-care products are widely available.

This extends to what you clean your house with, as well. I come from a long line of bleach slingers—the women of my family wash down the kitchen with bleach, and bleach, aside from smelling horrible, is poisonous. You can clean just about anything in your house with Borax, baking soda, white vinegar, and a bag of lemons; it's cheaper, environmentally friendly, and probably won't kill you. A large percentage of the Pagan population makes at least some effort toward a more organic lifestyle, but this doesn't just apply to what you eat.

Rites of Tea

The recent popularity of herbal teas and other remedies is rather prov-idential for Witches, as we are now able to find herbs more readily without spending a fortune. Even the simplest cup of tea can be a heal-ing ritual, and doesn't involve arcane ingredients or equipment, only hot water and a cup.

There are many blends available already made into tea bags, but you can also blend your own; this way you can buy your herbs in bulk and save money, and also control exactly what is in your mixtures and how they taste. I don't care what anyone says, or how effective it is, I'd rather have insomnia than taste valerian. It is often added into sleep-in-ducing mixes and completely ruins the flavor for me, but if I blend my own, I can leave it out entirely.

Having a cup of herbal tea in the morning or night is a very soothing and grounding ritual, and there are varieties available to just about every taste and for just about every physical discomfort. I have rather uncom-fortable menstrual periods, for example, but most over-the-counter anal-gesics and "PMS pills" make my stomach upset when I'm bleeding; I happened to stumble across something called Women's Moon Cycle Tea, and now it's become a part of my monthly moon rituals.

Like any other ritual, there are tools: a cup, a spoon, a special jar of honey, and so on. Set things aside for your magical teas. If you use a blend you make yourself, tea balls are handy and come in a variety of shapes, even moons. I have a cup that I only use for rites.

Here's an example to improve physical well-being using a tea blend that's a general tonic. The recipe is for a whole pot of tea, but you could combine the dried herbs and then steep a couple tablespoons of the mixture with one half-slice of ginger to make a single cup.

> 3 slices fresh ginger (a warming herb that strengthens the im-mune and digestive systems)
>
> 1 tsp. mint (good for digestion)

1 tbsp. chamomile (soothing, relaxing)

1 tsp. nettles (a tonic herb for the liver and kidneys)

1 tbsp. red clover (a blood cleanser)

1 tsp. rose hips (chock full of vitamin C)

Steep for fifteen minutes. As the tea brews, visualize its healing properties swirling into the hot water, infusing it as it will infuse your body. You can charge it with more energy, or simply let it do its work as is; the sugar or honey you add can symbolize renewed happiness and wellness. It's a simple thing, really, but tea has been used in ritual by the Japanese for centuries, and the process of heating water, measuring herbs, steeping, stirring, and sipping can be excellent therapy.

In fact, before I move on to the next section, I think I may have a cup of chai.

As She Made Us

I mentioned before that modern medical science's goal is to make people normal. If we were all exactly as "healthy" as we're supposed to be, we'd all be the same size, shape, and probably color and height, as well. One of my favorite T-shirts simply says, "Fuck your fascist beauty standards," and I'm beginning to feel that the standards of the medical community fit in here as well.

Granted, many health problems are just that, and cause pain and deterioration that medicine can help or even cure. The problem is, even when what's "wrong" with you is something that can't be drugged away or that doesn't hurt you physically, you're still made to feel that something is wrong with how you were born or how you grew.

How can we love our bodies if they don't work like they're supposed to? That's a hard question. If our bodies are so perfect just like they are, how do we explain so-called disabilities, deformities, and defects? What about the chronic problems many of us develop thanks to our lifestyles that just don't go away?

There is a reason for everything. Most of us have to believe this, or go crazy. There is nothing wasted in nature, and the Goddess does not create anything useless. The only conclusion, then, is that there is something we are meant to learn from what goes wrong with our bodies.

Like I said, sometimes we fall ill because our bodies are trying to get our attention, or force us to change unhealthy habits. Other times, it seems the gods of chaos have devoted their attention entirely to us, and things seem to fall apart for no reason whatsoever. What then?

I wish I could explain it. I wish I knew if there was a grand design, and why bad things happen to good Wiccans. I can't tell you what to believe, but I can tell you what I believe:

I don't believe that we are suddenly struck blind, or paralyzed, or molested as children, or given cancer as a punishment, or even as a test of faith; if we start questioning the divine will behind everything, we'll end up atheists, because sometimes, shit just happens. The Goddess granted us all free will, all of us, which means I can't always have my way; the universe runs on cause and effect, and frequently those causes and effects are too large and complex for my poor little mind to wrap around.

Rather than shaking my fist at the universe and asking, "Why me?" I would rather spend my time figuring out (a) what I need to take from the situation that will enrich my life, and (b) how to keep it from happening again, if at all possible.

That in mind, I have to say that whether your body is big or small, black or white or spotted, short, minus a leg, bald, bent, butt-ugly, or drop-dead gorgeous, it is beautiful, and you are a divine being no matter what. It may be that the purpose is to lead you to find compassion for others who are in pain, or to understand that the God and Goddess love you unconditionally and you should extend that same grace to yourself; but whatever you can learn from what you think is "wrong" with you, it's still right.

You may think that's easy for me to say, since I have almost all my original body parts and no terminal illnesses, and I'm a white, middle-class American. Maybe it is. But I've had my share of problems because of my appearance, and my share of ill fortune done to my body. I could give you a list that would turn your hair white, but I won't; though by the time you're through this book, you'll know a lot more about my past than you might have wanted to. I've taken a lesson, though, from the "disabled" people I've met who refused to wallow in self-pity or blame the universe for their bad fortune, and instead learned ways to live the best lives they can, which is really all any of us can do. We all have limitations, and physical ones aren't necessarily the worst: if you're reading this book that means you can read, first of all, so you probably don't live in a Third World country where people are starving wholesale and dropping from dysentery. You could be out on the street, hungry, cold, friendless, or a thousand other things that are arguably worse than not having all your limbs.

Often the Healer's most difficult task is overcoming our own mental state, and convincing us that life is worth living, and worth living well, no matter what.

Suffice it to say, knowing that everything happens as it should is easier sometimes than others, but at heart, I know it to be true. I heard it from the Lady's own mouth, and I'm inclined to believe her.

Goddesses of the Healer Archetype

We've already met one of my favorite Healers, a Celtic goddess, Airmid. She, along with her father Dian Cecht and brother Miach, tended one of the sacred healing springs of Ireland.

Airmid and Dian Cecht were by far the greater healers, and created chants and charms that were shared with the humans of the land. Miach grew jealous of their skill, and killed his father; from Dian Cecht's grave there sprung 365 herbs, each one matching a joint, sinew, or organ. Airmid, determined to preserve her father's knowledge, picked the herbs and arranged them on her cloak, each one laid out over the place in the body to which its powers applied.

Enraged at her temerity, Miach took up Airmid's cloak and shook it, confusing all the herbs so that their properties were lost; Airmid, however, was wise enough to remember them all, and so in order to learn the secrets of herb lore, Healers must petition her aid. The number of the herbs is said to be symbolic of the fact that their power is as true in winter as in summer, and that with time, the magic of the Goddess can heal any wound, cure any illness.

If you desire to learn more about Airmid, there are precious few stories about her in Irish myth, but taking what little is available you can certainly form an image of her in your imagination that can connect you to her. The image of the Healer is an evocative one, though most of the female deities of healing have been relegated to very minor roles.

AN INVOCATION TO AIRMID

I am Healer of nations, attired in growing green
Find me among the swaying blossoms, the sun alight in my hair
I will part the grass and touch the healing heart of the earth
I will lay my hand upon you and you will be renewed.
Here is my wisdom: the nodding head of coneflower,
The bitter bark of willow
The sweet scent of lavender.
Here is my raiment:
Edges woven of late summer wheat,
Pattern woven of verbena and thyme,
Thread of nettle, trim of sage.

Have you a year of days to give me?
Then I will lay my cloak over your shoulders,
I will speak the sacred names of that which grows upon it,
And in a year's time you may know them all.

SUGGESTIONS FOR EXPLORING THE HEALER

1. Make it a point to actually learn about human anatomy. A great many of us have no real idea how our bodies work, and don't bother learning until something goes wrong, rather like with car repair. A favorite book of mine is *Woman: An Intimate Geography* by Natalie Angier, which approaches the female body in a poetic and whimsical sense rather than using dry facts and statistics.

2. Sit down and make a list of all of your "health problems," from depression to weight to birthmarks to scars. Now, start another list of the parts of your body that work exactly the way they're supposed to—if you're alive, that means the second list is a lot longer than the first.

3. Find a method of alternative healing and learn something about it: Chinese or regular herbalism, flower remedies, aromatherapy, energy healing—the possibilities are endless. If nothing else, it will give you an appreciation for the wild variety of ways in which humans try to make their bodies work and feel better. People do everything from sticking wax tubes in their ears and setting them on fire to eating royal jelly (that's baby food for queen bees, to the uninitiated).

Recommended Reading and Resources for Chapter Five

BOOKS

Better Basics for the Home: Simple Solutions for Less Toxic Living by Annie Berthold-Bond

Herbal Teas: 101 Nourishing Blends for Daily Health and Vitality by Kathleen Brown, et al

Your Hands Can Heal You: Pranic Healing Energy Remedies to Boost Vitality and Speed Recovery from Common Health Problems by Master Stephen Co and Eric B. Robins

The Breathing Book by Donna Farhi

Wheels of Life: A User's Guide to the Chakra System by Anodea Judith

The New Age Herbalist: How to Use Herbs for Healing, Nutrition, Body Care, and Relaxation by Richard Mabey

Meditation Secrets for Women by Camille Maurine

Why People Don't Heal and How They Can by Caroline Myss

Women's Bodies, Women's Wisdom: Creating Physical and Emotional Health and Healing by Christiane Northrup

The Woman's Book of Healing by Diane Stein

MUSIC

The Essence by Deva Premal—contains a beautiful recording of the Gayatri Mantra as well as other mantras

WEB RESOURCES

Cranberry Lane, a site based out of Canada, sells kits and ingredients for making your own body-care and household products. <http://www.cranberrylane.com>

s i x

THE
lover

I know not how to praise you,
Oh my love,
Whose eyes hold mine across the fire,
I who am flame, dance only for you;
You burn me to ash with a glance.
How shall I touch you,
Oh my love,
Whose lips are sweeter than midsummer's mead,
River to sea beneath the milk-white moon
You baptize me in sweat of a thousand nights.
I wish only to know you,
Oh my love,
Whose laughter rings in me, dawn and dusk
Hands of a bard, calling song from my skin
You breathe the universe into my blood.

With what name shall I call you,
Oh my love,
Who rocks me like goddess,
Filling me like god,
Shadow to light, season to season,
My one, eternal, and my choice, for tonight.

If you're a wily little Scorpio like me, or a red-blooded female like most of us, you might well have turned to this chapter first.

I said before that the Mother archetype is the one who comes with the most baggage in terms of societal expectations and conflict; hot on her heels, however, is the Lover. Just walk outside your door and look at five billboards and a few newspaper headlines and magazine covers, and you'll see just how mixed our messages about sexuality have become.

According to mainstream religion, sex before marriage is taboo. Some even forbid contraception, I suppose on the theory that an over-populated planet is a God-fearing planet. Gay sex . . . well, if no one is allowed to have sex before marriage and gay people can't get married, they're doubly screwed . . . if you'll pardon the pun. There are even religious organizations dedicated to, and I kid you not, overcoming masturbation; these run off the logic that you can't have sex with anyone who isn't your lawfully married spouse—not even with yourself.

Right. Good luck wiping out that little habit.

Meanwhile, the second you turn on the television, what do you see? Sex. Who's doing it, what they're doing, why they're doing it, how they feel after they do it, what everyone they know thinks about them doing it, what they were wearing before, during, and after doing it . . .

Whatever the beauty "ideal" of our society, you can bet it's not being painted on canvas and hung in museums for posterity. It's glossed up, airbrushed, stripped to its undies, and used to sell everything from beer to tractor tires.

And regardless of our religious conditioning, no matter what the priests and health teachers tell us, the simple fact remains: we like sex. No amount of hate-mongering and Bible-thumping can change that about the human race. We are a sexual species, and we're damn proud of it . . . or, at least, some of us are.

The Virgin and the Whore

Sounds rather like an Aesop's fable, doesn't it? "Once there was a pale, wan young virgin and a buxom, happy whore . . ." The truth, however, is that these are the two sexual roles women are taught. We are, according to this outlook, either pure and devout, or we are temptresses of the devil, seeking to lure pious men into a den of iniquity through our amazing powers of Vaginomancy.

In this paradigm, it's only okay to enjoy sex if you're married, and even then, you don't talk about it—no matter what kind of weirdness your husband (and it has to be a husband, ladies, you know Jesus hates lesbians) (that's sarcasm, by the way) gets up to in the bedroom, it's between the two of you and perhaps your pastor . . . though I've never met a pastor I'd be comfortable telling that my Lawfully Wedded Husband liked to dress in my lingerie and yodel while spanking me with a trout.

Stranger things have happened, you know.

Think of the biblical accounts of Christ, and the two Marys therein: the Virgin Mother, and the Magdalene, a whore. There wasn't a Mary Only on Alternate Thursdays, a Mary Likes Leather, a Mary No Penis For Me Thank You. There was one woman who never had sex (or at least not until after Jesus was born—thinking that Joseph stayed with her all those subsequent years sleeping on the couch is pretty naïve), and another who did have sex and was therefore an outcast only a Savior would love. It's set up right there for all womankind, just like in Genesis.

Fortunately, in our modern world these two polar opposites have begun to show the full range of grey they hold between them. We've gone from a time in which any sex at all was secret to a time when ex-Presidents do Viagra commercials, and every other episode of Oprah is about who's doing it, what they're doing, how they feel about . . . you get the idea.

Still, the stigma remains against "alternative" sexualities, and we haven't even begun to broach topics like polyamory and S&M in common discourse. Gay characters are headliners on network sitcoms—but they never have long-term or healthy relationships, and certainly never get laid except in vague, off-camera terms. There are only a few programs, all of them on cable, that tackle the broad spectrum of sexuality with any sort of grace. Mention gay marriage, and conservatives panic like schoolchildren in an air raid. Slowly, slowly, sexual mores are changing, but there's still a long way to go.

So mainstream religious authorities say sex is almost always bad; politicians say certain kinds of sex are bad; advertising says it's good as long as afterward we buy cars and beer; our bodies say it's really, *really* good as long as everyone's consenting. With all these mixed messages, the Lover in us all has a hard time finding herself, let alone finding others of her kind. Too often she spends most of her life in hiding, afraid to show her head and risk ridicule, hatred, shame, or good old-fashioned prudishness. How, then, do we bring her out of the closet—whatever kind of closet we've built for her—and give her wings?

The Lover's role isn't just to govern the physical act of sex. Her sphere is much broader, much harder to define. The part of us that admires a painting, a vista, a woman in a tight skirt—that part is of the Lover, who is our sensual alchemist. She understands better than any other archetype what sensations bring us happiness, and not just with our clothes off. Any time you stand in the ocean reveling in the waves that buffet your legs; any time you run your hand over the back of a chenille sofa cushion; any time you close your eyes and inhale the scent of honeysuckle growing outside your window, you invoke the Lover.

Her hands always look for something warm and soft to touch. She lifts her chin, seeking the scent of afternoon rain. Her eyes flash across a crowded room, and people flock to her like a lone flame on a winter's night. Her power is that of connection; she binds hearts, bodies, and souls together, for better or worse.

Most importantly, the Lover in her truest expression has no shame and no fear of who she is and what she desires. She is perfectly well aware of the eyes that track her down the sidewalk. "Let them look," she says. "They should all be so lucky."

Bringing out the Lover, then, doesn't mean sleeping with anyone who nibbles your fancy; it means learning to appreciate and revel in our bodily sensations, especially as they bring us closer to others.

> I tend to be a wild woman, loud and rowdy—remember my name, you will be screaming it later!
>
> KYLARA

ADVANCED BODY AWARENESS—EXERCISE #1

We've already worked on becoming mindful of how our bodies feel at any given moment. This time, come up with a list of five sensations that you love. They have to be experiences you can have using your physical senses. For this example, I'll say one of mine is having someone brush my hair.

Now, close your eyes and do a check-in with your body. How do you feel? Breathe deeply for a few moments, allowing your awareness to fill your whole body, so that you really feel like you're in your skin. Imagine your consciousness is made of warmth, and slowly you warm every cell of your body; you could also imagine it as light, colored to each of your chakras, which filters out through you until you are all aglow from the inside.

Now, call to mind the first experience on your list. This will bring in your visualization skills, even though it's probably not a strictly visual image. Remember the feeling with your entire body, not just the part of you it affected. In my case, I feel the pull of the brush, the tickle on my scalp, the warm-fuzzies going all the way to my feet. I remember the feeling of trust, of physical comfort knowing that I've let someone get close enough to me to touch; I remember the occasional yank of a snarled hair in the bristles.

When the memory is as real as you can make it, gently let it go and move on to the next one. Remember to utilize all of your senses in the feeling of it.

To apply this skill to everyday, when something feels good to you, pause in your thinking, and feel. If someone runs a hand down your arm, feel it all the way through you and on your skin as well. Become completely present in your senses, and life will become richer—it's as if the colors of your world all deepen a shade.

Love Magic: Bespelling Yourself

"I want a boyfriend," she says to me. "Will you do a love spell for me?"

I give her my specialty, the Long Blink. "Um . . . no."

"But why not?"

I sigh; Witches get these questions way more often than we want to—which is never. "Do you want that alphabetically or chronologically?"

The most popular kind of magic out there is love magic. More spells have been written and more charms have been made to bring us lovers than anything else. We crave company, understanding, and good sex more than money, health, or status.

It's natural, after all. Human beings are not solitary creatures. Whether you're in favor of monogamy or other-gamy, you have to admit that no one likes to spend her life alone, and that we seek out companionship and prize it so highly that we're willing to put up with all sorts of bad habits, in-laws, and dirty clothes strewn over the floor in order to get and keep it. Friendship is vital, and we fight for it as well, but most of us want at least one person to wake up next to, at least once in a while.

When people come to Wicca, and to Witchcraft in particular, they are often immediately intrigued by the idea of casting a spell out into the universe and reeling in a true love. It's been my observation that love spells are usually the first kind new Witches cast—and the first they end up regretting.

There are problems inherent in most love magic. First of all is the most obvious: manipulating another's free will is not kosher among Wiccans, so that rules out doing a love spell on a specific person. From there it's hard to know how to proceed—how specific can you be without "accidentally" throwing a real person in there? But if you're not specific, who knows what the universe in its infinite humor might conjure up for you? "Let go and let God" isn't a popular motto for Wiccans; we usually feel that the gods have already given us their gift—the power to weave reality—and that to put every matter into their hands without working on our own behalf is a kind of ingratitude for that gift. We're given magic as a medium for change as much as speaking and walking; clearly we are not meant to leave it all up to deity.

Love, however, is one of those things that, if it's real and not some pathological codependent obsessive impostor, can be appreciated no matter how it comes. Who doesn't want more love in their lives? The second problem with love magic is tied into this—very often we cry to the gods for a lover when that's the last thing we need; it is nearly impossible to conduct a healthy adult relationship if both parties aren't healthy adults. If you haven't even started working on your own emotional issues, do you really want to pile someone else's on top of them? Magically speaking, like attracts like. A basket case will bring in basket cases.

Look at your life, if you're single—are you in a place where, if you attracted a person of comparable maturity and at a similar stage of personal growth, you would want that person? If you can't hold a job, you live off vodka and cigarettes, your home is a sty, and your daily life resembles nothing so much as a bad soap opera, what kind of lover do you think you will attract? Who in their right mind would want to jump into that kind of craziness? Exactly—no one in her right mind would.

A lover is not going to "fix" your life. Adding another person's needs and idiosyncrasies to your own makes things much more complicated. You may not be ready for that. It's not your lover's responsibility to take care of your problems or take care of you; it's not his or her (or their) responsibility to make you happy. If you can't find love and happiness within yourself, no one else can give them to you.

I can speak from experience on this. My first love spell, cast when I was nineteen, attracted a person who was exactly my match at the time. I spent two miserable years thinking I had botched my only chance at love, and I should hold onto this one no matter how horrible our relationship had become. Codependent, you think? Absolutely. So the guy I found was just as much a child as I was, and we made each other's lives hell.

This is not to say you can't have a love until your life is perfect. Your life, in case you haven't noticed, will never be perfect; you usually get a few months of smooth sailing before hitting a bump of some kind. But a sign that you're ready to deal with a relationship based on mutual trust, respect, and maturity is that when you hit the bumps, they don't knock you out of the wagon anymore. If you can't cope with conflict, trust me, you'd be better off with a dog.

They say you find what you want when you stop looking; I say, it helps if you send out a signal that you're about to stop, and that's where love magic comes in. When you reach a point in your life where you think you're ready for a relationship, work your magic, then stop worrying about it. Throw yourself into your life with gusto and live every moment, and your love spell will be cast first on yourself.

A LOVE SPELL

This spell is not designed specifically to bring you a mate. It may very well do that, but its primary purpose is to bring you love—from anywhere, everywhere. It is a spell to fill your life with love, whether that love is for yourself, from another, for your work, from your gods . . . love for your life entire, from your life entire. How it manifests will depend on what you need.

This is a case of being nonspecific in spellwork because however the answer comes, it's good. This isn't like a money spell wherein not specifying the source of your new income could result in a relative dying and leaving you an inheritance. About the only bad thing that can happen is that someone offers you love you don't wish to accept; to avoid this, you might focus on bringing only healthy, desirable love from those you could connect with, rather than leaving the door open for all manner of freaks and weirdos. It certainly isn't in keeping with "the good of all" for someone that you wouldn't kiss with someone else's mouth to fall for you, and then for you to break that person's heart, or even worse, to pretend to love them back and make both of you suffer.

One caveat, though—sometimes love can only come through pain. Sometimes we have to let go of the things and people who are keeping us from loving ourselves, or who are stifling our inner light—the beacon that draws love to us. If you are dead set on a good relationship and your life is chaos, you might have to go through the wringer and come out the other side before the spell will finish its work. The love you truly need and the love you think you want can be two wildly different things.

With that in mind:

Gather together one red or pink candle, preferably a short-burning one; something to carve the candle with; a small, empty bottle of whatever kind you like; sweet almond oil; essential oils of sandalwood, rose, cinnamon, and patchouli; amber incense, or another that you feel is symbolic of loving energy; a rose quartz small enough to fit inside your bottle; and red ribbon, beads, or other things to decorate the bottle if you like.

Cast a circle and invoke the Lord and Lady. Then state your intention:

I come before the gods tonight to work magic, that I may find love, and love may find me.

Spend some time meditating on what love means to you, and how you believe it would best manifest itself in your life right now. Think of the myriad varieties of love, which are all part of the same thing, and imagine as many of them as possible being increased in your life.

Carve a symbol of love onto the candle; this could be a heart, a rune, the word itself, whatever speaks to you. Then light the candle.

Now, carefully place the oils into the bottle as follows:

5 drops of sandalwood

3 drops of rose

1 drop of cinnamon

1 drop of patchouli

If your bottle is larger than a standard 2 dram oil vial, increase the amounts as needed. Then fill the bottle the rest of the way with the almond oil.

Take the rose quartz and drop it into the bottle's mouth. As it drifts to the bottom, visualize its energy infusing the oil, waking the properties of the ingredients: sandalwood brings spiritual love, rose brings romantic love, cinnamon brings comforting love, and patchouli brings passionate love. Cap the bottle and shake it. The stone will help the oils blend together. (An alternate way to work the spell, if you either don't have or can't afford the oils, is to do the same with several stones, putting them together in a small bag to carry; lapis could represent spiritual love, rose quartz for romantic, jasper for comfort, and carnelian for passion, or whatever combination you prefer.)

Decorate the bottle if you desire with ribbon, beads, and so forth; just be sure you can get the cap off again.

Charge the oil, holding it against your heart chakra, envisioning the chakra's energy bathing the bottle in a verdant green glow. Raise energy with a chant such as this one:

I call upon the Lover
I call upon the fire
I call upon the heartbeat
I call upon desire
I call upon the moonrise
I call upon the tide
I call to you, beloved
I call you to my side.

Allow the candle to burn out. Each day dab a drop of the oil over your heart; continue to do so until the oil is gone.

Being the Lover

The first person you need to be a lover to is, of course, you. How can you expect another to give you what you won't give yourself?

We wish for someone to take us to dinner and a movie, to go for long walks with, to make mad passionate love to . . . but we neglect to do these same things for ourselves. You are as deserving of your own love and attention as some phantom sweetheart. Don't forget that.

Invoking the Lover is more than calling for more bedroom acrobatics. It is a way of looking at the world, of seeing every part of life as a sensual experience. It is not just touching, it is *feeling*.

Wiccan spirituality leads us to view those in our lives—and in fact everyone—as a manifestation of the God and Goddess. Applying this to your love life can deeply affect how you treat people; it can also affect who you choose, or choose not, to associate with.

The Lover understands that she is goddess; she understands her lover is god, or goddess, or a combination of several, if she's up to a challenge. This means that she is careful who she sleeps with, because only those willing to treat her with the same reverence are worthy of her attention. If someone refuses to accord her the respect as he or she would a goddess, obviously he or she isn't ready to be initiated into her Mysteries.

When it comes to your sex life, keep this in mind: you are the Goddess, and "all acts of love and pleasure" are your rituals. Those whom you choose to honor with the gift of your body are blessed, and if they will not see that blessing, don't give it.

Which means, if you're about to have an interlude with someone and, for example, he or she tries to weasel out of safer sex precautions, kick him or her to the curb, and do so immediately. *You* decide what goes into your body—that goes for other people's bits as much as it does for food and drink.

At the same time, if you expect to be treated as the holy being you are, you have to reciprocate. People in our world play a lot of sexual mind games, and lie, steal, and cheat to get whatever they want out of others. Those of us who view the body as holy, and ourselves as sacred, are bound by our beliefs to walk a different path, the path of respect, compassion, and honesty.

Sex, Polarity, and the Divine

There was a time, back during Wicca's first days as a codified and more-or-less public religion, when covens, if not openly hostile to homosexuals, at least tried hard to maintain a strict male/female balance based entirely on heterosexual pairing. Homophobia aside, the reason was that

Wicca reveres a goddess and god as equal partners in creation, and that the universe is formed, and continues to move, out of the sacred interplay between opposites. How could a male/male or female/female pair create life? It took a man and a woman to make babies, a god and a goddess to make the world. Clearly a precedent had been established.

Fortunately, this prejudice didn't last. The minute Wicca invaded America, it hit the ground running, and one of the first places it ran to was California, where the feminist movement picked it up and gave it wings. Ecofeminist groups found in our spirituality the ritual framework and mythology that they craved.

You'd be hard pressed to find a feminist group made up entirely of straight women. Likewise, covens made up entirely of gay men began to form. As time wore on, the liberal nature of Wiccan philosophy and our belief that all forms of love are blessed by the Goddess transformed the traditional view, and now all manner of sexualities are represented in the Pagan community.

There is, in fact, a strange trend emerging—heterophobia. I've seen over the past few years that, in the Pagan world, if you aren't some kind of "alternate" you're looked on as less interesting, somehow, or less liberated from the patriarchy. The same thing goes for those of us who tend toward monogamy. I've found myself being given indulgent looks for my "vanilla" tastes. It gets, frankly, really damned tiresome. I will sleep with whomever I want to, thank you very much, in whatever numbers I like, as long as everyone is consenting, safe, and good at it.

> Who would give a law to lovers? Love is unto itself a higher law.
> BOETHIUS

While it's very true that the boundaries set upon our sexuality are constructs of a society based on restrictive Abrahamic beliefs, that does not mean that shedding those boundaries immediately turns you into someone else.

I'll say this now, out loud:

Being Wiccan, Pagan, or any other non-Christian faith *does not mean* you have to be bisexual, polyamorous, heterosexual, monogamous, homosexual, kinky, promiscuous, virginal, or anything else. It means that, as an embodiment of divine grace, *you must be true to who you are, no matter who that is.* It means you must be willing to stand up for your truth, and not be pressured by anyone, whether Pagan or not, to be anything but exactly who you are. *No one has the right to dictate your sexuality*—that's as true for fellow Wiccans as it is for Senators.

Wiccans have, as a group, a lot of sex, and rightly so. We instinctively feel and understand the holiness of the union of the masculine and feminine; that does not, however, in any way prohibit other combinations than man and woman. From a Jungian perspective, which many Wiccans adhere to, each of us has within her a combination of masculine and feminine qualities, neither of which is better or worse than the other; to be whole and complete beings, a balance must be found. Whether that balance finds you straight or gay is completely irrelevant.

It's my opinion that any pairing, or grouping, can be creative; breeding more humans isn't the only way to contribute or create, and in fact should probably not be quite so high on our priority list given the overpopulated state of the planet. A woman and a woman, or a man and a man, can embody Lord and Lady just as well as a man and woman; we all are born with the seeds of both.

Just looking at the pantheons and stories of the cultures whose myths we learn from, you find a wide range of sexualities, from crossdressing gods to gay cupbearers to islands full of warrior women who had absolutely no use for men. You find androgyny. You find deities who switched gender on a whim. If the faces of the God and Goddess can come in such wondrous variety, who are we to put a limit on the sexuality of humankind?

Sexuality is so much more than male/female, top/bottom, butch/femme. As Lover, it is our task to discover where we fit into the spectrum, but also to remember that love is fluid, changing like the moon. Your sexuality does not have to be the same forever, and it does not have to fit into one of the neat categories that humans have created to divide and conquer one another.

As Wiccans, we have set ourselves outside the restrictions of patriarchal culture—we no longer need to box ourselves into the limits that the establishment has dreamed up in order to have someone to hate and oppress. Like any arbitrary category or stereotype, distinctions of sexuality serve one purpose: setting up "us" against "them" and creating walls where there might otherwise be bridges. The dominant paradigm cannot tell you who you are or who to love.

> There is nothing wrong with going to bed with someone of your own sex. People should be very free with sex; they should draw the line at goats.
>
> ELTON JOHN

LAWS OF ATTRACTION—EXERCISE #2

Meditate for a moment on the people you have found attractive throughout your life. Think of celebrities as well as regular folk who have set your chakras to whirling.

Are they all the same gender? If so, try to imagine yourself with a lover of your own sex. What do you think would be different about a same-sex relationship—do you think it would be easier or harder?

If you've never slept with another woman, have you wanted to? Who with? What about that person attracted you? Was it purely physical, or was there an emotional or spiritual element to the attraction? If you've never felt such a thing, broaden your imagination: if you had to have sex with a woman, and could choose anyone you wanted to, who would it be? Why?

The point of this is that attraction doesn't always have logical reasons, and sometimes it makes no sense whatsoever. It may seem on the surface like a same-sex relationship would be easier, because you would know what makes the other tick; at the same time it may seem harder because you know what makes the other tick. The truth is, love and sex turn everyone into a fall-down mess no matter what sort of genitals are involved. All of us have the same problems and face the same fears and issues in relationships; at the same time, we all have the potential to create something beautiful together.

Self-Love, in the Biblical Sense

There are books and websites galore on how to be better in bed. This is not one of them. However, I will say that the only way to figure out what you enjoy sexually is through trial and error, and moreover, through speaking up. Just laying there staring at the ceiling isn't going to gain you any orgasms, and whatever you may think of your current partner, a lover worth his or her salt will get very frustrated with you if you refuse to communicate.

Imagine you've been sleeping with the same person for several months before they tell you they don't like being dipped in Nutella and hung upside down by their ankles. Wouldn't you feel like an ass? Part of the exchange of energy involved in sex is talking. If you're too embarrassed to talk about sex, don't have it. You're not a twelve-year-old, you're a grown woman who is hopefully learning to love herself and to value herself enough to make an effort to get what she wants out of life.

Good lovers take requests and direction—even if speaking up midstream is more than you can manage, you can at least grab someone's hand and move it for them. It's not so important *how* you communicate as it is that you do it effectively (and preferably with love and trust).

Sadly, many women have no idea what they really enjoy sexually. We're taught for so many years that "down there" is dirty and smelly and not to be discussed. Many of us don't even know how our reproductive systems actually work, much less how to make sex go from barely making the bed creak to peeling the paint off the walls.

There's only one way to find out. If you aren't with anyone, or don't want to be, or don't feel ready to enlist that person's help in your explorations, it's all up to you.

Contrary to popular belief, women masturbate. At last count something like sixty percent of those surveyed admitted to it; the other forty percent were lying. Some of us even start before we hit puberty—if it feels good to rub someplace, we do so, and no amount of outrage on the part of our parents can do away with the urge, even though we have no idea at the time why we like it.

We live in a wonderful age . . . a technological age. There are toys and devices for just about every preference you can imagine, and some you probably can't. It is my opinion based on years of personal research that every girl needs a vibrator—a vibrator never loses your phone number, doesn't steal the remote, and unlike ice cream, a vibrator won't leave you sick to your stomach unless you're using it in ways even I can't fathom.

Moreover, if you are between lovers and aren't in a place where having one would be a healthy idea, learning how to gratify yourself, whether with a chestful of toys or your own two hands, can help you blow off steam, which can keep you from making disastrous mistakes when it comes to choosing bedmates. If I'd had an Electric Boyfriend when I was nineteen, that love spell I mentioned earlier might have come out quite differently.

THE LOVER'S TEMPLE—EXERCISE #3

Arrange for a night when you have no commitments, no responsibilities, no place to go and nothing to do. You have plans—you have a date with yourself.

Start the evening off by treating yourself to a fabulous dinner, whether out or from your own kitchen. Sit at the table and leave the TV off. Eat by candlelight.

Then have a long hot bath, as in chapter 3, this time with the express intention of creating a sensual atmosphere. Light candles, drop a few rose petals in the water (a few so as not to clog the drain), add some oil or bubbles to the bath. Arrange a glass of wine and some chocolates within easy reach.

If you want to Witch it up a bit, spend a few minutes visualizing yourself as the Lover Goddess, stepping into the sacred hot springs attended by your nymphs, satyrs, and so on.

History has seen the rise and fall of the sacred harlot. There have been women who healed and worked magic with sex, who people from all over came to see. Their role was a venerated one, not stigmatized like the modern prostitute; the sacred harlot was an agent of the Goddess, and through her the Lady filled her clients with divine power and love. Imagine you are one of these women, perhaps in a bath surrounded by Greco-Roman marble columns.

Have your bedroom prepared to reflect your status. Before starting your evening, put clean sheets on the bed, preferably something luxurious that feels lovely under your skin. If you have a toy collection, have your favorites out on the nightstand. Burn incense and candles, and get into bed naked after rising from the bath. Now is a perfect time to start learning your body and what it responds to; there is no one here that you have to please but yourself, and you have all night, so take your time. Explore your body like a foreign country, even if you're already familiar with your own curves and sweetness. Imagine you are touching your flesh for the first time, that it is new-made and glowing in the candlelight.

I think the older I get and the more in tune I become with my body, the more I enjoy sex. I like my curves. I like the roundness and softness of my body.

METIS

You may feel a little silly doing this sort of thing just to jill off, but that's exactly why you need to do it; there is too much embarrassment, shame, and self-consciousness in our sex lives today, and it's time to let it go. A priestess of the Goddess is not ashamed of her body or her desires.

While we're on the subject of shame, I think it's important to touch on the concept of "going skyclad." There is a certain stigma in parts of the Pagan community toward people who don't want to take their clothes off, whether in ritual or just for the hell of it. I say again that no one has the right to tell you what you can and cannot do with your own body, as long as you're not hurting anyone. I've seen people laughed at for wearing a bathing suit in the pool; I've actually had people tell me that wearing clothes is a sign of being enslaved by the patriarchy. Still others have told me that you can't do effective magic with clothes on because they get in the way of the energy.

I'm sorry, but if you can't raise enough magical energy to overcome a sixteenth of an inch of fabric, I don't think the clothes are your problem. As to the rest, I've seen enough sunburned scrotums, ant bites, and poison ivy to know that there are times when clothes are a very good idea. Often it takes a while for newcomers to be comfortable enough to wander the campground in their skivvies, so if you want to try it but aren't quite ready, you might go slowly, such as going topless at the revel fire or in a circle once or twice to see how you feel. Staying dressed doesn't mean you are ashamed of your body—it might just mean you're cold. So if you want to go skyclad, by all means do so, but don't let others pressure you into it, and don't pressure others either.

End rant.

Sex and Magic

Sex magic is thousands of years old, embraced and explored by many cultures, though more popular by far in the East. The basic theory behind it is that two can raise energy more powerfully than one, especially when those two are having sex, since erotic energy can be frighteningly strong. Most forms of sex magic involve control of the breath, and of orgasm, to build the energy and then release it at the right moment and at peak intensity.

Sound theory. I'm sure it works for a great many people. I, however, am apparently not meant to be a sex sorceress.

It's not that I can't focus my intention—my history as a Witch will tell you I'm perfectly capable of laserlike concentration on a goal. It's not that I'm bad in bed—I am known to some as Sylvan the Headboard Slayer. The problem, for me, is that if I try to do both, I end up either with lousy magic or lousy sex.

I've decided that sex and magic are both activities that deserve my utmost attention, so I keep the two separate, though I'm certainly not above playing with my lover's chakras or having fun with the energy that builds. That sort of thing, however, is meant to enhance the sexual experience for its own sake. I prefer my magic to do its own thing.

If you are interested in learning sex magic, however, there are a wealth of techniques available. Most of us are familiar with the positions of the *Kama Sutra* (familiar in that you've *seen* them—I know few people flexible enough to perform most of them, and I'll be damned if I'll ever twist myself into something called Two Monkeys Fighting Over a Banana, or whatever), but even something as simple as breathing in tandem and visualizing your energy as it merges and spirals higher is a good start. Again, this doesn't have to have a "higher" purpose—sexual pleasure is a high enough purpose in my book.

If you can manage it, though, you can do some amazing magical work. My experiences are just that, and yours can be in another universe entirely.

The Lover's Shadow

Samhain, 2001, just a month after the World Trade Center fell, I was at one of the largest Pagan gatherings in Texas, surrounded by almost a thousand of my brethren from a hundred different traditions. It was Saturday night, and the revel fire had just been lit.

If you've never been to a Pagan festival, particularly this one in Texas, I'll tell you up front: if you don't get laid there, it's because you weren't trying. "Camp-out encounters" are an interesting tradition in the community: sometimes they lead to long-term affairs, but for the most part they stay at the festival grounds where they were born. That weekend I'd had at least a half-dozen propositions—none from anyone I'd actually bed, but it does make a girl feel all warm and fuzzy knowing she's appreciated.

I was walking back to my campsite alone, my companion having gone off to someone's tent for the evening. Our campsite was on the outer loop, away from the heart of the festivities. There were portable toilets spaced out along the path. As I passed one, a rather drunken fellow clambered out of one, dressed in a cloak and nothing else. That being fairly commonplace at said events, I was not alarmed. Nor was I alarmed when he asked if I could help him straighten out his cloak.

I wasn't especially surprised that he made a move on me; I was surprised that he didn't listen when I said, "No." I fought, but shock and terror crippled me—I am not used to violence. I had never been beaten before. Fists made no sense to me.

My back hit the muddy ground; over his shoulder I could see the moon. I stared up at the smoke-smudged night, my face hurting and vision swimming where he hit me, thinking, "So this is it." At that moment, when he rolled off me and disappeared, I felt something in me die. Reeking of beer, covered in mud, bleeding and bruised, I went back to my tent, and told no one.

Sex is one of the most powerful forces in nature. Whereas love itself cannot be perverted, lust can be, and often is; it makes a handy and reliable weapon, especially against women, who have already been beaten down and beaten down for our biology for centuries and are taught to close our eyes and think of England, no matter what.

Like many thousands of other Pagan women, I am a survivor. This story isn't the only one I could tell; unfortunately, it is also not unique. In my case, the setting was very rare—only once in a great while does violence occur at Pagan festivals, and then usually when the number of attendees is so high that nobody has any idea if the people there are actually Pagan, let alone whether or not they'll keep to the Rede or any ethical code whatsoever. In our enthusiasm to draw our people together, we have begun to realize that no matter how spiritual people are supposed to be, in a group of a thousand people, there are going to be at least a few dozen complete bastards.

A lot of women come to Wicca, and to goddess-related spirituality in general, out of a need to reclaim the sanctity of our bodies. The brutality of others has thrown us bloody and broken to the ground, but rather than remain victims forever we seek out ways to find our way back to ourselves. In many ways, this book is the culmination of that search in my own life; three years ago if you'd told me my body was holy I would have laughed in your face.

The first thing you have to remember, if you have been assaulted or abused, is that *you did not ask for it*. I don't care what you were wearing; I don't care if you were dancing naked; I don't care if he's your husband. Whether you tried to fight back or were too petrified to move, whether you did what you were told at gunpoint, it is not your fault—whoever hurt you made that choice, taking your choice away. No one ever has the right to force you to have sex with them. *Ever*. You do not owe anyone the gift of your body, because it is just that, a gift; if someone thinks otherwise, he is a thief.

The second thing I have to say is that being raped or molested does not make you damaged goods; it does not destroy the sanctity of your body unless you let it. It can shake you, tear your life to shreds and strew them to the winds, but it can only break you if you allow it to. A woman is free until she gives herself willingly—if you choose to let your attacker keep a part of you, you will never be free again. Only you can take it back.

The third thing is that it doesn't matter what anyone says or what they expect. You have the right to heal at your own pace, on your own terms. A few people tried to rush me into "letting it go," and made it clear they were weary of my problems—if anyone tries to do that to you, tell them to shove it, and find new friends who understand. You will probably feel more alone after being raped than at any other time in your life; try to connect with other women who have stories like yours and you'll see that there are many voices, some who have been heard, but many who have not. But as long as you are doing the best you can to get through it, and as long as you don't give in to your fear and retreat into a cave forever, you will eventually make it; true friends may not be able to relate to what you're going through, but they will give you room to breathe as well as a shoulder when you need it.

Lastly, tell someone. Tell the truth, all of it, as soon as possible. I believe sex crimes should be reported and prosecuted to the full extent of the law, but I also remember being too ashamed and scared to say a word, so I know it may be tempting to pretend nothing happened. Don't do that. If you can't go to the police, go to a friend, a mentor, someone. There is nothing to be gained from your silence. I was silent, and the truth ate at me for months until I couldn't live with it anymore. There is help out there, and people who care about you, if you'll let them.

It will most likely be a while before you feel up to resuming your religious and magical life—I know that it was months before I wanted to say anything to the Goddess, much less do any sort of healing or cleansing rituals like the ones you can find in women's spirituality texts.

The one thing it's probably very tempting to do is hex the perpetrator. Don't. Why not? It has nothing to do with some lofty notion of compassion for those who are sick enough to hurt us, although in time you may begin to feel just that. It's not even an ethical reason, to be perfectly honest. It's pragmatism.

Raising energy out of hatred is bad for you. Black magic is about as good for your body and spirit as shooting up heroin—and in the end, it does about as much good toward your long-term healing. You have already been through enough; dealing with the repercussions of such magic, as well as the side effects of channeling so much negative energy, is neither useful nor wise. Even a binding is tricky; when you bind someone, you bind your own energy to theirs whether you mean to or not, and as long as they are bound you are still connected to the spell. When you are trying to recover from trauma, you don't need anything else to drain your energy.

If you want to take magical action against your attacker, the best thing to do is to simply call for justice—ask that the scales be balanced, and remove your own desires from the equation. You have to be prepared, and accepting, for whatever comes; the result might not be the painful bloody death you had in mind, but once called, the gods rarely ignore a call for justice. Invoke the Dark Mother and get the hell out of the way.

THE PATH TO HERE—EXERCISE #4

No matter how sordid a sexual experience has been, there is something to be learned, something you can take away from it enriched.

Think back to your first encounter. For most people it's a bit awkward and bumpy, usually with a lot of fumbling about and, "So . . . are you done?" How was yours? How old were you? What did you learn from that moment about being a lover? How did that experience shape those that were to follow?

When was your first orgasm? Did someone else contribute or was it all you? If you've never had one, why do you think that is? The answer to this question may require a lot more than a few moments' thought and meditation; it can even require therapy and doing battle with the demons of fear and shame.

In your mind, journey along your sexual history and consider all the lovers, all the relationships, all the sex you've ever had. This may take more time and effort for some of us than others. If you can't remember a particular period, think about those interludes that stand out in your memory for being spectacular, horrendous, or just plain funny.

Each of us brings more than one body to bed when we take a lover. You bring with you all the people who have ever touched you; each time, you shape the way you think about love, sex, and connection. The entire timeline of your adult life has affected the passion you create now. Has that influence been largely positive, or negative? Have you allowed the past to make you bitter and ashamed about sex, or have you taken the lessons you needed from your past so that you could make better choices today?

A Few More Thoughts

I could spend a lot of time talking about sex in the Pagan community, and about various forms of kink and alternative sexuality, but I'm less concerned with what you do in bed and more concerned with how you feel and think about it. It's very hard for someone who hates her body to be a good lover or to enjoy the efforts of others; if you are too busy worrying about what you look like naked, there's a good chance you're missing the fun.

Your body has an infinite capacity for pleasure—as with magic, the gods gave us this flesh as a gift, and not to explore our utmost potential would be wasteful. In the Wiccan worldview, any kind of consensual sex, as long as the people involved approach each other with reverence and respect, is a blessed and beautiful thing. Properly appreciated even a quickie in the broom closet can be a reverent act.

There are a few additional things you should keep in mind:

There is, as they say, no such thing as absolutely safe sex. Sex can never be safe—aside from the risk of babies and diseases, when you allow someone to touch and enter your body you are showing that you trust that person at least for the duration. Perhaps you can't always predict the consequences for your heart, but you can do something about possible consequences for your body; that means condoms, condoms, condoms, and any other applicable precautions as well.

If the person you are with refuses to put on a condom or demands that all the responsibility for contraception and prevention is yours, put your boots back on and walk away. A real Lover will care about you enough to do anything he or she can to ensure your safety; anything less is an egregious lack of respect and is unacceptable.

The same holds true for someone who is unwilling to reciprocate when it comes to pleasure. Sex isn't everything, but it should be something—even if you care very much for your lover, an inability to please you—or, rather, a refusal to even try—does not bode well for the future of your relationship. That doesn't mean that if your eyes don't roll back every single time, you should dump the guy or gal; it means that first of all, you need to communicate your needs. Second, they have to hear you. If you've tried and tried to no avail, it might do you well to reconsider. For example, do you really want to spend your time and possibly your life with someone who, to quote Roseanne, "gets in the elevator but won't go down?"

Your body's desires should be a high priority for you. As we've discussed, denying the importance of your body is denying the importance of the manifest world, and therefore the earth; as a Wiccan, a reverence for the natural world has to include honoring your own needs. If you're determined to get high-quality exercise and high-quality food, you should also include high-quality sex. All the aspects of your physical being should matter.

> I can say that a spirituality focused on Earth instead of setting its sights on the unknowable and unseen has allowed me to experience my body and its sensations in a meaningful and spiritual way rather than merely taking them for granted.
>
> ANISE

Goddesses of the Lover Archetype

Gods and goddesses of love are pretty popular; you might never have heard of Acuecucyoticihuati, but I'd bet money you've heard of Aphrodite.

Another widely known and venerated Lady of the Heart is Freya, one of the chief Norse goddesses. Freya was considered the most beautiful of the goddesses, and was petitioned in matters of love and sexuality throughout history and today.

The blue-eyed Freya is said to ride in a chariot drawn by cats; she wears an enchanted necklace that is a symbol of either the stars or the fecundity of the earth, and it enhances her beauty even further. Taken as a hostage to the realm of Asgard, she taught the gods there the secrets of magic; her husband, Od, is believed by many to be either another name for or an aspect of Odin, the Lord of Lords in the Norse pantheon.

She shared Odin's love of battle, as well, and it is said they wander the battlefield and divide the slain between them. Odin's warriors go to Valhalla, where they fight all day and feast all night; Freya's chosen, most often those who have left behind loved ones on the earth, are eventually reunited with their families and spend their time being entertained in Freya's hall, Sessrumnir.

Freya is as fierce a lover as she is a warrior; her way is to take risks and stand up for those you love, as well as for yourself.

In the Tantric tradition, the Lover is personified as the goddess Shakti. She is the active principle of the universe—without her, life cannot exist and nothing can be created. Shakti is the first cause, from whom all effects arise. Because women are the direct embodiment of Shakti, they are considered the embodiment of life itself.

In some traditions, Shakti is a goddess; in others, particularly Hinduism, she is often a mystical force without a specific face. Her union with the god Shiva, and their sexual fulfillment in each other, is how the world is impregnated with life and possibility. The two are often invoked in sex magic, in rites similar to Drawing Down the Moon, which imbue the magicians with the powers of creation.

Remember that, Tantric or not, every sexual encounter you have holds the potential to create anything from an accidental baby to a deliberate relationship. Sex is the fundamental creative act; it has power, and beauty, and is how we all originated. It is a force that demands respect, an experience that transforms, a form of entertainment better than Monday night football (and often just as baffling to some people). Your body seeks out pleasure, and the Lover suggests you let it have its way.

SUGGESTIONS FOR EXPLORING THE LOVER

1. Surround yourself with sensuality. Turn your bedroom into a lush haven of texture, scent, and color; to bring the Lover's influence out, give her things to play with. That includes people as well—if you have a lover in your life, pretend you're starting from scratch, and have to completely relearn each other's bodies. Explore the contours and curves that you may have grown to take for granted; imagine each time is new, and you'll never get bored.

2. Have a goddess feast, as we discussed in chapter 4; this time have everyone wear clothes that make them feel sexy, whatever that means to the individual, and serve only foods that can be eaten with your fingers. If you're on familiar enough terms, feed each other; you could also give each other massages, or simply recline in a hot tub if one's available, drinking wine and telling tales of each other's sexual exploits. My personal favorite is the "strangest places you've done it" game. You'll be surprised at how adventurous your friends really are.

3. Educate yourself on the ins and outs of having female parts. Find one of the books in the end section of this chapter and see how much you don't already know. The complexity and elegance of human reproduction is pretty amazing, especially given that people are capable of having sex without laughing their asses off. ("You want to put that *where?*")

4. Buy a sex toy. No, really. The website listed below is owned and operated by women, and they have great recommendations for first-timers; they ship in discreet packaging, and you don't see "Giant Dildo Emporium" or anything on your credit card statement. If you're embarrassed at having a vibrator around the house, there are even models disguised as household objects—my personal favorite is the I Rub My Ducky, a waterproof vibrator shaped like a rubber duck. I've heard overwhelmingly positive testimonials about the friendly, handy Mr. Ducky.

5. If you're straight, don't depend on men to take care of your safer-sex precautions. Actually this applies to lesbian and bi women too—expect your lovers to be willing to contribute, but never assume there will be a condom in your boyfriend's pocket when you stop for a shag in a truckstop bathroom. (Um . . . no, I've never done that either.)

Recommended Reading and Resources for Chapter Six

BOOKS

Tickle Your Fancy: A Woman's Guide to Sexual Self-Pleasure by Sadie Allison

Sex Tips for Straight Women from a Gay Man by Dan Anderson

Looking Queer: Body Image and Identity in Lesbian, Bisexual, Gay, and Transgender Communities by Dawn Atkins

Big Big Love: A Sourcebook on Sex for People of Size and Those Who Love Them by Hanne Blank

Zaftig: Well-Rounded Erotica by Hanne Blank

Aphrodite's Daughters: Women's Sexual Stories and the Journey of the Soul by Jalaja Bonheim

Goddess in the Bedroom by Zsuzsanna Budapest

Sexual Ecstasy and the Divine by Yasmine Galenorn

The Survivor's Guide to Sex: How to Have an Empowered Sex Life after Child Sexual Abuse by Staci Hanes

Enabling Romance: A Guide to Love, Sex and Relationships for People with Disabilities (and the People Who Care about Them) by Ken Kroll and Erica Levy Klein

The Sexual Healing Journey by Wendy Maltz

The Whole Lesbian Sex Book: A Passionate Guide for All of Us by Felice Newman

The Clitourist by Karen Salmansohn

WEB RESOURCES

Good Vibrations
<http://www.goodvibes.com>
Be sure and visit their Antique Vibrator Museum.

working half from the ideas of others and half from brute instinct that called out from my blood, my bones, and my feet. I had no idea what I was reaching for, only that I had to reach.

There is a state you aspire to in trance dancing that Roth calls the Silver Desert, but the simplest description is simply ecstasy—you are no longer the dancer, but the dance, and the world falls away. The cosmic pulse beats through you, and suddenly the body that seems so solid and concrete becomes a vessel to a far-off, yet very immediate place deep within your self and somewhere within the heart of God.

The first few times I reached this state, I noticed that when I came down, I had the distinct feeling I was being watched.

Then one night, there was some indefinable shift in my consciousness, and energy flooded through me like a tsunami, leaving me exhausted and about to pass out, on my knees on my living room floor. The feeling of presence intensified, and my heart pounding out of what I can only call recognition, I looked up from under my sweaty hair . . .

. . . and there he was.

I've never been prone to visions or prophetic dreams; my psychic skills are not extraordinary, though I have been known to do some pretty nifty things with fire and weather when I'm not trying too hard. The gods were known to me through feelings, a change in the air . . . but never a full-out apparition in front of my couch. The vision was vague, moving in and out of focus, but a few details registered: male, dark hair and eyes, a tattoo around one arm that is never the same image twice. A wry smile. Beardless, slender, tall. And, at the risk of sounding blasphemous (which thankfully we don't have in Wicca anyway), unbelievably hot.

I would have dismissed this as a hallucination or the product of a tranced-out mind, nothing more, but then I saw my cat on the arm of the couch. He was standing, eyes huge, his back fur on end.

I looked back at my visitor, unable to frame even the simplest question.

He held out his hand, and his voice vibrated through all seven of my chakras and off the fabric of space and time itself. "I am the Lord of the Dance," he said. "Shall we?"

Life hasn't been the same since.

I can only communicate with the Lord when I'm in an ecstatic state, and most of the time it's little glimpses and flashes, nothing as dramatic as that first time. Often he's just a voice in my head, so there's every chance I'm just crazy—but it's a good kind of crazy.

He's a god on a mission—there are things, he says, he is here to teach me. One of those things was learning to share my experiences with others, so I've been developing workshops and essays and so forth to help people find their own Spirit Dancer. However it is expressed in your life, however you find your ecstasy, the Dancer is your guide to a deep, cell-by-cell union with deity.

> God respects us when we work but loves us when we dance.
>
> SUFI PROVERB

The Dancer archetype is, in a way, an extension of the Lover. She spins the give-and-take of erotic energy that powers the universe and gives it expression on her feet, rather than on her back (or up against the wall, or . . . never mind). The Dancer is movement, both for our health and for a higher, or rather deeper, purpose: spiritual ecstasy.

As I have mentioned, in Wicca we generally believe that the ecstasy of the spirit can be found through the body rather than in spite of it. The Lover can take us to that ecstatic state, but the Dancer is truly the shaman of mystical union.

The Dancer is the priestess whose great work is healing the Great Divide. Only by filling the body with the radiant energy of spirit can we know how it feels to be complete, unified beings without a split down the center; once we know that feeling, we can begin to manifest it every day as much as possible.

Naturally, we can't live every minute in a state of spiritual ecstasy; we'd starve to death and never get anything done. We can, however, bring an ecstatic appreciation to our "mundane" lives, treating every action of our bodies as a prayer of the soul, nurturing our connection with the Lord and Lady as often as we can. Living without the Divide is truly living. Otherwise, no matter how much we fill our lives with purpose and activity, something will always be missing.

I don't know where I would be, or if I would even be alive, if it weren't for dance. You would never believe it to look at me, but I've practiced trance dance for years now; it has, in fact, saved my life on more than one occasion when the mundane world was closing in on me, and it was either dance or be crushed beneath the weight of my own existence.

It's ironic, really, because I hate to exercise, as I imagine many of you do. From childhood, exercise is forced on us whether we want it or not, often in the most humiliating settings possible. Who could forget those god-awful gym uniforms, the indignity of group showers, or being forced to run in endless circles around the football field while a succession of sadistic coaches blew their whistles?

We forget the thrill of playing freeze tag or Red Rover, or simply of wandering through the woods for hours on end. Moving our bodies becomes a punishment, something we do because we're not "fit" enough. I have seen more people spend twenty solid minutes bitching and moaning on a Stairmaster three times a week about how much they hate the Stairmaster. My question is, why on earth do they do it?

Well, they say, because it's good for you.

Right. Being miserable is good for you. I don't buy that for a second. I believe that the gods put us on this earth and into our lives to find joy, and it's up to us to seek out places where joy might live. Life already has enough opportunities to suck without us pushing ourselves into even more, so it seems to me that spending hours and hours a week engaged in yet another activity we don't enjoy is going counter to our life purpose. We already lose so much time in the rat race, running in circles after the Almighty Dollar to finance the real part of our lives.

We've talked about the value of self-nurture, and the importance of making choices that are healthy and enriching. It's not enough to fuel your body with care and attention—you have to move it with care and attention, as well. Our bodies weren't made to sit for eight hours at a desk, staring into a glowing box while we type with one hand and hold the phone with the other. Our bodies weren't meant to be confined to cars, stuck in traffic on a gorgeous spring day. Our first occupation as a species wasn't having board meetings—it was hunting, gathering, and running away from big critters with pointy teeth. From the first hairy homo sapiens down to the present homo sedentary, our bodies were made for action.

Were we, then, made to go to the gym and spend our time running, walking, biking, and jumping to nowhere? To jog on a treadmill reading magazines about other people when our focus should be on ourselves? I really don't think so.

We Westerners have become too goal oriented in our thinking. We fix our eyes on that target weight, that measurement, that number of reps. The end result is all that matters to us nowadays, and the faster we get there the better—just thirty days to a brand new you! We don't bother taking joy in the journey, because there are too many more "important" things to do, like get there *now*. Besides, what joy is there to be found on a treadmill?

Ever watch a hamster run around in his little wheel? Kind of sad, isn't it?

The bottom line is, in order to have a healthy body by most reputable sources' standards, you have to get off your ass and move once in a while. The mindless sort of exercise most of us do, however, forces the mind and body even further apart, as we are thinking about anything but what we're doing—unless, of course, it hurts. If you are not fully engaged in what your body is up to, you are only working your muscles, not your being. That old cliché about a "human doing" versus a "human being" comes into play here; we are far too busy doing, without being.

Of course, if you're the sort who gets a charge out of free weights and the Stairmaster, by all means, have at it. Body joy can come in all sorts of forms. Just be sure that, of all the ways you could be moving your body at that moment, it's the one you really want to be engaged in.

FINDING YOUR MOVEMENT—EXERCISE #1

Take a moment to think about the physical activity you do every day. Moreover, think of all the various forms of "exercise" that have been foisted on you since childhood, from dodge ball to aerobics. Write them down.

Now go back through your list and think about how each of these activities made you feel, both physically and mentally. Even as a child, was there a particular game that you really enjoyed? Why? In your adult life, what kinds of movement make you feel good? By "good," I don't mean, "I pulled every last muscle, so I'm a good girl," but rather, that feeling of satisfaction afterward, knowing that you've done something for yourself that was genuinely healthy for your body, your mind, and your spirit?

Imagine you are in perfect physical shape (whatever that means to you) and money is no object. What kind of physical activity would you try then? Mountain climbing? Hiking the Appalachian Trail? Swimming every day? Tae kwon do?

Imagine spending an hour or two in this activity. How do you feel during, and after? Even if you can never afford that trek up Everest, this can give you an idea of the kinds of things to look into.

The things that give you body joy aren't necessarily going to be traditional exercises. You may find your ecstasy gardening, playing tag with your kids, walking your dog, cleaning your house. As long as it's something that gets you up and moving, and it's something you feel more than a passing interest in (or hatred for), that's what matters. Whatever exercise you do, a little bit with your mind and body working together is better than hours on end of boring, repetitive motion that leaves your brain and heart asleep.

It's entirely possible you have never felt this way about any kind of movement whatsoever. I can relate. Up until I realized that dancing didn't have to mean going through a prescribed series of steps and wearing a leotard, I hated anything that made me sweat. Fat girls generally don't like to sweat in front of other people; it's yet another chance for embarrassment in an already scrutinized life. You only have to be laughed at once to lose all your zeal for exercise, which is why you don't see a lot of big girls in gyms.

If you've never felt body joy, try to imagine what it would feel like. Think of really great sex (assuming you've had that), and translate that glowy sort of fuzzy feeling (or craving for Taco Bell, in my case) into other activities. Can you think of anything you could do with your body besides sex that would make you feel like that? Imagine yourself in a variety of different situations, including those we'll talk about in this chapter, and see if any "click" for you.

> Movement never lies. It is a barometer telling the state of the soul's weather.
>
> MARTHA GRAHAM

Moving the Body, Healing the Soul

Many people live in a state of chronic inertia. We wander through life on autopilot, never feeling like we're really getting anywhere; day in, day out, same old same old. Work, eat, sleep. Work, eat, sleep. Throw a ritual in there somewhere. Add in the occasional vacation.

Depression and despair are both born of inertia. Inertia is, in essence, stuck energy. Something in ourselves stops moving, and an imbalance is created at one chakra or another, causing all the others to malfunction as well thanks to a lack or overload of energy.

For example, remember the function and purpose of the third chakra. If you're feeling powerless or feel the need to exert your power over others, energy gets backed up at the solar plexus and everything above it starts to starve. Your compassion for others suffers. Your sense of truth and your inner vision become weak, and your spiritual life is stunted. In addition, the chakras below the solar plexus become clotted with that stagnant energy—power-hungry people often use the emotions and sexuality as weapons, or ways to feel superior.

Then one day you reach the crisis point, when all of that sluggish and stuck energy has backed up as far as it can. Something has to give. That's when people go into meltdown and start doing extremely unhealthy things. Some medicate their pain with drugs, alcohol, or food; some disengage themselves from that part of their lives entirely; some go insane. However it manifests itself, the implosion of stagnant energy can cause lasting damage to your psyche and to your relationships with other people.

Being a Scorpio, I have a tendency toward moodiness; being me, I have another tendency toward bottling my emotions. I have spent years shoving anger and hurt further and further down, on top of buried memories and suppressed pain. I wore a brave face for the world while I was basically rotting inside. I've had several episodes of major depression, and have come damn close to suicide a number of times, all because I had no idea how to get that painful energy flowing so that I could release it. I held onto it all, but there's only so much room in one person's heart, and eventually it was bound to go boom.

And boom it did. When I was twenty-six, I lost a family member through tragic circumstances, and that loss was all my psyche needed to fall completely apart. Years and years of pent-up emotion and memories dating back to my childhood came flying out, and I went into a period of black despair that came complete with a crisis of faith—I spiraled into what is commonly termed "a dark night of the soul."

I could have stayed there, wallowing in my own misery, but my years of Wiccan practice taught me at least one thing: the only certainty in this universe is change. Things will change regardless of what we do—our task, then, is to decide *how* things will change. I could have drowned in that place and eventually become suicidal, maybe even died this time; I chose otherwise. Eventually I called a halt to my self-pity and decided that I would *act*.

One of the most important lessons I have learned from my gods is that the Wheel of Life turns around again and again, bringing us back to the same places over and over—but each time we return, we return changed, and so does the universe. I was a different person this time from the last time I dealt with depression, and I made my choices rather than letting things happen however they happened. I got up, got out of bed, and danced.

There's only one cure for stuck energy: movement. The energy must be made to flow again if we ever want to be healthy and self-actualized people. There are a number of ways to get your energy moving, but among the most efficient and effective is this: move your body.

Think about the ways that Wiccans raise energy in ritual. Most of them involve movement of some kind, if only movement of the breath. To raise the most energy, you have to give yourself over completely to the act of raising it, which can be difficult to do while holding a magical purpose in mind; it takes practice to handle both at the same time, but if you've ever had a cone of power blow the roof off your circle, you know it's possible.

We raise energy through dance, of course, but also through chant, which involves the vibration of vocal chords and the movement of lips. We raise energy through breathwork, through drumming, through sex—it's so much harder to accomplish anything by simply thinking, isn't it? Have a circle of women imagine a spell working and it might work; have a circle of women dance a whirl of magic into the future, and a positive outcome is almost guaranteed.

Spiritual energy, therefore, responds to physical motion. Even something as simple as a gesture can be a very powerful symbol in ritual; we trace pentagrams in the air at the quarters, we draw the circle itself with a hand or wand or athame. The power moves through us, and we can feel it in our bodies, whether as a change in temperature or a prickly sensation or a sound. The most important magical tools, after all, are your hands. Second only to that are your feet.

TAKE A WALK—EXERCISE #2

As soon as you finish reading this passage, put this book down and take a walk. Five minutes, ten, thirty, it doesn't matter; just get up and move. Go outside and greet the first living thing you see with a "Hi, there," and a "Blessed be."

As you walk, feel your connection to the earth through your feet. Feel the presence of our precious planet holding you up as you take each step. Feel the air moving gently in and out of your lungs. Feel the sweat start to form on your skin. Feel the sun in its daily turn overhead. Feel yourself as a nexus of the elements, from the earth of your bones to the fire of your heartbeat.

Spend the rest of your walk just walking. Become mindful of the motion of your muscles and bones moving past each other, of your lungs expanding and deflating. Be mindful of the way you walk on this earth—hunched over? Straight and tall? With quick, tiny steps? In a long-legged strut? What might that say about how you live in your body, and how you relate to the world around you?

Try to hold the mindfulness of your body as you shift your primary focus to the environment. Where are you? Think outward—block, street, neighborhood, city, state, country, hemisphere, planet . . . and so on. Look, really look, at the buildings and trees and people you see. How is your understanding of them subtly changed by your awareness of yourself?

Why You Should Get Up and Move Now

Assuming you haven't been living under a rock for the last ten years, I'm not going to spend a lot of time harping on the health benefits of exercise. Almost every reputable (and even those who aren't) source "in the know" about the body agrees that exercise is vital to a healthy body. Granted, they disagree wildly over how much, what kind, and when, but at the very least it's common knowledge that our modern sedentary lifestyle is part of what's turning Americans in particular into pasty pudding people.

We might argue for hours about whether being "overweight" is really as deadly as the "experts" say, but even a staunch anti-diet gal like myself has to concur that the eight-hour workday in front of a computer monitor followed by four hours in front of the television is killing us. We suffer from what are known as diseases of affluence—illnesses that people in nations that don't have our technology, industry, and leisure time have a much lower occurrence of. You're probably not going to see a lot of Masai tribesmen with lung cancer and heart disease, for example, any more than you're likely to see a Pygmy on Prozac. In America, however, our lifestyle is slowly destroying our collective health. Whether you're fat or thin, being sedentary could well be the death of you.

The most recent information (subject to the whims of medical science) is that even a moderate amount of exercise several times a week will help you maintain your health. From a metaphysical perspective, of course, this makes sense; as I said, moving your body gets your energy moving, which keeps your chakras from becoming sluggish. Not only does this benefit you physically, but it helps the whole system to stay in good working order. You don't have to work with spiritual energy, or even believe in anything, to see that exercise is good for the mind as well as the muscles.

One of the most common excuses I hear (and have used, to be honest) is, "I'm too fat to exercise," or, "I'm in such bad shape, I'm too embarrassed to go outside." I can understand that. I've been honked at by passing cars. Assholes love to laugh at sweaty fat girls, and there's nothing quite as detrimental to your health habits as tripping over your two left feet in aerobics class and taking a nosedive into the floor.

The fact is, however, that if you let this excuse keep you from moving, you're doing yourself a great disservice and feeding into your negative body image issues without even realizing it. We get into a mindset that becomes a nasty little circle: I'm too fat to exercise, so I won't exercise, so I won't feel good about myself, and I'll feel too fat to exercise. So many of us put things off that we really want "until I lose weight," and that day simply never comes; we waste so much time on someday that we lose the now.

I'm hoping that by this chapter you have started to at least think of yourself a little differently, but regardless, I'll say it again: *You are a sacred being, an expression of the Lord and Lady's grace, and you are worth taking care of.* Add that to your affirmation list and repeat as necessary. You deserve every possible opportunity to be happy and fulfilled, and putting off making positive changes and taking care of yourself is denying your inherent sanctity as a child of the gods. If you value the gifts that deity has given you, if you as a Wiccan have vowed in any way, shape, or form to care for the earth and all her creatures, you must tend to yourself as you would tend to any of the Lady's creatures.

A DUMB RITUAL

No, it's not what it sounds like. I just thought it was a funny name, as well as appropriate.

Most of the time, when we do rituals with others, there is a lot of vocalizing—explanations, invocations, chants, et cetera. Then when we get home and cast circle alone, many of us don't speak at all; our invocations are all thought, and our actions have to be symbolic without the help of audible commentary.

To become aware of how vital movement is in ritual, the next time you have one, make it a point to not speak. Pay close attention to what your body is doing when you cast, when you invoke, when you do whatever it is you've come to circle to do.

Then, create a ritual that is intentionally silent, preferably one to do with other people who have some experience with Wiccan ritual so you won't have to spend an hour beforehand explaining everything. When you create the ritual, spend time exploring what the gestures and movements mean to you, if they have purpose or are just done out of habit—why do you hold your athame that way? Why do you pick up the salt, and what do you do with it?

That can translate into a whole new way of doing things, at least for this ritual. You might try doing one as if the people in your circle didn't have any experience—how would you have to change your movements to make it clear what you were doing? Become the Wiccan mime for a moment (just try not to hate yourself the way people seem to hate mimes).

There are certain postures and gestures I use often that have deep significance for me. One in particular is a cornerstone of my practice, and other people have commented that it looks and feels pretty amazing. It was born out of the "Ritual of Gestures" in Scott Cunningham's *Wicca: A Guide for the Solitary Practitioner*, but soon took on a life of its own.

THE DANCER'S DEVOTION—EXERCISE #3

Stand facing north, if possible. Spend a moment breathing deeply, bringing your full attention to the moment and to your body.

The following steps should be performed in a slow, fluid continuum from one to the next, with short pauses in between, if you like. Practice them one at a time until you get a sense of their meaning.

First, raise your hands to about waist level, with your elbows still at your sides. Hold your palms flat, facing the ground, and imagine you are pressing your hands into the earth and you can feel its strength and solidity. If you are normally a verbal person, think to yourself the word *earth*.

Open your arms out into a downward-facing V, fingers spread. Imagine you are standing on a cliff or mountain peak and the wind is blowing through your fingers, catching your hair. Think the word *air*.

Bring your hands around in front of you, palms out and angled toward the ground as if you are warming yourself before a campfire. Feel heat and energy in front of your hands. Think: *fire*.

Draw your arms up into a circle (imagine holding a huge beach ball in front of you). Hold your palms upward and visualize either rain falling through the circle of your arms, or an ocean contained in them. Think: *water*.

Next, shift into the traditional God posture, arms crossed over your chest, one hand on each shoulder. Visualize the God in whatever way he comes to you. Feel his presence within and around you, and think: *Lord*. (Or substitute the name of your patron God.)

Move your arms up into a V, the traditional Goddess posture, open toward the heavens. Visualize the Goddess as you normally do. Try to feel her presence. Think: *Lady*.

Pull your hands down and touch them to your forehead, then open them out to the universe, offering yourself and your actions for the benefit of all, in the service of the Divine. Then bring your hands back to your sides where they started.

It sounds complicated, but is really fairly simple and elegant. I generally do this before every ritual; it is very grounding, and gives me a feeling of balance. It is also a powerful trigger for my spirit that something sacred is about to begin, and helps shift me into the frame of mind necessary for good ritual. If you don't like the gestures I described, come up with your own; the point is that the devotional is silent, grounded in the body, and meaningful to you.

The same thing can be accomplished with yoga postures or tai chi forms, if they are more to your liking. Both are designed to promote healthy energy flow, which is exactly what you're after. You'll be amazed at the difference in how well your rituals work once you spend some time beforehand moving your body and aligning your energy.

In Hinduism and Buddhism, sacred gesture is elevated to an art form, the mudra. The word "mudra" means "seal," or "sign," and can include everything from a single hand position to a full body posture. Mudras can also make use of the symbolism of each finger of the hand; starting with the thumb, the fingers represent each of the five elements in Eastern philosophy, and their contact with one another in mudra synthesizes the elements and brings one closer to the divine.

One of the more common mudras, the Anjali mudra, is familiar even to most Westerners: the hands pressed together at the chest, the "prayer position" typical of many spiritual paths. The Anjali mudra is often used at the beginning and end of yoga classes, for example, along with the greeting "Namaste," which translates loosely to "I bow to the divinity within you from the divinity within me." The Anjali is said to unite the two hemispheres of the brain, as well as the heart.

Ritual gesture is common to almost all religions; one of the most well known is the sign of the cross used in Catholicism. The sign is considered both an affirmation of belief and an invocation in and of itself, calling upon the Holy Trinity. Even in Christian traditions, the body and movement are vital to divine communion, even if the experience is considerably less intense than ecstatic drumming or dancing.

A variant a little closer to home is the Kabballistic Cross used by ceremonial magicians, which draws upon the Hebrew tradition but in effect accomplishes the same thing as the Catholic sign: it reinforces the connection between the practitioner and deity. I have seen a number of Pagan adaptations of these practices, most involving the pentagram and/or the chakras. You could develop a variety of gesture rites for a variety of purposes ranging from blessing and invocation to protection and even more mundane magical needs.

A PENTAGRAM BLESSING—EXERCISE #4

This simple little rite, much like the previous one, involves no speech; it has the added advantage that it is easy to perform even in chaotic situations and mixed company.

First, touch your dominant hand to your forehead, visualizing your third eye, throat, and heart chakras alight; the pentagram will essentially be drawn over the three, uniting vision, expression, and emotion. Draw your hand (use one finger, the whole hand, whatever is comfortable; you could probably come up with all sorts of symbolism relating to using a certain number of fingers, but that's up to you) down to your left breast, then up to your right shoulder, across to your left shoulder, down to your right breast, and back up to your forehead. I like to end it by touching my hand to my lips; I have no particular reason for that, other than it feels complete. Play with the gestures until you arrive at a sequence you like—I started with the left breast because the traditional invoking pentagram for earth would look that way if it were directly out in front of me, but you might want to reverse that as if someone were watching from the outside.

It might take a little practice to be coordinated enough to do this quickly. Once you are able to do it without really thinking about it, add in a silent invocation like the following one, attaching one line to each movement of your hand:

(Start at forehead) May I be blessed
(Down to left breast) by the strength of earth
(Up to right shoulder) the wisdom of air
(Across to left shoulder) the passion of fire
(Down to right breast) the compassion of water
(Back up to forehead) and by the grace of the Lord and Lady.
(Touch your hand to your lips) So mote it be.

Even little things like mudras and the pentagram above, when incorporated into your daily practice, can help you bring the aspects of your self more in line with one another. Every little bit helps.

> A ritual wouldn't be a ritual to me without some kind of movement and music.
>
> METIS

Becoming used to moving your body during religious activity, rather than simply sitting in a pew as many of us are accustomed to, can help make it easier and more effective when it comes time to let the Dancer come out and play.

Ways to Move Even If You Hate Moving

Cultures the world over throughout history have managed to create techniques that unite body, mind, and spirit. Systems combining movement and meditation, along with energy work, appear in a wonderful variety of forms in the East; a few have even developed in the West, in spite of the dominant culture's insistence that the only way to find God was to pretend our skin was an impediment to holiness rather than holy in and of itself.

If you are a confirmed old exercise-phobe like I am, I recommend that you look into some of these systems; many are easily tailored for those of us who aren't Tae Bo instructors.

Walking

Of course, the simplest exercise is walking. It's pretty much a universal. Most people make walking into just another workout, another chore to be gotten through, steps ticked off on the old pedometer.

In Buddhism, however, the mindfulness practice we've talked about applies to walking, which becomes a form of meditation all its own. As you saw in the second exercise in this chapter, walking provides an opportunity to attune with your environment as well as your legs.

Walking meditation has the distinct advantage of being something most people can do with minimal expense and minimal coordination; a pair of good shoes and the earth are really all you need. Even if you are unable to walk, just going outside and moving through space in whatever way you can, being mindful of the parts of your body that are in motion, can do a world of good.

Drumming

Drumming in and of itself isn't a form of exercise, but it often accompanies others, especially trance dance (see below). Drumming is, however, a beautiful way to commune with the Divine physically—your hands and arms and heart all fall into the same rhythm, and soon the whole universe is sharing in the beat. Working with a drum is an excellent way to raise magical energy for any purpose; it has been employed in so many cultures that the sheer variety of drums and methods available is mind-boggling. Middle Eastern and Native American drums are the two most popular that I have observed in the Pagan community.

There is something so visceral about drumming, a perfect synthesis of earth and fire—from the time we're children, we like to bang on things, and even without the fun of making a lot of racket guaranteed to annoy your parents, drums carry us deep within the heart of the Mother, somewhere between the core of the earth and the core of our being. If rhythm is our mother tongue, drumming is its voice.

Don't have a drum? Use a bucket. Have a drum but don't know how to play? Listen. There are myriad drumming CDs out there (my personal favorites are listed at the end of the chapter), and sometimes the best way to learn is to close yourself in a darkened room with the stereo and your drum, with no distractions. There may also be classes available in your area, or drum circles you can attend where you will most likely happen into at least one person willing to give you a crash course.

There is a special etiquette to drum circles that I won't delve too far into here, but there are cardinal rules: One, don't try to lead if you're a neophyte. There are usually one or more people who become the natural leaders in a circle, so listen carefully to them, and when in doubt, go with the bass line. The second rule is not to "drop" the dancers, which is Paganspeak for knocking someone violently out of trance, either by physically touching them or by screwing up the rhythm. This naturally brings us to:

Dancing

You have probably experienced something like ecstatic (trance) dance without even realizing it, if you've ever been to a club and been caught up in the DJ's spell. Our ancestors of spirit danced to bring the rain, to call the gods, to move the world and bring magic into being; modern rave culture is an attempt to bring back that magic, though in that context, "ecstasy" takes on a whole new meaning.

The good thing is, you don't have to indulge in better living through pharmaceuticals to reach an ecstatic state with music; it's remarkably easy, once you let go of the part of your ego that insists you look like an idiot or you're too fat/skinny/clumsy/old/whatever to dance. As my Lord has said to me, "How many times do I have to tell you, child—I don' t care if you weigh four hundred pounds and have to be set on your feet with a forklift, as long as you're moving."

(My God is a snarky God.)

There are no steps, no rules, except this—do what feels good. Whatever your body says, however it wants to move, is the right way to dance.

I practice trance dance fairly regularly in an informal ritual structure, and I generally dance alone unless I'm at a bonfire. As I said, I met God in the dance, so my rituals usually revolve around our relationship. I started out using the wave method created by Gabrielle Roth, which describes five essential rhythms and how they affect our souls; you do not, however, have to go by anyone's ideas but your own.

A DANCE RITUAL

This is basically how I do my rituals, but you may prefer more ritual or less, from a full-out circle casting to just pushing "play." Occasionally I cast circle during dance rituals, particularly if there are other people there or if I am raising energy for a particular purpose rather than simply connecting with deity. You may find that casting to music leads you to move in different ways for each element, which can be very evocative.

Imagine for a moment how you would move if you were to invoke fire just with your body. How would that differ from water? Air? How could you call the Goddess?

It's important to choose music for ritual that draws you into trance and doesn't distract you, but this varies wildly from person to person. One of my friends can only trance out to industrial and techno; I lean more toward electronica or world beat, particularly anything with a Middle Eastern flair, such as Loreena McKennitt's "Santiago" or "Marco Polo." You may find that straightforward rock gets your mojo working. Don't try to force yourself to use music just because it "sounds Pagan." If what's playing doesn't help you get your groove on, there's no point to it.

Before beginning a dance ritual, I usually anoint myself on the third eye, hands, and feet with a special oil blend I created, and then perform an offering rite as illustrated later on in the chapter (Exercise 5). A word of caution—if you use an oil, be absolutely certain it does not contain ingredients that will irritate your skin, and only use a tiny bit, if any, on your face; the last thing you want is to have to stop midritual because the sweat has carried oil right into your eyes. My favorite recipe is a combination of sandalwood, frankincense, rose, and patchouli, blended in sweet almond oil (the proportions are a matter of personal taste).

Begin in a candlelit room with ample floor space. Make sure the candles are up off the ground, so that you don't go blundering into one and knock it over. Burn incense if you like, but be mindful of the fact that you will be breathing hard, and might not want to gulp great breaths of smoke.

I also have a special towel set aside for dance ritual; I don't use it for anything else. (Yes, it gets washed.) Be sure you have a glass of water nearby. In this ritual, that glass is your holy chalice—but so are you, a vessel waiting to be filled with divine energy.

One last important point before you begin is that the object of this kind of ritual is to commune with deity, not kill yourself. Be careful not to overexert or injure yourself, particularly in the beginning of your practice. Program your stereo to play two or three songs at most the first few times, and as you get used to moving this much and your stamina increases, add more.

Start the music and stand in the center of the ritual area. Become aware of your breath and your heartbeat, and notice where they are when your body is at rest. You might ground and center at the start and end of the ritual. I typically have a track at the beginning of the ritual where I just stretch, getting my muscles ready for motion; stretching is very important, as it will keep you from straining or worse.

Close your eyes for a moment and let the music flow through you. Sink into it and feel its beat echoing through your body. Listen with your whole being, not just your ears—how does the music move through your skin, your bones, your limbs? Let yourself start to move however you feel comfortable. Sway at first, feeling energy start to travel up through your feet. Draw the energy all the way up to your head, passing through and waking up each chakra in turn. Then let go, allowing your body to move in whatever way it desires. Don't think: let your body talk. It knows what to do, where tension is knotted and where blocks are obstructing your energy. When you feel completely present in the moment and your body, let yourself be danced.

Feel the dynamic power of the world around you, the force of the music, the response of your muscles. See the world dancing with you:

grasses swaying in a field, the leaves on the trees fluttering in the wind, sand dunes sweeping across a desert. See people the world over moving with you: children playing tag, mothers rocking babies, lovers finding one another.

Become an ecstatic breath of the Goddess and release all the boundaries that seem to separate you from all else that lives. Let the rhythm of electrons and sound waves and the ocean and seasons fill you, move you, carry you home. Feel the energies of the Goddess—that which receives, nurtures, and transforms—and of the God—that which activates, animates, and enflames—flowing through you and around each other, the two halves of your being turning around and around in an endless spiral.

Finally, slow down—gradually—and breathe deeply. Allow the energy that has risen in your body to ground out through your feet, but don't sit or bend over until your heartbeat begins to calm, otherwise you might pass out. Eventually, when your body tells you it is time to come to Earth, touch the ground with your hands and forehead, offering up the last excess energy to the benefit of all. Be certain to drink plenty of water afterward, and stretch as you did in the beginning to keep your muscles from getting in a twist.

Yoga

Yoga is all the rage nowadays, and so is its cousin, pilates, which is essentially yoga with the spirituality removed. The word "yoga" is from a Sanskrit term meaning "to yoke or bind," and is often interpreted as meaning "union." Yoga has been around for at least two thousand years, and has spread like wildfire in the last few. Its original purpose was spiritual enlightenment, though most Westerners use it almost entirely for its considerable physical benefits.

Most people identify yoga with hatha yoga, which is only one branch of the philosophy. Hatha yoga consists of a series of postures (called asanas) that are designed to align the parts of the body and create harmony. There are other branches of yoga, such as bhakti and tantra, with a different focus; even within the umbrella of hatha there are different styles, some of which are combined with the other branches. Iyengar yoga, for example, focuses on holding each asana for a longer period of time, whereas Ashtanga yoga moves fairly quickly through a flowing set of postures.

You don't have to embrace any of the Eastern gods in order to practice yoga, which is a philosophy, not a religion. You also don't have to be some skinny yogini who can twist herself into a human pretzel—even large and inflexible people can benefit from yoga practice. At the very least, yoga can help you to relax and release stress, as well as become stronger and more flexible. There are even yoga videos designed specifically for people who don't fit the stereotypical rail-thin vegan image of a yoga practitioner.

I have tried a variety of yoga methods and have found it isn't really my thing, mostly because I need more rhythm in my workouts and yoga has a tendency to bore me. I have, however, used a morning yoga practice video to help gear up for the day, and a corresponding evening video to relax and prepare for sleep. But even if you don't enjoy the traditional hatha yoga taught in most studios, don't give up until you have tried different styles and branches; chances are there's one that will appeal to you.

Tai Chi

Tai Chi, also known as Tai Chi Chu'an, is a gentle martial art that arose from Taoist philosophy. Tai Chi is a series of movements that flow together with breathing exercises and spiritual and mental intent that help you move into a spiritually receptive state. The movements of Tai Chi help balance the yin and yang aspects of the self (often translated as feminine and masculine, although this definition is a little too simplistic) and facilitate the flow of chi, or life energy, through the energy body.

There's something very calming and spiritually soothing about watching a group of people do Tai Chi in a park, all of them moving in unison, a ballet of energy. I enjoy Tai Chi, as it feels like a slow and meditative dance. It is also a lot more physically demanding than it seems—I was surprised to find that halfway through a session I was sweating buckets. Tai Chi demands a lot of attention to detail, with subtle changes in hand position and posture that require focus and practice. It's also performed almost entirely on your feet and doesn't call for all the bending and contorting that yoga often does. If you appreciate the discipline of yoga but are looking for something more lyrical, give Tai Chi a try.

Whirling

You probably didn't know this, but as a child you may well have been a mystic. Did you ever hold your arms out and spin and spin and spin until you fell over? That is similar to the practices of the whirling dervishes, who were mystics of the Sufi sect of Islam. Sufism was founded by the poet Rumi, whose writings reflect a deep and personal relationship with God through lyrical metaphor. Rumi founded Sufism in the thirteenth century; it was considered rather radical because Islam forbade most sacred music.

The dervishes (dervish means "doorway") perform a centuries-old ritual known as a *sema*, in which they wear long white robes with voluminous skirts and whirl, both around their own axes and around each other. The whirling is said to reflect the turn of the earth around the sun. The dervish holds the right hand palm up, and the left palm down, in order to receive the energy of God; through their spinning they reach a trance state in which divine communion occurs. In this way they are said to stand between the material and cosmic worlds, representing the union of the physical and spiritual.

If you would like to try whirling, even just out of curiosity to see if you can get past the dizziness factor, I would strongly suggest making sure you have plenty of clear floor space without anything to crash into.

Bruises and concussions aren't terribly conducive to spiritual practice. Generally the dervishes didn't end their rituals by toppling over like six-year-olds, but in the spirit of "mirth and reverence," if there's enough cushion around it might be fun to punctuate a prayer with a good laugh.

Sex

As you might expect, sex is one of the tried-and-true ways to connect body and spirit, as well as to raise energy. Having spent an entire chapter on the topic I won't belabor the point, but suffice it to say that sex is one of the more entertaining forms of exercise out there, but comes with plenty of warning labels for safety and health. If you are interested in working with sexual energy in a more directed way, I suggest learning about tantric philosophy; while tantra is not a purely sexual art, the energy it utilizes is distinctly erotic in flavor and can send your chakras into orbit.

In all of the above ideas, the important thing to keep in mind isn't so much the action as the attitude. Any act, no matter how seemingly mundane, can be an act of prayer if you allow it to be. Whether in the middle of a drum circle or at the weight bench, think of it as an offering: you are giving your time and energy to maintain the vessel of your soul, and in doing so honoring the gods.

> I move my body in many ways. My favorite is in dance with another person. Whether that dance is vertical or horizontal doesn't matter. Once I have reached the level of intimacy that allows me the freedom to dance I want to revel in the feeling of my body sliding and moving against my friend or lover's body and energy.
>
> JEWEL

THE OFFERING—EXERCISE #5

Before you begin any workout, pause a moment to ground and center in whatever way you feel most comfortable doing. Become aware of your breath, and reflect on how that breath will carry you through your work, changing its cadences to draw in as much energy as you need.

Become aware of each part of your body, briefly, and think about what it will contribute to the activity you are about to engage in.

Then, think or say the following prayer:

Lord and Lady,
Here I make an offering of myself,
A prayer in sweat and motion.
Bless my efforts this hour and always
That I may honor and serve you in health and in joy.
Blessed be.

After the workout is finished, conclude with a short prayer of thanks for the arms and legs and heart and any other part that the God and Goddess have blessed you with that assisted you, and give thanks also for your health—even if it's terrible, it could be worse. If you're working out at all, obviously you're alive and not in a coma or full body cast, so be grateful.

Alternate Ecstasy

Ecstasy through the body doesn't just come through movement, and in the last decade or so we've seen the rise of other forms that were once relegated to the "freak show" category. No discussion of physical ecstasy would be complete without mentioning body modification.

Tattoos and piercings are becoming more and more common, and for most people they are little more than fashion statements, a way of being a conforming anticonformist. Many Pagans, however, take a different view, and permanently alter the body to reflect the indwelling spirit—or vice versa. We are a lot less likely to get tattoos and the like on a whim, because at heart we understand that when you change your outer form, you change the inside as well.

Body modification can be an invocation, a rite of passage, a declaration, or any other kind of ritual you can think of. Perhaps you got a pentacle tattoo to mark your entry into Wicca, or have the image of your power animal on your body to connect you more fully to its energy. You may also have gotten some sort of ink to create a similar change in your-self; for example, you could get a tattoo of a bindrune (a combination of runes that together create a magical working) for protection, self-love, or spiritual growth.

There are modifications of all kinds ranging from the relatively sim-ple tattoo or piercing to elaborate holes and implants. I've seen women's backs embedded with loops of metal that could be laced up like a corset; I've seen men with horns, women with tails, people with spikes protruding from their faces and who hung themselves from hooks in their skin. You might flinch at the thought, as I tend to do, but I've come to understand that there is a lot more than vanity at work here.

Apart from the initial purpose behind the modification, a great many of those who undergo such rites find that the pain they engender is a potent form of ecstasy all on its own. Pain, like pleasure, releases endor-phins in the body that can lift the mind and spirit up out of ordinary consciousness and into realms beyond.

It's well known that for some, tattoos and piercings become addic-tive; once you've felt that transcendence that is at the same time so completely physical, you want to go back again and again. After having my first tattoo at age nineteen, I started looking at my entire body dif-ferently, now as a canvas of blank skin, much the way a sculptor might look at a chunk of marble—what was within waiting to be released? What lurks beneath the surface that only a needle can set free?

I probably don't need to tell you this, but choose such alterations with care. Practically speaking, be sure you have the time and patience to take care of the mark or hole until it is healed, and to treat it gin-gerly as much as possible. Also be absolutely sure of the location and type of alteration and how it will fit into your life as it stands now. It's all well and good to get your lip pierced to symbolize your commit-ment to the truth, but are you prepared for that truth to land you in the unemployment line if your boss is a little too conservative for your tribal sensibilities?

Most importantly, consider well the possible effects of the alteration. You are calling upon powerful primal forces of nature when you call upon pain to change you in body or mind. Allowing your holy vessel to be changed irrevocably should require a good deal of meditation beforehand. Plastic surgery isn't just a day procedure or walk in the park; neither is a tattoo. Ask yourself: who am I getting this done for? Is my authentic self crying for the change, or am I allowing outside opinions to determine what I look like?

And please, please, *please* don't pick flash off a tattoo artist's wall—you know, the predrawn pictures that are the equivalent of the candy rack at the supermarket, designed for impulse shoppers. Your body deserves a lot more forethought than that. Again, I speak from experience: I picked a premade design on a whim, and I lucked out in choosing a fairly simple and fairly small tribal-designed butterfly. As I mentioned in my last book, that choice brought an onslaught of transformations in my life that are still not finished eight years later.

I was fortunate, though. My college roommate's best friend picked a flash tattoo off the wall but failed to look closely at the picture she'd chosen despite the tattoo artist asking three times, "Are you *sure* that's the one you want?" Two hours later she got home and realized the butterfly on her back was actually a winged penis.

The moral of the story: choose body modifications wisely, and soberly, particularly if you're a nearsighted eighteen-year-old lesbian.

Warrior's Marks

There is an old Scottish proverb: "Never give a sword to a man who can't dance."

The Dancer has another face, who uses movement in a slightly different way: the Warrior, whom we spoke of briefly in chapter 3. Rather than using the power of motion to achieve spiritual ecstasy, the Warrior transforms it into protective magic, discipline, and emotional expression.

The Warrior's primary task is to transform anger. You'll find that if you work with movement spiritually, your emotions will start to arise in the course of your practice, and you have two choices: bottle them up, or let them out. Obviously the latter is healthier, but it is the Warrior who chooses how your emotions are best dealt with through the body.

You might expect that the Warrior causes us to get into fights, but in fact the greatest Warriors are the ones who don't have to fight; they find other ways to deal with conflict, and never, ever lift a sword out of anger. Anger can cripple your judgment and cause you to act rashly, doing things you'll regret, from hacking someone to bits with a battle-axe to riddling a loved one with verbal bullets.

The Warrior takes anger, lets it move through her body, and out. She might use dance or other movement to encourage that flow, or might take up a martial art. Above all, she makes sure that she is in charge of her own self-expression, and chooses the circumstances and form in which to act, not react.

There are entire spiritual systems devoted to the path of the Warrior, but for Wiccans, her job is to protect and transform within the boundaries of the Rede and our own worldview in which everything is sacred. She must find a balance between, "Harm none," and, "What did you just call my mother?" and know when to engage. Despite the common interpretations of the Rede, Wiccans are not expected to be complete pacifists; when something precious is in danger, or has been violated, we have to consider the consequences, our options, and then act, not sit waiting for things to simply unfold in a way we'd like.

The Dancer's magic is tapping into the divine universal energy and using it to transform herself from the outside in. The Warrior takes that same energy and pushes it outward when needed, to form shields, protective circles, and occasionally offensive actions as well. Most Warriors never strike first, but when they do, they do so with the intent to end the conflict right then and there.

It is the Warrior who gives you that weird prickly feeling you get walking alone at night, encouraging you to put up magical barriers, get your keys out and ready, and become aware of your surroundings. The Warrior works very closely with the self-preservation instincts of the root chakra as well as the fiery power of the solar plexus.

Your body, being holy, is not only worth reverence, but worth defending. Women often pretend we have no inner Warrior, that "nice girls don't hit." We're taught passivity and surrender, not to make a lot of noise, and we even apologize to inanimate objects we bump into. Just as we give and give until we have nothing left, we let ourselves be walked over and pushed around.

My advice: stop being ladylike. This is not a nice world to be a woman in; being ladylike can get you hurt. It is possible to be female, considerate, and compassionate, and still not take any crap. You didn't create the societal definition of womanhood, anyway. That definition turns strong, independent Pagan Amazons into demure servant-girls. Which would you rather be? You're the one who gets to decide what a woman is; allow your own definition to include the willingness to kick a bit of ass.

Gods and Goddesses of the Dancer Archetype

There are many deities associated with movement. One of the lesser-known is Atlanta, a Greek huntress similar to Artemis, who we have already discussed. Atlanta's father was so disappointed he had a daughter that he left her out in the wild to die; she was found by a band of hunters who raised her as their own, and became a formidable member of their tribe who could bring down even the toughest game. Later, she vowed she would only marry the man who could beat her in a foot race. The man who managed it could do so only by deceit— Melanion sought the aid of Aphrodite, who helped him trick Atlanta into falling behind so that she lost the race and had to marry him. In reality, or at least in a fair contest, she was never truly beaten.

Personally I would have been a very unpleasant spouse if the man I had to marry had won me by cheating. I can't imagine Atlanta was too thrilled about it, either.

Though not associated with movement per se, another deity who comes to mind with regard to the Dancer archetype is Dionysus, the god of wine and ecstasy. Dionysus was strongly linked with Mystery schools that taught transcendence of the mundane world through physical and spiritual intoxication. In many accounts, Dionysus was treated rather harshly; he was considered by some to be a dangerous latecomer to the Greek pantheon who destroyed his enemies and encouraged violent and lascivious behavior, a distinct counterpoint to the other, more "civilized" gods of Olympus (you know, the ones that liked to rape women and then turn them into cows).

In fact, the female devotees of Dionysus, the maenads, were depicted as madwomen who left their domestic chores and family life to go live in the woods and participate in orgiastic and bloody rituals. The maenads were said to accompany the god through his travels and devour the raw flesh of animals. They are often shown in paintings clothed only in fawn skins, dancing with the abandon of ecstatic union with nature. Whether these accounts are true or simply sensationalized stories to discourage women from engaging in socially unacceptable behavior, when the maenads at last returned to their homes they were exhausted, and never spoke of what had happened during their run with the wild god.

The god that I encounter in my rituals is a loose combination of Dionysus and another deity well known to trance dancers: Shiva.

Shiva was third of the great triumvirate of Hindu gods; he was seen as the Destroyer, but also given regenerative powers. In his form of Nataraj, he was lord of the dance of cosmic cycles, the rhythms of birth and death. He is often paired with Shakti, the great feminine force we spoke of in the previous chapter, with whom he dances the universe in and out of existence.

In many schools of thought, all female divinities of the Hindu pantheon are thought of as emanations of Shakti energy. Shiva then is paired with Parvati, and also with Kali, the Black Mother.

Kali is a fascinating goddess in and of herself, as one of the most fully realized dark goddesses—and one of the few female deities of any sort who can boast an unbroken line of worship up to the present day. At first glance she appears terrifying, with her necklace of skulls and skirt of severed arms, her bloodlust and her fierce eyes. Her devotees, however, see her as a mother figure, and a liberator—she offers freedom from all fear and ignorance, and maintains the cosmic order.

There are several versions of the birth of Kali, but most would agree that she was created in order to fight a demon or demons that no other god had the power to defeat. Kali emerged ready for battle and made short work of her enemies, and then began to dance to celebrate her victory—what she didn't realize, however, was that in her ecstasy she was essentially dancing the universe to death. All existence would have been annihilated by her exultations, but just in time, Shiva threw himself beneath her feet. In Hindu culture, touching someone with your feet is considered a sign of egregious disrespect. When Kali realized what she had done, and was about to do, she stopped—it is said that Kali's face in many paintings, shown sticking out her blood-red tongue, is an expression of embarrassment at her ill-considered actions. Regardless, there will come a day when Kali will dance and nothing, not even her consort, will be able to stop her from ending time.

The feminine principle in Hinduism is actually the active aspect, while the masculine is seen as passive. In fact, the creative energy of Shakti is represented by the "i" in Shiva's name, without which his name would mean "corpse." The union of masculine and feminine is what drives the dance of the universe.

A great many Pagans invoke Kali thinking they want change in their lives, without really considering the consequences. Kali does not screw around—her way of changing your life can be likened to a forest fire.

In the wake of destruction, new life can grow, but first comes the inferno. As I said, Kali's devotees are fortunate in that there is plenty of literature and ritual already in existence for her, so you can go to the source materials such as the *Devi-Mahatmya* to learn more. I don't recommend working blithely with Kali—devote some time to studying her and her culture before calling for her help, or you deserve exactly what you get.

Dance, then, is often associated with both creation and destruction as in the myth of Shiva and Kali; with positive energy and that which tears away boundaries and borders, in the case of Dionysus. The flow of life that pours through us when we move our bodies is the same flow that causes day to flow into night into day. As in the story of Atlanta, physical motion also confers freedom—being able to outrun anything with legs meant that she was free from constraint, until, of course, she was duped into matrimony.

The Dancer is the child of the Wild God and the Dark Mother; she is the full realization of our unbridled physical selves, whole and complete, able to dance the universe to life and to death with each step we take.

SUGGESTIONS FOR EXPLORING THE DANCER

1. Pay attention to the ways you move your body throughout the day, everything from brushing your teeth to a romp in the sack. Are you allowing your body to move freely, or do you restrain yourself, hold still when you would rather be up and running? What effect does that restraint have on your health—for example, sitting for eight hours at a desk can cause a number of problems for your back, knees, and the size of your butt.

2. Find ways to incorporate more movement into your day—take the stairs instead of the elevator, don't circle the parking lot fifty times for a spot up front.

3. Count the number of steps you take in a day. Recent research suggests that 10,000 steps a day is the number we should aim for to maintain good health—how far short of that mark are you? (If you're me, that's pretty far, so don't feel like too much of a slacker.)

4. Pay attention to how people express their inner selves through their bodies. How do your friends walk? Look at posture, body language. You can learn so much about someone before they say a word to you; there are books and courses out there on how to "read" people that way, which I've found is a combination of their body language and their energy language. How would you compare the way a confident and self-secure person moves as opposed to someone who hates her body? Try mimicking the former for a day and see how it makes you feel.

5. Dance. Go somewhere crowded where you don't have to feel like you're being stared at, and get your groove on like there's no tomorrow. Nobody's watching, and you know what? If they are, and they think it's funny, they're assholes you don't want to know anyway. Forget them. Anyone worth knowing will love the way you dance.

6. Take a self-defense class, or train in a martial art. You don't have to be Jackie Chan to employ the Warrior's arts, especially when it comes to taking care of yourself. Just be sure that you learn practical applications of your skills; breaking ice blocks with your hands is impressive, but it doesn't help a lot when you're held up at knifepoint.

Recommended Reading and Resources for Chapter Seven

BOOKS

Moving into Ecstasy: An Urban Mystic's Guide to Movement, Music, and Meditation by Jivan Amoda

Stretching by Bob Anderson

A Woman's Book of Power: Using Dance to Cultivate Energy by Karen Andes

The Wiccan Warrior by Kerr Cuhulain

Crafting the Body Divine: Ritual, Movement, and Body Art by Yasmine Galenorn

Great Shape: The First Fitness Guide for Large Women by Pat Lyons

Real Fitness for Real Women: A Unique Workout Program for the Plus-Size Woman by Rochelle Rice

Sweat Your Prayers: Movement as Spiritual Practice by Gabrielle Roth

Sacred Woman, Sacred Dance by Iris J. Stewart

Office Yoga: Simple Stretches for Busy People by Darrin Zeer

VIDEO/DVD

The Ecstatic Dance Collection—a set of three videos by Gabrielle Roth, illustrating three different "workouts" with her Wave Method

The Goddess Workout with Dolphina—a really groovy belly dance workout video

Yoga for Round Bodies

Yoga for Inflexible People

MUSIC

As I said, you can do trance dance to any kind of music that moves you, but my favorite artists for ritual movement are:

Dead Can Dance

Deep Forest

Delerium

Deva Premal

Krishna Das

Loreena McKennitt

Rasa

Gabrielle Roth and the Mirrors

Some artists whose CDs feature drumming:

Mickey Hart

Steve Gordon

Ubaka Hill

e i g h t

THE

crone

Old One, weaver of the shining web,
whose hands spin the thread of life and death . . .
This dark moon is your night,
And on this night,
I pray to you.
Help me find the strength to end what must be ended
to stand up for myself and no longer look away.
Guide me from this place to another,
Where the moonlight shows the path before me
And I walk unafraid.
I wait in your darkened wood where the three roads meet
One back to this same place again,
One down into the shadow,
One up the spiral mountain to the stars.
Give me the courage to walk

And not look back
But only onward, into your face.
By your grace,
So mote it be.

Of all the archetypes we have explored, of all the parts of our lives that we must bring together in order to be whole, the face of the Crone is the one we seem to fear most.

Sex is a muddle of contradictions; nurturing is full of stereotypes; the Reflection is distorted . . . but it is the Crone that we run from, clinging desperately to what, in the end, must be released.

On the far side of the circle, at the center of the spiral, she awaits our passage through the years, closer and closer to her side—and no matter what surgery, drugs, and cosmetics we cover and fill ourselves with, eventually we will return to her. There is no other way. The Crone will not be defied.

We sure as hell try, though. In fact there is an entire subset of the beauty industry and hundreds of products devoted entirely to fighting age. The rhythm of our bodies is an enemy to be conquered, like everything else in Western society, and we'll fight with whatever weapons are handy: lotion, facelifts, calcium supplements, you name it. There are probably more anti-aging concoctions out there than there are weight-loss products, and if preying on our fear of fat is a successful marketing scheme, preying on our fear of death and decay is sheer genius. There may or may not be a lot of naturally thin people, but everyone ages, so the money-making potential is vast.

As you might expect, the Crone laughs outright at all this foolishness. "You might as well try to hold back the tide," she says as she peers into her cauldron. "Nothing made of flesh can stay."

The Crone is a multifaced, paradoxical archetype, for she rules over aging and death, but also over the forces that enable women to create life: the Blood Mysteries. The cycle of the moon that moves within us every month is her exclusive domain. In fact, all physical rites of passage interest her. At heart, her watchword is simply "change," the continual and irreversible growth and evolution that moves through our bodies from birth until death.

You might think that such things would be the province of the Mother, and it's true, you could look at it that way—but the Crone stands at a place of complete understanding, both of how our bodies change, and why. The Mother's specialty in the Blood Mysteries would of course be childbirth; menarche, menopause, and all the other moments in between are not her concern. The Healer may ply her trade on the pain and discomfort inherent in a female body, but overall she has no say in how things flow. The Lover is not interested in procreation; that's the Mother's job. She's in it for the fun and the ecstasy, just like the Dancer, so all the messiness of bleeding just ends up getting in the way.

The Crone is an old wise woman, and yet she is ageless. She is the cycle itself, which never ends, even though our individual lives do. When this earth-walk is over and this body is dust and our souls have moved on to another, the Crone will remain, standing at the center, waiting.

Bette Davis once said, "Old age ain't no place for sissies," and the Crone was speaking through her, for certain. The Crone's lessons are not easy ones. They require us to face our deepest fears of growing old and dying, which, in our society, are way up there on the phobia list. Under her tutelage you will learn the impermanence of living and the eternal nature of life, all held within the spiral, turning and turning and returning again.

We are a culture terrified of aging. I've seen women start looking for crow's feet at twenty-five, and heard

How can we be fully and completely balanced when all we are taught is to turn aside the wisdom of our elders and to reject the natural ebb and flow that happens within our bodies as we move through each stage of our lives? Our modern society has robbed us and our mothers and their mothers before them of a cherished heirloom. Unfortunately, no one had any idea there was a thief among us.

JEWEL

more than one person say, "Oh, I'll die before I'm fifty. I can't stand to get that old."

What is it we're really afraid of? Is it aging, death, both? Along with the fear comes a certain contempt, for we know at heart that no matter what we buy and what we put on our faces, we're moving a breath closer to the cliff every second of every day. We like to think we're in control of our lives, and we are to an extent, but we are not in control of nature. The Crone makes sure of that.

Her way is that of ultimate acceptance. To truly embrace life, you must embrace all of it, which means giving up the need to stay thirty and "stop having birthdays."

Wiccans and other varieties of Pagans might have it a little easier; we see in the world around us that everything has its cycle, and an end is a beginning as well. But it's hard to let go of our conditioning with aging, as with everything else. We give reverence to a variety of Crone goddesses, so we see that there is honor and wisdom in the latter half of life; that doesn't mean we're quite ready to jump just yet.

> You are as young as your faith, as old as your doubt; as young as your self-confidence, as old as your fear; as young as your hope, as old as your despair.
>
> DOUGLAS MACARTHUR

There is absolutely nothing wrong with enjoying your youth—I'm finally enjoying mine, yet I still wouldn't take eighteen again if you paid me—but if you live that youth in fear of age, you rob yourself of some of the ease and grace of today with constant worry about tomorrow. Half of what ages us "prematurely" is our obsessive need to not age.

THE CRONE IN THE MIRROR—EXERCISE #1

Look into a mirror and examine your face. Then visualize it as it looked when you were a child; how have you changed?

Now imagine the years passing, and each year showing in the mirror, up to today, and beyond that. Imagine how you will look—realistically—at forty, fifty, sixty, and onward. How do you feel about the face in the mirror?

Consider whether the love you are creating for your body will extend to old age. If not, why not? Is your body somehow less holy as the years go by?

What do you fear about aging, if anything? Do you worry about a loss of ability, making the activities you enjoy now harder and harder? Do you worry about being in pain, sick, dying?

Why?

I know, it's a strange question. Who wouldn't be afraid of death? It's so . . . final.

But you're a Wiccan, remember? Nothing is final in nature. Nothing ever truly dies. As with every other natural law, you are not immune to this. Once you're done here, you get to go on to another grand adventure.

Humans are the only creatures in nature who try to outwit her. Our intellect and self-awareness have led us to a certain arrogance, thinking that we have dominion over the earth, the water, and life itself. The advances of medical science have made many believe that eventually we'll conquer aging the way we want to conquer disease.

No matter what new plastic surgery or drug comes onto the market, however, we know better, and it scares and angers us so much that we pretend that getting older is optional. We surround ourselves with images of young, toned women with the bodies of children, and are determined to hide away those things that remind us of the inevitable.

Respecting Your Elders

Our dread of getting old isn't just a dilemma for ourselves. It has affected the way we think of the older generation in general, and how we treat those who have lived longer than we have. In the East, elders are thought of with a capital E, considered wise and blessed to have lived so long. They are treated with honor and dignity, and accorded a high place in the household, where they live out their whole lives and die among family.

There aren't a whole lot of nursing homes in Japan. You won't find grandmothers lying in hospital beds staring at the walls, wondering when their grandchildren are going to visit. You won't see old people shut away from public eyes, where we don't have to think about them or what they represent about our own mortality. You certainly won't find them on the street because their Social Security isn't enough to pay rent with. The very idea is akin to blasphemy in the East.

The same goes for many native and tribal cultures the world over, owing to a time when making it past sixty was borderline miraculous. In a way, the medical technology which enables us to overcome disease and to live longer is to blame. Growing old is no longer viewed as special, because anyone can do it without much effort, provided they don't stress their way into an early grave or honk at the wrong person in traffic. The same advances that have rendered influenza "no big deal" have made our elders "no big deal."

It seems to me that regardless of how easy it is to reach a ripe old age in our modern times, living through decades of tumultuous change commands a certain level of respect. Think about it: the people you know right now who are eighty lived through the Great Depression, several wars, a dozen presidents, the evolution of America from industrial to technological, the birth of television, computers, and a thousand other things we take for granted now. To have seen so much, and survived so much, deserves at least a little consideration, doesn't it?

Where are your grandparents? Are they still alive? If so, how often do you see them? How often does anyone see them?

I personally have a deep and abiding fear of nursing homes, but I figured out a few years ago that it has nothing to do with the elderly. Nursing homes are basically houses where people lie around waiting to die. When I walk into one, it's as if all the hope and energy is sucked out of me. The staff treat the inmates like children; there's a pervasive air of futility and weariness. I cannot imagine spending the sunset of my life in a place like that, but that's exactly what we expect people to do. This is what we earn by working hard and staying healthy enough to last?

Imagine living eighty years on this earth, seeing war and fire and flood, enduring poverty and enjoying prosperity, raising children and bouncing grandchildren on your knee, being a productive member of society . . . and then being pushed away from the world, off to a place where people hate to come visit you. Imagine being thought of as useless and feeble because of a number on a birthday card.

It's not all that different from being considered weak and inferior for being a woman, really. As the world wants to forget that women are powerful, it wants to forget that old people aren't finished yet.

When I was in Girl Scouts, we used to occasionally adopt an old person—we found people in nursing homes who didn't have any family, and made it a point to bring them gifts, visit at least once a week, read to them, and anything else a twelve-year-old had the power to do. As much as I hated it at the time, I wish we'd done it more often and for much longer. Consider having your coven or study group, or you as an individual, do something similar; we can decide not to take on the shameful attitude of most Westerners that the elderly are best kept out of sight, out of mind, and out of life.

> You could not pay me to be one minute younger than I am today! I think the preoccupation with youth in the culture today is disgusting and weird . . . everyone is supposed to look like a child and act like an adult. I'm proud of my gray hair.
> SHANA

A RITUAL TO HONOR YOUR ANCESTORS

Rituals like this one are often performed at Samhain, when the year is waning and sailing toward its own death. At that time, deep in autumn, we pause to remember the lives that have touched ours and then gone across the veil.

We have ancestors all year, though, just as there are hungry people when it isn't Christmas. There are older folk and the beloved dead every day of the year, so it's always appropriate to give them honor.

Choose a person in your family, or simply someone who was an ancestor of spirit, regardless of when they died; on the dark of the moon, go to his or her grave. (You probably can't do this at night without getting arrested, so daytime is fine, preferably at dusk.) Bring a sprig of rosemary or a flower known for its association with memory and rebirth, such as chrysanthemum, white rose, or carnation.

The old Mexican traditions of Dia de los Muertos are still practiced, and in Texas at the beginning of November you often see marigolds and sugar skulls left along headstones; families take time out to trim grass, reset stones, and in other ways straighten up the grave sites of their family plots, then leave the flowers and candy as offerings. Elaborate altars are set up for the dead; traditionally, November 1 is the day for repairing and cleaning the cemetery, and November 2 is a day for family reunions with a much more festive flair.

To reflect these old traditions, spend some time tidying up the grave if it needs it before having a seat next to the headstone. If you're lucky enough to live somewhere with a large Hispanic population, you may be able to get your hands on a sugar skull, which I think of as symbolic of the paradox of life in death, sweetness in sorrow. Lay your flower or herbal offering on the ground. If there's anything you wish you could say to that person, say it; hopefully they aren't still hanging around the graveyard, but honor their memory regardless, for yourself if for no other reason.

You might wish to repeat this ritual yearly for a particular person, or more generally, commemorating all the people in your life who have gone on ahead. It doesn't have to be performed on Samhain or even in the autumn, though a dark or waning moon is most symbolic.

The Blood Mysteries

Beneath the civilized trappings, we are all basically animals with shoes. Deep within our bodies we still feel the call of nature as the Crone stirs her cauldron and, in its waters, the cycle of time. Our lunar flow is one of the ways we are still intrinsically connected to the wild world and to our essential selves. When it hits us, we regress from the illusion of sophistication to a more elemental version of humanity, in which our bodies and hormones are in charge. This is usually viewed as a bad thing, probably because, like aging, we can't control it like we wish we could.

Time is not linear, though we usually perceive it that way. The year turns back around to its beginning; the moon waxes and wanes and waxes again. We are born, we live a while, we die, we are born. We start our lives without bleeding, then we bleed, then we finish our lives without. All things move in circles, of which the Divine is both center and circumference.

I have always thought that aging is part of life, every line in your face whether from laughing or crying you have earned and they tell the story of where you have been and what you have done. I think our culture is ashamed of aging, that is why there are so many people in the business of staying young; people sell their souls and go under the knife rather than look in the mirror and see crow's feet or laugh lines.

KYLARA

Human beings are still connected to the source; we simply choose to ignore that connection most of the time. Wiccans and other Pagans have chosen to remember. We renew our link to the earth, and in doing so realign with the sacred beat of the Mother's heart. As women, we have yet another connection, this one to the moon.

Remarkable things happen to women. Have you ever spent a lot of time with a group of other women and found that after a while all of you had the same cycle? Given time and interaction, especially magical work of any depth, we synchronize. If you've paid any attention to this, try working magic on a night when you are all bleeding and see if you notice a difference. The common take on it is that our psychic and spiritual gifts are most powerful during our periods, even more so if they fall on a full or new moon.

Equally amazing is the fact that with a bit of help from dad, a whole entire human being can grow in our bellies and push its way out, capable of breathing, thinking, and growing into anyone at all. The potential inherent in the female body is endless, however we choose to invoke our creative power.

CHARTING THE MOON—EXERCISE #2

This is a long-term project, but can give you important insights about your body as well as other aspects of your life. A great many Wiccans already do this sort of thing.

Find a lunar calendar; by this I mean one of the sort that shows what phase the moon is in every day. The one I have isn't even set up like a standard calendar, but has each month as a line of moons. If you can't find one, you can make do with a regular calendar as long as you write in the lunar phases in as much detail as possible.

Also, acquire a blank book of some sort to keep with your calendar. Each month, note the days of your period on the calendar, and in the book write down details such as how you felt emotionally, if you had any weird food cravings, what sort of flow you had, and so on.

Expand this to include the week before your period; this can be very helpful if you have problems with PMS, as it can give you signs to watch for so you know what to expect. Write down how your libido is doing, too; I've found that the week before my period I turn into something of a nymphomaniac and spend a lot of time with the Electric Boyfriend, otherwise I end up chewing the tires off my car.

In addition to physical data, in this book write down how you feel in terms of spiritual and magical power. You've probably noticed that there are times you feel much Witchier—you have extremely successful rituals and meditations, your skill at divination soars. Other days you'd be doing well to cast your way out of a paper circle. You may find a pattern emerging, and it may be one linked to your menstrual cycle or to the lunar calendar itself.

Aside from getting you in touch with your body, this information can do wonders for your magical life as well. From here you can plan rituals based on your internal cycles; if you find that you're too tired on your period to do spells, you'll know not to plan anything major during that time.

I'm on My Euphemism

There are few areas of female life subject to more misconceptions, stupid taboos, and general disdain than menstruation. Even the word itself makes us giggle, or blush, or clam up in a hurry. We've come up with all sorts of creative metaphors: Aunt Flo, the "monthlies," moon time, surfing the crimson tide, Witching time, technical difficulties, crying a bloody river, big red, code red, being "sick," courses, that time of the month, seducing vampires, up on blocks, on the rag, Miss Scarlett, falling to the communists, the eve of St. Menses, riding the cotton pony, and my personal favorite: the curse. (Well, that's not entirely true. My real personal favorite is saying, "I'm on my euphemism.")

Hilarious as these may be, having read most of this book, what do you think the implications are of giving such a name as "the curse" to one of the most intimate and fundamental biological processes of womanhood? You can most likely trace that one back to biblical times again, to the pronouncement that as her punishment dear old Eve would suffer pain in childbirth.

Eve wasn't our only problem, though. Women have a variety of interesting negative reactions to their periods, ranging from a regretful sigh to outright contempt. "Damn it, not again!"

In fact, the only time we seem glad to see our blood is when it means we're not pregnant. You've never had a sweeter period than the one after the condom breaks.

Regardless of our religious conditioning, we're raised to view bleeding as nothing more than a messy, painful inconvenience that keeps us from enjoying life to the fullest. It interrupts our busy schedules with its slow, sluggish pace; it makes us pay attention to our bodies whether we want to or not. For those of us who don't want children, it's doubly frustrating, because there doesn't seem to be any point to it; those who are trying to have children hate it, too, as it signifies another month without conception.

Historically speaking, a lot of men have been terrified, fascinated, and disgusted with menstruation, which they have generally written about as a disease or form of pollution. After all, men don't do it, so it must be abnormal, right? All sorts of explanations have been put forth, including the idea that since the uterus is the weakest organ of the body (of course—babies just fall out, you know, it's all about gravity, and all that screaming is just us thinking about changing diapers for the next couple of years), blood naturally collects there and then leaks out, thanks to the inferior physical construction of a woman's body.

Pliny the Elder actually wrote of menstrual blood, "Contact with it turns new wine sour, crops touched by it become barren . . . the fruit of trees fall off . . . hives of bees die, even bronze and iron are at once seized by rust, and a horrible smell fills the air; to taste it drives dogs mad and infects their bites with an incurable poison . . ."

I'd like to know who exactly has been getting that friendly with her dog, for one thing. For another, how exactly do hives of bees come in contact with menstrual blood? There's a mental image nobody needs. To hear Pliny tell it, we just leave puddles all over the place for pure, innocent, superior men to drop their swords in.

There are all kinds of laws and recommendations in religions the world over regarding menstruating women, the consensus of which seems to be, "Don't touch her, don't talk to her, lock her in a room, and don't let her sit on anything you like." Apparently a prophet or two left the toilet seat up while his wife was bleeding, and her ensuing wrath scarred him for life.

Turkish Muslim women, for example, aren't allowed to enter the mosque, touch the Koran, or join in the Ramadan fast if they are bleeding. (I'm kind of on board with the antifasting thing—I think I'd be afraid of a flock of hungry hormonal women, too.) There are similar taboos in Judaism as well.

We'd like to think we live in a progressive, forward-thinking society; you need only tell someone you're on your period to see that we're not. Western menstrual taboos might not be strictly religious in nature, and we might not be required to undergo purification rituals before we're allowed back up on the furniture, but we've got our own unspoken set of rules.

For instance, if you sneeze into a tissue, you simply throw it away, but tampons and pads have to be wrapped at least three times in toilet paper and stuffed into the most remote corner of the trash can we can reach without standing up. People will tell you it's because of the smell. Since when are bathrooms known for their pleasing scent, anyway?

There's also the Pink Rule—everything having to do with periods has to be wrapped in pink, preferably with lame little flowers on it. I remember being in my aunt's bathroom and noticing she had pads that came wrapped in blue plastic instead of pink; closer inspection of the package revealed they were for incontinence, and behind them was a package of prerequisite pink, kept contritely under the sink where no one would ever see them and, perish the thought, think someone in the house was on her period.

We sit around and dish about sex like it's going out of style, but if someone says the word "period," she'd better be talking about punctuation or the conversation will grind to a screeching halt. It's a little better in all-female groups, but even then there are so many euphemisms batted about that as a preteen I was convinced that every month my mother got some kind of stomach virus that only women could catch.

And if you want to see a man squirm, ask him to pick up some tampons while he's at the store. Of course, I have to applaud modern men for their willingness to give it a go, especially given the vast array of products to choose from in the girly aisle. Women aren't a lot better about it, actually. We try to sneak our supplies in amongst our other purchases as if they aren't really there. Unfortunately it's hard to hide a big rustling plastic bag of plastic pads with a gigantic logo in flowing script down the side, so about the only thing that can cover it up is tractor tires. There aren't a lot of stores that sell both.

I have noticed, also, that there's a trend to make menstrual products as small as possible, ostensibly for our comfort, but more likely to avoid the embarrassment of people finding out you're a woman like every other woman and your body does exactly the same thing theirs does. Advertising for period products tends to be annoyingly vague, depicting women walking down beaches and riding horses; those ads that aren't made entirely of metaphor always emphasize how easy their items are to conceal.

For a long time menstrual pads and tampons were sold under the hazy designation of "feminine hygiene," along with all sorts of fun sprays, powders, and insertables whose purpose is to completely cover up the fact that you're bleeding and make sure you smell like a basket of roses instead of a woman. Nowadays the aisle is also lumped in with the condoms and lubricants under the even hazier "family planning" title. Everything potentially embarrassing in the store is found right there, so no matter which end you're browsing on, you're screwed. I feel kind of sorry for guys in this case, because for the more skittish among them it's impossible to pretend to look at something else when people walk by if all that's on the aisle are tampons and spermicide. About the only thing they can do at that point is say loudly, "Hmmm, I just don't see the Super He-Man-sized Trojans; guess it's back to using duct tape."

The human body is a messy, untidy thing. We expel a variety of strange and unwelcome substances, and we get dirty and gross on a regular basis. People seem desperate, or rather, Americans seem desperate, to hide as many of our natural functions as we can. Other countries don't seem to have our preoccupation with body odor, for one thing—we've got products for everything from underarm funk to foot funk to period funk to breath funk.

In Japan, tampons are sold with little plastic finger gloves so that women don't have to touch themselves "down there." Sound stupid? What are applicators for, then? I think a lot of women would be happy if they came equipped with tiny cannons we could fire from a distance.

Women tend to be even messier than men, what with all that childbirth and bleeding and mammary glands craziness. This has helped reinforce the stigma against having a female body; as I said, the standard for what is "normal" has long been men's bodies, and any difference is seen as a flaw.

Just for the record, I've seen plenty of gross things come from men, but you'll notice there aren't a lot of TV ads for men's crotch spray or jock wash. Because we are largely uneducated about our anatomy, and would prefer not to deal with our own biology if at all possible, it's easy to dupe us into buying unnecessary and sometimes dangerous things. Did you know that in the 1950s Lysol was marketed as an "antiseptic douche?" It was said to prevent pregnancy, and after you used it to flush out your vagina, you could use it to clean the toilet bowl. How convenient! You could probably save time by using the same brush for both areas!

Strange as it may sound, I was genuinely shocked to discover that there were other options besides commercial pads and tampons out there. It wasn't until I went through my strident feminist phase that I heard of such a bizarre thing as reusable menstrual supplies—imagine! I don't know what I thought women did before the advent of the maxi with wings, but once it occurred to me that Tampax hadn't always existed, I did a bit of research and found that women have used everything from wads of cotton to paper tampons to just letting themselves bleed all over the place. I wasn't quite ready to go that far, but I did come across some interesting ideas: sea sponges, for example, used as tampons and then washed out and put back in; cotton pads with snaps and Velcro that can be washed in hot water and reused; something called the Keeper, which is essentially a rubber cup you stick in that catches the blood. (That option isn't any good for the number of women I know with latex allergies, but it's an intriguing idea all the same.)

The problem most women have with these ideas is that they require getting up close and personal with one's bits, as well as one's bodily fluids, and we've been raised to think that's absolutely disgusting. We don't want to touch ourselves unless absolutely necessary, as if our genitals are only meant for other people to have fun with, let alone maintain. And for some reason the idea of a bowlful of blood-soaked rags has a higher ick factor than a trash can full of them; maybe if they made pink plastic wrappers for reusable pads, they'd be more popular.

The first concern people have is hygienic; they don't think anything made of fabric can be disinfected as thoroughly as plastic that came out of a machine. Makes you wonder how the female species didn't die out all those hundreds and hundreds of years before we had disposable tampons. Powerful laundry detergent is another pretty modern invention.

Never mind that cotton pads are less irritating, more environmentally sound, way more comfortable, and can come in all sorts of fun colors; 80 percent of the women who have found out I use that sort of thing have exactly the same reaction: "Ew." I reply, "Believe it or not, soap gets almost anything off your hands. And by the way, when you made those hamburgers earlier, you were up to the elbows in bloody animal flesh. Why not be up to the elbows in your own? At least you know where it's been."

Menarche, the Non-Rite of Passage

Think back to the day you got your first period. Now, if you lived in a tribal culture or in many other countries around the world, that day would have been marked with celebration, or at least a little attention. Perhaps your mother would have taken you out for dinner and bought you something "adult," like earrings, in order to mark your step over the divide between childhood and what lies beyond. Or maybe the elder women of your village would seclude you somewhere and ritually pass on the secrets of women's magic, sex, and growing up.

If you were Jewish, your mother might have slapped you in the face—don't laugh, it's a real custom, and though it's not written anywhere in Hebrew law, it's still practiced today. Most women who follow it, in fact, don't really consider the reasons why; it's just tradition, perhaps linked to the Curse of Eve, perhaps to something else entirely. (Maybe it's a way of saying, "You might be a woman now, but I can still kick your butt.")

So what did happen? Anything? If you're me, you had already seen The Period Film in school, so you knew what to do: call Mom. (Actually, the film also recommended we talk to a school nurse or minister, and I have no idea what a Southern Baptist minister or a woman who I choose to believe has no genitals could tell me that would be useful.)

Mom came in the bathroom, took one look at my panties, and said, "Oh honey, I'm sorry."

Thanks. What a momentous way to join the tribe of womankind.

For most of us, menarche wasn't much of a celebration. There seem to be two schools of thought among preteen girls these days: one set can't wait to menstruate because it will make them "grown up," and the other set can only think about the fun stuff, like the mess and cramps and PMS.

As a society, we have failed girls when it comes to the Blood Mysteries. First comes that awkward talk; a great many parents just let the schools handle that part, which is probably the greatest mistake they can make. Acting like puberty and sex are some sort of secret, forbidden thing not only makes girls ashamed of themselves as they start exhibiting signs of adolescence (I remember some horrific months that revolved around my burgeoning bosom, which went from nubbins to casaba melons in what felt like two days), it leaves them wondering what's so hush-hush about it all . . . what are their parents hiding? From there, they start exploring on their own, and who is the first person they ask? The official class "bad girl" who knows about this sort of thing, even if she doesn't really. Lady only knows what misinformation they might get this way.

A lack of openness about sex has contributed to a lot of our "moral decline," as the conservatives like to put it. Teenage pregnancy, promiscuity, STDs . . . all of these could be avoided if parents and kids talked about sex honestly.

I know, it's awkward as hell, and no parent likes doing it. That much is obvious. But aren't our daughters worth it?

Even if you don't have children, chances are there is or will be a young woman in your life who will reach that moment while you know her. Think about how you wish your entry into womanhood had been, and do what you can to help her find it.

Wicca has been around long enough that we're starting to see a lot more kids raised in the religion, though the number is still low. We have a unique opportunity to create and instill traditions in our younglings that can become a healing force in society to help us overcome the divide and raise mature, self-actualized girls and boys. A great many families, covens, and other groups have developed rituals to mark menarche and other rites of passage for young people, some of which our ancestors-of-spirit might not have thought of, such as getting your driver's license and going off to college.

THE RITES OF MENARCHE—A MEDITATION

Imagine for a moment that you are an elder woman in your community. Your status as Witch and Priestess of the Goddess means that you are often called upon to lead rituals for handfastings, funerals, and other milestones. In your years in the Lady's service, you have seen babies born into the world, children grow, and wise men and women pass to the Summerland.

You are not surprised, then, to hear that one of the village girls has been gifted with her first blood, and it is time for her to at last enter the circle of women.

All the adult women of the village are called together. You divide them into two: in one group are the women who still bleed, and in the other are those who, like you, have left childbearing years behind. The younger women take the girl out of the village, off to the blessed springs to bathe and be anointed; while they dress her in the bright red robes of the Maiden, they tell her women's secrets. She learns what herbs to use to lessen aches and pains; she learns that her moon time will bring her great power and perhaps visions, dreams, and deeper intuition.

Then the girl is brought into the house of the moon, where women of the village can spend their bleeding days secluded in peace and meditate away from the labor and stress of everyday life. Afterward, they bring her to the elders, to you.

One by one, the elder women give the girl their advice. Finally, you step forward and take her hands. "The Great Mother has blessed you with tremendous gifts," you say to her. "Yours is the power to bring forth life—creation is begun in the womb of a woman. Whether you give birth to babes, song, craft, or ritual, know that you have now joined the circle that connects every woman to every other, and that ours is the sacred calling to create beauty and joy in the world."

With that, you present her as a woman to her clan.

The House of the Moon

A consequence of our modern lifestyle is that we are no longer able to fully withdraw from the world into a moon lodge or other women's retreat every month when we bleed. Even so, I have heard many women say that during their periods they feel "fuzzy-headed," very meditative, and a little removed from normal life; our blood calls out for honor, even if our lives don't permit it.

Perhaps you can't disappear for five days a month, but you can quite easily create your own rituals to commemorate the Mysteries of your body.

I've read in various places that if we truly celebrate menstruation instead of hating it, and we embrace our blood in Witchy style, all our "symptoms" will vanish into thin air—no more cramps, no more PMS, no more bloating, all because of a change in attitude.

Unfortunately, this seems to be wishful thinking, at least in part. It's true that how we perceive life influences how we live it—going into every period with a string of curses and revulsion toward the whole process will make you miserable no matter if you're bloated or not.

Certainly I've found that changing how I feel about my cycles has gotten me more in touch with my body, my femininity, and my connection with the Goddess; the physical symptoms, however, haven't gone away just because of my attitude. It does help that coming from a more holistic perspective, I tend to seek out gentler remedies instead of throwing a whole bottle of Advil at the problem; listening to your body and learning what aggravates cramps and irritability will go a long way toward easing them.

While we're on the subject of natural alternatives, there is some evidence (untested, primarily because success would mean that Midol would stop selling so well) that using painkillers for cramps and other menstrual discomfort actually makes them worse. Even if you don't believe that, it's studies have shown that too much caffeine just before and during your period makes all your symptoms, especially cramps, increase. I thought that was crazy until I stopped drinking sodas and coffee three or four days before I started, and immediately noticed a huge difference in how I felt; now I typically cut way back on caffeine for those few days and drink lots of water, which is another way to ease cramps, bloating, and backaches.

Granted, the relief of altering your diet or drinking herbal "women's tea" or any of the other natural remedies isn't as rapid or as complete as taking a handful of ibuprofen, but try not to think only of this month; sometimes it takes a couple of cycles for natural methods to really show their benefits. Our quick-fix world gives us blinders against any idea that takes more than half an hour to work, but like with exercise, drinking water, and taking your vitamins, the body has its own clock and calendar, and it doesn't especially care that we're in a hurry.

Plenty of people have told me that the way to combat cramps is to exercise; well, if I exercise on my period, I tend to pass out. If that counts as pain relief, then I guess they're right. No two women have exactly the same set of experiences—you may crave red meat for three days while I want nothing but chocolate. Honor your body's desires, especially now, as when you bleed your body is speaking from a much deeper place and from much more primal needs.

Likewise, you can look at your blood as a chance for your body to cleanse and renew itself. A lot of women find that all their bodily functions seem to speed up and intensify, as if their bodies are trying to purify themselves of the toxins we take in on a daily basis as well as the stress of the last month. Instead of getting pissed at your body for feeling as weird as it does, think about why it might be feeling that way—what purpose does it serve for your health and your spirit?

What sort of rituals do you enact every month? You may not realize you have any, but you probably do, even if it's just getting wasted every night and being too hungover to care about cramps. I've always had very painful periods, unless I was on birth control pills, so over the years I developed a sort of Sylvan moon lodge all my own, though it's pretty mundane. If at all possible, if Cramp Day lands on a weekend or I can snag a day off from work, I curl up in bed with my heating pad, a cup of Yogi Tea's Moon Cycle blend, my MP3 player with angry feminist and/or trance music ready to go, my cat at my side, and the phone turned off. I take the hottest shower I can stand, bundle up in the blankets, and usually fall asleep with my headphones on. By the time I wake up, I feel like a new woman, not only because the pain's gone, but because I have taken time out to listen to my body's language and heed what it has to say.

A MOON-TIME RITUAL

On a more spiritual note, aside from your sacred pampering, consider a short ritual each month to honor your cycle. You could consecrate a special red candle to burn for that ritual, and have it on your altar all four to seven days of your period.

Each month, sit before your altar for a while and meditate on the mystical meaning of our lunar rhythms. Visualize yourself as part of an endless spiral of women throughout thousands of years of human history; your blood connects you to everything that is female, including every woman ever born. In the animal kingdom, the human cycle is the closest match to the exact length of the lunar month; as daughters of the Goddess, our bodies wax and wane as does her face.

You could raise energy to charge a charm or talisman to help with physical discomfort or to increase your psychic abilities during this time; if moving too much energy while you're bleeding makes you feel all wonky, like it does me, simply allow your consciousness to drift down into your belly, and float there in silence for a while, essentially communing with your womb.

I know of women who use menstrual blood as a spell component for just about everything—they'll slap that stuff all over the place. I'm not really okay with that idea personally, but not because of any perceived ick-factor; blood, I feel, is one of the most powerful magical substances there is. It is the essence of our life force, and menstrual blood carries even more weight in that regard. As such, I think it should be treated as a magical can of whoop-ass, and only used in ritual when you truly want to invoke the primal first-chakra energies that live within it.

The Mansion of the Dark Moon

If our menstrual cycles are so intrinsic to womanhood, what happens when they finally stop? Menopause suffers from a great many negative stereotypes, too; women are shown on television "going crazy," having hot flashes like nuclear reactors while their moods swing from one extreme to another faster than a presidential candidate.

Our national fear of aging translates very easily to a fear of menopause. After we stop bleeding, the attitude is, we're no longer as female as other women are. In order to keep our status as real women we have to fight every last wrinkle and hot flash, and try to "look years younger" at all costs. After all, once you get old, you've outlived your usefulness, so it's best if nobody has any idea how old you actually are, otherwise it's the old folks' home for you, ma'am. You might as well stock up on denture cream and adult diapers.

As I am writing this, I am at the ripe old age of twenty-six, so menopause isn't really something I've had to live personally, though plenty of relatives and friends have, with varying results. One thing I have learned is that hormone replacement therapy is scary. Another thing I've learned is that older women are not asexual, or any less women than those of us still unfortunate enough to be under thirty. If anything, they are *more* women, because they have had time to not only live, but to start to understand what that life has meant, and continues to mean. They have the entire experience of womanhood to learn from, and can take a broader perspective on the whole grand affair.

My favorite expression of the Crone's attitude toward aging is the now-famous poem by Jenny Joseph that begins, "Warning: When I am an old woman I shall wear purple . . . With a red hat which doesn't go and doesn't suit me . . ." My mother always says that the one thing she enjoys about aging thus far is that the older she gets, the less of a damn she gives about what other people think of her.

I learned about older women watching *The Golden Girls*, and because of the sexy, energetic, and hilarious characters on that show, I've never equated menopause with losing your femininity. Seeing how other people react to the end of their cycles, though, I wish more people had watched the show.

The thought that without periods you're not a woman is the same sort of doctrine that makes us think that you're not a real woman unless you have children. As I've said, giving birth isn't the only way to be creative, and it's certainly not the only way to be a woman; therefore losing the ability to conceive is only a biological loss, and in no way compromises our creativity.

It can, in fact, do just the opposite. Upon reaching menopause, symbolically, women no longer have to live for anyone but themselves; their children are grown, and no more will come, so they suddenly have a whole new freedom from the social responsibility and baggage attached to female fertility. After stepping over the divide into Cronehood, our creativity belongs to no one but ourselves, and we have, in a way, left the last of the confining and contradictory roles that society has created for women behind.

The waning half of life, as with the waning half of the year, is a time to look within for lessons instead of seeking them out in the maddening crowd. In autumn and winter, we withdraw from the frenetic pace of the waxing year, and our focus shifts to a quieter, darker, more meditative state of mind. The same can be said of the Crone's time of our lives; no longer so concerned with the opinions and needs of the outside world, we can become more authentically ourselves than ever before.

This shift, I believe, is part of what causes people such problems with aging. We reach a point where our bodies are changing much faster than our minds seem to—we still feel thirty inside, though the wrinkles and creaking bones say otherwise. As our world is so focused on the outside of the body rather than its inner wisdom, seeing that change can be a source of panic. We think that feeling young must also mean looking young, so women on the threshold of Croning are a large market for plastic surgeons. A facelift may be an effort to make the outside match the inside, but it comes from the mistaken belief that once you start to age, you have to be *old*.

I am one of the few young women I know who can't wait to be thirty. As long as I can remember, I have always connected more with people at least five years older, perhaps because I had two older brothers growing up. Even without that, though, I have found it's hard to be taken seriously when your age still starts with a two. People expect our generation to be rash, irresponsible, and immature; I would like to think I am none of those things, except when it comes to my apparent stupidity with money.

I've heard my mother, as well as other women, say a number of times that she didn't actually feel like a real adult until she hit thirty-five, because at that point she knew who she was, where she was going, and what she wanted out of life. The older we get, the more we understand ourselves, and that understanding isn't something that can come without the passage of time and the true embrace of life.

The elder matriarchs of my family have always been respected; my grandmother was a venerable lady to whom everyone turned for comfort and advice. People just don't often do that when you're twenty-six; people are generally surprised when they find out my age. A part of me can't wait to be sixty—I plan to be an eccentric, succulent, wild badass in a red hat who can out-shop, out-magic, and out-drink women half my age.

In the Pagan community, there is a higher degree of respect for elders than in general society; I have attended a number of rituals in which a woman steps up to take her place among the Wise Women and shows she has earned a new title, in addition to Priestess and Witch. To be named Crone in our community is to be part of an inner circle, without which the outer circle could not turn.

The Crossing

No discussion of the Crone would be complete without touching upon death, our final—and first—rite of passage. Again speaking as a fairly young person, I haven't quite gotten to that making-peace-with-death place, as I feel I have a lot to do before I'm ready to turn in my body and check out a new one. It helps, however, knowing that death is not the end of anything, and is in fact the start of a whole different adventure.

The Wiccan concept of the afterlife is a bit vague; it reflects the diversity of belief that our theology allows. The only constant is a belief in some variety of reincarnation. What that entails and how it works, nobody seems quite sure of, though we have plenty of theories. As long as we know we'll be back, we don't really worry too much about the afterlife. The present life becomes that much more important, knowing it will influence what happens next, and that we were born to live, not to be afraid of dying. So we live life like we mean it, and plan to worry about the next one when we get there.

BEYOND THE VEIL—EXERCISE #3

Spend a while meditating on your idea of the afterlife. What do you think happens after we take that last step? How did you arrive at this conclusion? Has your idea of death changed since you became Wiccan?

Do you believe in the Summerland, or some variation thereof? What do you think its purpose is? How long do you get to stay there? Do you choose your next life consciously or let the gods do it for you?

I am writing this in October, when Samhain is around the corner and death is much on our minds. What do you do for Samhain? Is it a time to honor ancestors, to communicate with the departed, to look into the darkened glass of the future? In your rituals, do you leave offerings for the dead, or enact the journey to the Underworld as in the stories of Persephone and Inanna?

Up until this year, my Samhain rituals were always very theoretical. Then I lost a brother, and suddenly the idea of death took on a whole new importance; I choose to believe that my brother basically hit control-alt-delete on his life and now will have another chance to do things differently, hopefully without going down the same path. This year I will send my love through the Veil, to wherever he's at now, and hope that it's felt.

Unlike a lot of people, I don't believe that the departed hang around to talk to us for very long after leaving. They have better things to do, like being reborn and getting on with things. I do think we have options, though, and if we need to stick around for a while and pop into a few dreams to reassure our loved ones, or right the wrongs we left behind, we can. Eventually, though, we have to let go and move on, otherwise we end up ghosts, too afraid or attached to the old to face the new.

What do you think? Do you think we can come back as animals, or only as humans? Either gender, or only the one we are now?

A great many Wiccans put a lot of energy into finding out all about their past lives. I've never been particularly interested, as I feel that my job here is to take care of this life, not dwell on my history. You can, however, learn from your prior mistakes if you do past life regression. I don't recommend doing so lightly, however, as stepping back in the spiral of time can be hazardous if you get swept up in what happened long ago and become confused as to how to return. My advice, if you want to look back, is to enlist the help of someone who has experience with regression and do it as a guided meditation, so that you have an anchor to your body and the present and someone completely conscious who can talk you through it if you need help.

Goddesses of the Crone Archetype

In Mexican culture, the patron of Dia de los Muertos is a skeletal figure known as *La Muerta*, Lady Death. The traditions of the holiday are descended from an Aztec commemoration of Mictecacihuatl, who governed death and children, as well as more modern Roman Catholic rituals. The celebration of La Muerta is inspirational for a better outlook on death; rather than the fearful attitude that gave rise to the demons and evil spirits of Halloween, Dia de los Muertos is centered around family, on love and honor for the ancestors rather than appeasing restless spirits. My favorite Samhain rituals have been a combination of the traditional European-based Wiccan customs and ones that reflect the North American old world.

We are used to seeing a number of Crone goddesses in Wiccan ritual and liturgy, most often including Cerridwen and Hecate, but also the Norns, Grandmother Spider, and Baba Yaga. Also sometimes put into the same category, though not a Crone herself, is Persephone, Queen of the Dead; while she was most often seen as a young woman, her role as wife of Hades and ruler of the Underworld has a distinctly Crone-like feeling to it. Any myth, in fact, which involves journeying to the Underworld and returning again is a favorite of the Crone.

Among several Native American tribes, Spider Woman, sometimes known as Grandmother Spider, was the Creatrix of the universe, spinning it out of her web. She also spun time itself, a theme carried over to the three Fates in Greek mythology. The Fates spun, measured, and cut the thread of every individual's life. The same image is found in Norse lore with the three Norns. In meditation I have seen Spider Woman, who often sends her children to act as messengers when there's something I should be writing but am procrastinating, as an old woman sitting at a spinning wheel, rocking back and forth and singing to herself. She later evolved into my current patroness, who often appears wearing a robe made of shadows and spider webs, and who sits at a great loom instead of a wheel. The concept of a weaving goddess whose craft becomes the fate of all humankind is a widespread one.

Most popular among the Crones is, of course, Hecate, the Greek lady of the crossroads. She was seen as either having three heads or simply three aspects, which made her a perfect candidate for embodying the Triple Goddess. Each of her heads was said to look in a different direction. Crossroads have long been associated with fate, as you stand at one and must choose which direction to take.

Hecate's stories from Greek myth are sparse, but her best-known role comes from the Hymn to Demeter, in which it is Hecate who brings to Demeter the truth about Persephone's abduction. Once the compromise with Hades is made, ensuring that Persephone will spend part of the year in the Underworld and part on Earth with her mother, Hecate is said to act as a guide, leading Persephone to the land of the dead and back again every year. Her association with the Underworld led her to eventually be treated as a goddess of evil Witchcraft in European literature, including *Macbeth*, in which the Three Weird Sisters invoke her to aid them in their nefarious arts.

Wiccans call to Hecate as the Dark Mother, who walks the graveyards beneath the dark moon, her ghostly hounds at her side. She is often invoked for justice, banishment, and other "dark" purposes. She is patroness of all those who stand at the crossroads of life, death, and rebirth: healers, midwives, Witches, and Crone women themselves. She is our guide into the darkest parts of the self, down the spiral that winds from past to future and around again, and lends us her vision to see between the worlds, learning that death is not to be feared, nor is life to be squandered.

SUGGESTIONS FOR EXPLORING THE CRONE

1. Research your family history, particularly that of the women of your kin. You may find some surprises, and at the very least will get a greater sense of where you have come from.

2. Among your family, or out in the world, try to find a woman (or more than one, if you're lucky enough to know them) who embodies the kind of Crone you want to be when you "grow up." Look to her for inspiration on how to walk gracefully through the years.

3. Pay more attention, and give more reverence, to your own rites of passage. The physical ones that are commonly celebrated aren't the only ones that matter; a divorce, new career, or even a new car can be a turning point in your life. We go through many versions of ourselves just in a single incarnation; how many have you been through so far? How many have you honored, and how many have slipped past without your knowing?

4. Take a moon retreat. Schedule a weekend that coincides with your menstrual period in which you can stay home, or go somewhere else away from responsibility and everyday life. Spend time in circle, meditating; howl at the moon; and most of all, find silence, and really listen to your body. You could even take other bleeding women with you and do rituals together to explore your connection to each other and to the web of women throughout human history.

Recommended Reading and Resources for Chapter Eight

BOOKS

Blood, Bread, and Roses: How Menstruation Created the World by Judy Grahn

The Curse: Confronting the Last Unmentionable Taboo: Menstruation by Karen Houppert

Goddesses in Older Women: Archetypes in Women Over Fifty—Becoming a Juicy Crone by Jean Shinoda Bolen, MD.

Crossing to Avalon: A Woman's Midlife Pilgrimage by Jean Shinoda Bolen

WEB RESOURCES

<http://www.menstruation.com.au> An Australian site has menarche greeting cards, other interesting merchandise, and articles about all things menstrual.

<http://onewoman.com/redspot> The Red Spot is a neat little site with a few articles on menstrual taboos and rituals.

Glad Rags cloth menstrual pads

<http://www.gladrags.com>

CONCLUSION

Hear the words of the Lady of a Thousand Names, she whose body is the greening earth as well as the flesh you wear:

I am the Woman whose hands sculpted all things; in the time before your birth I smoothed your face into its final shape, and named you daughter. You were called up out of the dust of the stars, out of the fallen leaves and the first light of morning, to be exactly who you are, and to become who you choose to be. Choose, then, to walk with your spine unbent, to dance no matter what fool's eyes may be watching. Choose love for yourself, and for those who see the radiance and wisdom I have clothed you in. Choose compassion for those who are blinded. Choose to live by the truth of who you are, and you will know the path before you and walk unafraid.

Look into the mirror if you would see beauty; look into your own eyes if you would find divinity. My blood flows through your veins and your heart beats in time with mine. Not one of my daughters shall ever be apart from me, for I brought you forth, and I abide in you always. For I dwell within you from birth unto death, as far away as your own bright spirit, and as close as your own skin.

BIBLIOGRAPHY

Recommended reading can be found at the end of each chapter. The following works were used as general references for *The Body Sacred*:

Books

Bonheim, Jalaja. *Aphrodite's Daughters: Women's Sexual Stories and the Journey of the Soul.* New York: Fireside, 1997.

Davis, Elizabeth, and Carol Leonard. *The Circle of Life: Thirteen Archetypes for Every Woman.* Berkeley, CA: Celestial Arts, 2003.

Galenorn, Yasmine. *Crafting the Body Divine: Ritual, Movement, and Body Art.* Berkeley, CA: Crossing Press, 2001.

Johnston, Anita A., PhD. *Eating in the Light of the Moon: How Women Can Transform Their Relationship With Food Through Myths, Metaphors, and Storytelling.* Carlsbad, CA: Gurze Books, 2000.

Judith, Anodea. *Wheels of Life: A User's Guide to the Chakra System.* St. Paul, MN: Llewellyn Publications, 1987.

Maine, Margo. *Body Wars.* Carlsbad, CA: Gurze Books, 1999.

Monaghan, Patricia. *The Goddess Path.* St. Paul, MN: Llewellyn Publications, 1999.

Roth, Gabrielle. *Sweat Your Prayers: Movement as Spiritual Practice.* New York: Putnam Publishing Group, 1998.

Russell, Stephen. *Barefoot Doctor's Guide to the Tao: A Spiritual Handbook for the Urban Warrior.* New York: Three Rivers Press, 1999.

Other Sources

The Encyclopedia Mythica, consulted continuously throughout my work, is one of the greatest sources of cross-cultural mythology on the Internet. <http://www.pantheon.org>

Human Body Facts. Funology.com. July 10, 2004. <http://www.funology.com/thatsodd/odd_humanbody002.htm>.

Young, Shana. *Kali Pages.* The Tribe of Ancient Ways. August 20, 2004, <http://www.tribeofancientways.com/kali.html>.

INDEX

Free Magazine

Read unique articles by Llewellyn authors, recommendations by experts, and information on new releases. To receive a **free** copy of Llewellyn's consumer magazine, *New Worlds of Mind & Spirit,* simply call 1-877-NEW-WRLD or visit our website at www.llewellyn.com and click on *New Worlds.*

☽ LLEWELLYN ORDERING INFORMATION

Order Online:
Visit our website at www.llewellyn.com, select your books, and order them on our secure server.

Order by Phone:
- Call toll-free within the U.S. at 1-877-NEW-WRLD (1-877-639-9753). Call toll-free within Canada at 1-866-NEW-WRLD (1-866-639-9753)
- We accept VISA, MasterCard, and American Express

Order by Mail:
Send the full price of your order (MN residents add 7% sales tax) in U.S. funds, plus postage & handling to:

> **Llewellyn Worldwide**
> **2143 Wooddale Drive, Dept. 0-7387-0761-9**
> **Woodbury, MN 55125-2989, U.S.A.**

Postage & Handling:

Standard (U.S., Mexico, & Canada). If your order is:
$49.99 and under, add $3.00
$50.00 and over, FREE STANDARD SHIPPING

AK, HI, PR: $15.00 for one book plus $1.00 for each additional book.

International Orders (airmail only):
$16.00 for one book plus $3.00 for each additional book

Orders are processed within 2 business days.
Please allow for normal shipping time. Postage and handling rates subject to change.

The Circle Within

Creating a Wiccan Spiritual Tradition

DIANNE SYLVAN

Anyone can put on a robe and dance the night away at a Sabbat, but it takes courage and discipline to be a Wiccan twenty-four hours a day, seven days a week, for the rest of your life. Every act can be a ritual, and every moment is another chance to honor the Divine. This book shows you how to do just that.

The Circle Within guides the practicing witch toward integrating Wiccan values into his or her real life. The first part of the book addresses the philosophy, practice, and foundations of a spiritual life. The second part is a mini-devotional filled with prayers and rituals that you can use as a springboard to creating your own.

0-7387-0348-6

216 pp., 5¾₆ x 8 $12.95

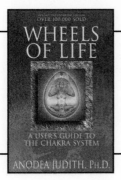

Wheels of Life

A User's Guide to the Chakra System

Anodea Judith

An instruction manual for owning and operating the inner gears that run the machinery of our lives. Written in a practical, down-to-earth style, this fully illustrated book will take the reader on a journey through aspects of consciousness, from the bodily instincts of survival to the processing of deep thoughts.

Discover this ancient metaphysical system under the new light of popular Western metaphors: quantum physics, Kabbalah, physical exercises, poetic meditations, and visionary art. Learn how to open these centers in yourself, and see how the chakras shed light on the present world crises we face today. And learn what you can do about it!

This book will be a vital resource for: magicians, witches, pagans, mystics, yoga practitioners, martial arts people, psychologists, medical people, and all those who are concerned with holistic growth techniques.

0-87542-320-5

480 pp., 6 x 9, illus. $17.95

To order, call 1-877-NEW-WRLD

Prices subject to change without notice

The Goddess Path

Myths, Invocations & Rituals

Patricia Monaghan

For some, finding the goddess is a private intellectual search, where they can speculate on her meaning in culture and myth. For others, she is an emotional construct, a way of understanding the varying voices of the emerging self. Then there are those for whom she is part of everyday ritual, honored in meditation and prayer. All are on the goddess path.

If you have never encountered the Goddess outside your own heart, this book will introduce you to some of her manifestations. If you have long been on this path, it will provide prayers and rituals to stimulate your celebrations. *The Goddess Path* offers a creative approach to worship, one in which you can develop and ritualize your own distinctive connection to her many manifestations from around the world.

1-56718-467-7

288 pp., 7½ x 9⅛, illus. $14.95

The Urban Primitive
Paganism in the Concrete Jungle

RAVEN KALDERA & TANNIN SCHWARTZSTEIN

Modern neo-paganism is primarily an urban movement, yet few books exist for city pagans, specifically city pagans on a budget. *The Urban Primitive* shows how every disaffected urban pagan can use magick to survive and make good in the city.

Find practical recommendations not found anywhere else, including how to protect your back in the combat zone, defend your house from intruders and lousy energies, find jobs, keep your car running, locate good parking spaces, and use the city's energy for sorcery. There are even chapters on body decoration, urban totem animals—such as sparrows and cockroaches—and old gods in new guises, including Skor (goddess of dumpster treasures) and Slick (god of fast talking).

0-7387-0259-5
288 pp., 6 x 9, illus. $14.95

To order, call 1-877-NEW-WRLD
Prices subject to change without notice

Solitary Witch

The Ultimate Book of Shadows
for the New Generation

SILVER RAVENWOLF

This book has everything a teen Witch could want and need between two covers: a magickal cookbook, encyclopedia, dictionary, and grimoire. It relates specifically to today's young adults and their concerns, yet is grounded in the magickal work of centuries past.

Information is arranged alphabetically and divided into five distinct categories: (1) Shadows of Religion and Mystery, (2) Shadows of Objects, (3) Shadows of Expertise and Proficiency, (4) Shadows of Magick and Enchantment, and (5) Shadows of Daily Life. It is organized so readers can skip over the parts they already know, or read each section in alphabetical order.

0-7387-0319-2

608 pp., 8 x 10, illus. $19.95

To order, call 1-877-NEW-WRLD
Prices subject to change without notice